The Annotated *Laozi* 老子

SUNY series in Chinese Philosophy and Culture

Roger T. Ames, editor

The Annotated *Laozi* 老子

A New Translation of the *Daodejing* 道德經

PAUL FISCHER

SUNY
PRESS

Cover art: Image courtesy the Metropolitan Museum of Art. Unidentified artist. In the style of Gao Kegong 高克恭 (1248–1310). China, Ming (1368–1644) or Qing (1644–1911). Bequest of Edgar Worch. Accession Number: 54.193.

Published by State University of New York Press, Albany

© 2023 State University of New York

All rights reserved

Printed in the United States of America

No part of this book may be used or reproduced in any manner whatsoever without written permission. No part of this book may be stored in a retrieval system or transmitted in any form or by any means including electronic, electrostatic, magnetic tape, mechanical, photocopying, recording, or otherwise without the prior permission in writing of the publisher.

For information, contact State University of New York Press, Albany, NY www.sunypress.edu

Library of Congress Cataloging-in-Publication Data

Name: Fischer, Paul, author.
Title: The Annotated *Laozi* : a new translation of the *Daodejing* / Paul Fischer.
Description: Albany : State University of New York Press, [2023] | Series: SUNY series in Chinese Philosophy and Culture. | Includes bibliographical references and index.
Identifiers: ISBN 9781438493992 (hardcover : alk. paper) | ISBN 9781438494012 (ebook)
Further information is available at the Library of Congress.

10 9 8 7 6 5 4 3 2 1

見素，抱樸，少私，寡欲。

Manifest purity, embrace simplicity, reduce selfishness, and decrease (contrived) desires.

—*Laozi* 老子 chapter 19 (ca. 400 BCE)

凡道無所，善心安處：心靜氣理，道乃可止。

Generally speaking, the Way has no fixed place, yet in a competent mind it will securely abide: if the mind is tranquil and the body is principled, the Way will then be able to settle.

—*Guanzi* 管子 chapter 49 (內業) (ca. 400 BCE)

It is only when he discerns beauty itself through what makes it visible that a man will be quickened with the true, and not the seeming, virtue—for it is virtue's self that quickens him, not virtue's semblance. And when he has brought forth and reared this perfect virtue, he shall be called the friend of god.

—*Symposium* 212a (ca. 380 BCE)

孰能以無為首，以生為脊，以死為尻？孰知死生存亡之一體者？吾與之友矣。

Who can take formlessness as their head, take life as their spine, take death as their rump? Who knows that life and death, abiding and loss, are all a single body? I will be their friend.

—*Zhuangzi* 莊子 chapter 6 (大宗師) (ca. 300 BCE)

人何以知道？曰心。心何以知？曰虛壹而靜。

How do people know the way? With the mind. How does the mind know? With openness, focus, and tranquility.

—*Xunzi* 荀子 chapter 21 (解蔽) (ca. 250 BCE)

博學之，審問之，慎思之，明辨之，篤行之。

Extensively learn it, critically inquire after it, carefully apprehend it, percipiently discern it, earnestly practice it.

—*Liji* 禮記 chapter 31 (中庸) (ca. 200 BCE)

致知在格物。

The extension of knowledge lies in the investigation of things.

—*Liji* 禮記 chapter 42 (大學) (ca. 200 BCE)

There is no wisdom for a man without harmony, and without harmony there is no contemplation. Without contemplation there cannot be peace, and without peace can there be joy?

—*Bhagavad Gita* chapter 2.66 (ca. 200 BCE)

達於道者，反於清靜；究於物者，終於無為。以恬養性，以漠處神，則入於天門。

Those who understand the Way return to purity and tranquility; those who examine things end up in non-contrivance. Those who use calmness to nourish their nature and use silence to dwell in spiritousness will enter the gates of Heaven.

—*Huainanzi* 淮南子 chapter 1 (原道) (ca. 139 BCE)

People are disturbed not by things, but by the views which they take of things.

—*Enchiridion* (ca. 125 CE)

菩提本無樹，明鏡亦非臺：本來無一物，何處惹塵埃？

Enlightenment is not contingent on the person; percipience likewise is not contingent on the mind: originally there are no individual things, so where exactly might ignorance abide?

—*Platform Sutra of the Sixth Patriarch* (六祖壇經; ca. 670 CE)

Thy mystery of migrating butterflies, the mystery of gravity and dreams are but operating arms of the Great Mystery, the perpetuation of which maintains us all.

—Tom Robbins, *Another Roadside Attraction* (1971), 26

Contents

Acknowledgments	ix
Introduction	1
Key Concepts	11
Translator's Note	33
The Annotated *Laozi*: Translation and Explanation	37
Appendix: The Chinese Text	285
Index	299

Acknowledgments

In college I majored in religion and minored in philosophy. There I was introduced to the *Laozi* (thank you, Prof. Anderson) and was even able to take a course dedicated to it (thank you, Prof. Moeller). In that *Laozi* class, none of us could read Chinese, but we read the text side by side with the Chinese anyway. Then I worked for a few years refinishing hardwood floors (thank you, Steve). In 1989 I left to travel around the world. In an old army surplus rucksack I carried the *Laozi* (as well as Plato's *Symposium*, the *Bhagavad Gita*, *Enchiridion*, *Platform Sutra*, and Tom Robbins). Since this was before the internet or cellphones, I spent many hours reading these books on beaches in Fiji, mountains in New Zealand, deserts in Australia, the Kokoda trail in Papua New Guinea, volcanos in Indonesia, across the mountains in Borneo—more or less the usual route described in the Lonely Planet books (thank you, countless youth hostel owners). Two years later, when I ran out of money, I went to Taiwan to teach English and learn Chinese (thank you, Tsao *laoshi*). It was there that I bought my first *Laozi* in Chinese and the other books I carried began to take a backseat. After two years in Taiwan, and after mailing home half a dozen modern Chinese translations of the *Laozi*, I continued my way west across Asia until I got a letter via poste restante from my mom, asking me to come home for my folks' fiftieth wedding anniversary in October 1995, which I did. In 1996 I started graduate school at the University of Chicago, where I studied classical Chinese and early Chinese intellectual history (thank you, Prof. Shaughnessy). Before graduating in 2007, I had gone back to Taipei (thank you, Prof. Chen Guying 陳鼓應) and Beijing (thank you, Prof. Li Ling 李零) for classes on ancient Chinese thought and in both places the *Laozi* was central to our inquiries. As a teacher, I've taught the *Laozi* several times in my Daoism class (thank you, students). So the *Laozi* has been a part of x | Acknowledgments

my life for quite a few years now, both personally and professionally. I'd like to thank everyone who helped me on the way, from Gia-Fu Feng at his Stillpoint retreat, so long ago, to Seymour Glass, who, I suspect, left a quote or two from the *Laozi* for his siblings on his bedroom wall.

Introduction

The **aim** of this book is to translate and explain the *Laozi* 老子 to a college undergraduate or general audience. The method used is more philosophical than historical, by which I mean I have analyzed the text for those interested in it as a narrative in a "living" tradition that can have meaning for them now, rather than primarily as a historical document to be solely, or even primarily, situated and understood within its own historical context. This approach is rather easy to do with a text like the *Laozi*, since it makes no reference to any historical people or places; thus, it is not *obviously* situated anywhere (though, of course, like all texts, it must have been at one time). No one knows for certain who the original intended **audience** was, but there are two likely candidates: either it was written to persuade contemporaneous rulers to be less aggressive, or it was written to poetically describe to individuals how to situate oneself within the cosmological paradigm presented by the author. (Or both or, perhaps, neither.) Since I suspect my audience will include relatively few aggressive rulers, and since I am not writing this primarily for history students, I focus on the situating of oneself within the cosmological paradigm presented in these pages. This kind of "situating" was called, in early China, "self-cultivation" (修身).

No one has established a firm **date** for the *Laozi*, but my guess is about 400 BCE. Because of the Guodian 郭店 manuscript finds of 1993, we can be certain that at least parts of the *Laozi* were written down by 300 BCE. Maybe those "parts" were added to over time to create our current eighty-one-chapter version, or maybe those parts were extracted from an extant eighty-one-chapter version. Tradition holds that the author was an older contemporary of Kongzi 孔子 (551–479; aka Confucius), so that gives us a traditional date of about 500 BCE. One could do worse than split the difference at 400 BCE (but if you are interested in dating ancient texts, by

2 | The Annotated *Laozi* 老子

all means, look into it).[1] The most important archeologically recovered *Laozi* manuscripts discovered in recent decades are the three Guodian manuscripts, the two Mawangdui 馬王堆 manuscripts (excavated in 1973 and dated to pre-168 BCE), and the Beijing University manuscript (purchased in 2009 and dated to ca. 100 BCE). Though I do not focus on most of the textual variations contained in these manuscripts, they and several other *Laozi* exemplars have informed this translation, and thus I will refer to them, when relevant, in the footnotes. The appendix details these texts, along with other sources used in deriving the Chinese text translated herein, for the interested reader.

There are two primary ways of **contextualizing** the *Laozi*: as a "religious" text among other religious texts, assessed from a modern point of view (perhaps for a comparative religion course in college), or as a "Scholars text" (子書), which is to say, a "philosophical" or "intellectual history" text, as considered from (at the latest) a ca. 100 BCE royal librarian's point of view (perhaps for a philosophy or history course in college). Within the context of Christianity, Islam, Hinduism, and many other "world religions"—or, to be more precise, the more traditional, conservative, and literal iterations of those religions—the *Laozi* stands out for promulgating a very different cosmic paradigm. Whereas these other traditions posit anthropomorphic deities amenable to prayer, heaven(s) and hell(s), and an immortal soul that will come to reside, for eternity (in Christianity and Islam), in one of these cosmic destinations, the *Laozi* has no deities, no inhabitable heaven (explained later), no hell, and no immortal soul. For this reason, some students will see this text as, prima facie, more "philosophical" than "religious" and, in fact, it is so categorized and taught in East Asian universities.[2] Nevertheless, for comparing different cosmological paradigms, the *Laozi* provides an excellent counterpoint to those found in the world's major religions.

A more historical way to contextualize the *Laozi* is not with Christianity and the others (religions that the *Laozi* author had certainly never heard of), but as Sima Tan 司馬談 (d. 110 BCE) did. Sima Tan is the first royal

---

1. One good place to start with the question of dating is Sarah Allan and Crispin Williams, eds., *The Guodian* Laozi (Berkeley: Society for the Study of Early China, 2000).

2. However, a third way of contextualizing the *Laozi* is as a religious text within the tradition of "religious Daoism," a tradition that began several centuries after the heyday of "Scholars texts," and that appropriated the *Laozi* for its own, decidedly supernatural, ends. I address the difference between "philosophical Daoism" and "religious Daoism" in Paul Fischer, "The Creation of Daoism," *Journal of Daoist Studies* 8 (2015): 1–23.

Introduction | 3

historian that we know of in East Asia. He described six traditions that we might call "schools of thought."[3] They are: Yin-Yang (i.e., cosmology), Ruism (aka Confucianism), Mohism, Rhetoric, Legalism, and Daoism. In describing Daoism he cites, without attribution, two brief phrases that are now found in the *Laozi*.[4] A century later, the royal librarian Liu Xiang 劉向 (79–8 BCE) listed the *Laozi* under the "Daoist" heading in his library catalog.[5] I won't take the time to describe these six schools of thought here, but they offer a much more historically accurate way of contextualizing the *Laozi*.[6]

The two earliest descriptions of the *Laozi* come in the form of descriptions of its eponymous **author**, Laozi, that is, Scholar Lao or, if one thinks that "Lao" was not an ancient Chinese surname, the Old Scholar(s).[7] In any case, tradition holds that Laozi's real name was Li Er 李耳, as we shall see later. Whether or not Laozi really was the author of the *Laozi* is hard to say. It's like asking if Abraham, Moses, or Jesus were real, historical figures: if you ask an American (about 70 percent of whom are Christian), they will probably say, "Yes, of course." But if you ask a Chinese person (about 3 percent of whom are Christian), they will likely say, "I don't know; given that their stories involve miracles, probably not." And, I suspect, if you asked the same question about Laozi in those two locations, you might get the same answers in reverse proportions. By and large, people tend to

---

3. Some scholars object to the "schools of thought" nomenclature because they think it implies physical school buildings or articulated teacher-student lineages. I imply neither of these and use the term loosely.

4. His opening two sentences appear to include paraphrases of *Laozi* chapters 37 (or 48) and 70. For a translation of this part of Sima Tan and his son Sima Qian's 司馬遷 (145–86) *Shi ji* 史記 (Scribal records; 91 BCE), see William Nienhauser, ed., *The Grand Scribe's Records*, vol. 11 (Bloomington: Indiana University Press, 2019), 320.

5. Liu Xiang's library catalog is preserved in Ban Gu's 班固 (32–92 CE) *Han shu* 漢書 (Han history; 92 CE) chapter 30 "Yiwen zhi" 藝文志 (Literature record), but it remains untranslated. The *Laozi*, or rather four different annotated *Laozi*s (all lost, unfortunately), appears in the standard Chinese edition on page 1729.

6. For more on five of these six schools (minus the Rhetorists), see Benjamin Schwartz, *The World of Thought in Ancient China* (Cambridge: Belknap Press of Harvard University Press, 1985).

7. *Zi* 子 means "scholar," "master," or "teacher." *Lao* 老 means "old" or "experienced." One might transcribe the Chinese as "Lao Zi" rather than "Laozi" to show that the last two letters are in fact an honorific, but convention, and a desire to not give the impression that Zi is a surname, conspire to put them together. This is the case with the names of all early Chinese scholars, like Kongzi, Zhuangzi, and Mozi, whose names end with *zi*.

4 | The Annotated *Laozi* 老子

believe that their own ancient cultural heroes are real, while other people's ancient cultural heroes are mythological (at least when miraculous events are involved). And the further back in time you go, the harder it is to find corroborating evidence to support the narratives about the people in question. There are no miraculous events in the *Laozi* (as I read it; however, some bits, read literally rather than metaphorically, can be construed as describing the miraculous), but Laozi's earliest biography (which we will look at shortly) says he *may have* lived to 160 or even 200 years of age. So, while there is nothing necessarily "mythological" in the *Laozi*, the biography of Laozi is a little suspect, by modern standards of historicity.

Aside from the potentially miraculous part of a biography of Laozi written centuries after his death, some scholars assess the eighty-one chapters as "reading like" an anthology written by different authors. I might agree with the "anthology" description, since the ca. 300 BCE Guodian manuscripts order their chapters differently from the received version, and the 168 BCE Mawangdui manuscripts reverse the two halves of the text (but otherwise mostly keep the same chapter order).[8] But since the text reads quite coherently to me, philosophically speaking, I remain unpersuaded by the "several different authors" claim. Nevertheless, if the *Laozi* has taught me anything, it is the wisdom of fallibilism (discussed later), so maybe there was no historical Laozi, and maybe the *Laozi* was written by many authors and redacted into a single text by a later editor or several editors. It doesn't really matter to a philosophical appreciation of the book. In any case, I shall refer to "Laozi" as the author, even while not claiming that an individual named "Li Er" wrote the book. One thing is certain: given all the variora among exemplars, the exact wording of the text has certainly changed over time. I address authorship further in the appendix.

The two earliest **descriptions** of Laozi come from the *Zhuangzi* 莊子 and from Sima Tan (or his son, Sima Qian). The *Zhuangzi* also has an eponymous author, Zhuangzi, Scholar Zhuang, and was also categorized as a Daoist text by Liu Xiang. The first chapters of the *Zhuangzi* are often dated to about 300 BCE, but it is the last chapter that has the description of Laozi that we are interested in. This chapter also has a description of Zhuangzi himself, which suggests that he did not write it. So just *when* it was written is unclear; sometime between 300 and 8 BCE, when Liu Xiang noted it in his library catalog. I'll tentatively date it to 250 BCE,

---

8. The first "half" is constituted (in the standard, received version) by chapters 1–37, and the second "half" by chapters 38–81.

Introduction | 5

since it shows no indication of the 221 BCE Qin unification of China, a unification that changed the tone of scholars who succeeded the scholars in pre-Qin schools of thought.

Zhuangzi chapter 33 refers to Laozi as Lao Dan (we'll find out why later).

> Lao Dan said: "Know the male, but preserve the female: be a 'mountain stream' for the world; know the white, but preserve the black: be a 'valley' for the world."[9] And: "People all choose to be in the lead, while I alone choose to follow: this is called accepting the misfortunes of the world. People all choose full-ness, while I alone choose emptiness: I do not hoard, therefore there is more than enough, manifestly more than enough!" He (i.e., Laozi) carried himself calmly yet efficiently, uncontrivedly yet with cheerful skillfulness:[10] "People all seek wealth, while I alone am 'bent, then whole': this is called 'carefree avoidance of ruin.'" Using depth as his root and moderation as his standard, he said: "Rigid, then ruined; sharp, then blunted." Abidingly tolerant toward all things, without thereby reducing humans, he may be said to have reached the zenith.[11]

---

9. This is almost identical to a quote from *Laozi* chapter 28, except in the received text there is an explanatory sentence between the two halves marked by the semicolon, and the received text has "model" (式) instead of "valley" (谷), though "valley" is used in the next line in the received version. Thus, the *Zhuangzi* chapter 33 author could have been paraphrasing the *Laozi*, or they could have been quoting a different version.

10. Most scholars read "uncontrivedly yet with cheerful skillfulness" as "uncontrivedly and laughed at cleverness." The difference results from how to parse the grammar: I read the sentence as "topic (其行身) + adjectives X而Y + adjectives X而Y," while other scholars read it as "topic (其行身) + adjectives X而Y" then "topic (無為) + verb-object." Both readings are possible. Moreover, "skillful / clever" (巧) is used negatively in *Laozi* chapters 19 and 57, but it is also used positively in chapter 45. And *Zhuangzi* chapter 19 describes Woodworker Qing as "skillful" in a positive sense, so it seems plausible that the author of *Zhuangzi* chapter 33 would also use it positively here.

11. The first three sentences, as well as the second half of the fifth and sixth sentences, all seem to be quotes from Laozi, but only the first matches an existing passage, so it seems likely that the author of *Zhuangzi* chapter 33 had access to sayings of Laozi that did not make it into the final, received version of the text. Or perhaps this author was paraphrasing the *Laozi*, insofar as most of these sayings *do* have echoes in the received *Laozi*. For example, for the second sentence, see chapters 7, 66, and 78; for the third sentence, see chapters 3, 38, and 44; for the fourth sentence, see chapters 20, 22, and 9; and for the fifth sentence, see chapters 59, 4, and 6.

6 | The Annotated *Laozi* 老子

老聃曰：「知其雄，守其雌，為天下谿；知其白，守其辱，為天
下谷。」「人皆取先，己獨取後，曰受天下之垢。人皆取實，己
獨取虛：無藏也故有餘，巋然而有餘。」其行身也，徐而不費，
無為也而笑巧：「人皆求福，己獨曲全，曰苟免於咎。」以深為
根，以約為紀，曰「堅則毀矣，銳則挫矣」。常寬容於物，不削
於人，可謂至極。

This description, however, does not really tell us much about the text that
we would not have learned from reading it. The second description, however, from Sima Qian, does. Remember that if we date the *Laozi* to ca.
400 BCE, and Sima Qian finished his (and his father's) work ca. 91 BCE,
three centuries had elapsed.

> Laozi was from Churen village in the Li district of the Hu prov-
> ince of the state of Chu. He was surnamed Mr. Li, given-named
> Er, and style-named Dan. He was a scribe in the Zhou archives.
> When Kongzi went to the state of Zhou to ask Laozi about
> protocol, Laozi said: "The people of whom you speak, both
> their persons and their bones, have all already withered away:
> only their words still remain. Moreover, when noble people meet
> with the right time, then they ride in a carriage, but when they
> do not meet with the right time, then they move like tumble-
> weeds piling up. I have heard that the full storerooms of clever
> merchants appear empty, and that the countenances of noble
> people who are full of virtuosity appear stupid. Be rid of your
> arrogant manner and many desires, your proud demeanor and
> excessive willfulness: these are all of no benefit to your person.
> That is all I have to tell you."[12]

老子者，楚苦縣厲鄉曲仁里人也。姓李氏，名耳，字聃。周守藏
室之史也。孔子適周，將問禮於老子，老子曰：「子所言者，其
人與骨皆已朽矣，獨其言在耳。且君子得其時則駕，不得其時則
蓬累而行。吾聞之，良賈深藏若虛，君子盛德容貌若愚。去子之
驕氣與多欲，態色與淫志：是皆無益於子之身。吾所以告子，若
是而已。」

---

12. To "ride in a carriage" implies having a job in government, which was socially
esteemed, well paying, and provided an opportunity to help the community; while to
"move like tumbleweeds" is to wander around, presumably without stable employment.

Here we learn that Laozi's "style name," or "pen name," is Lao Dan and three things about him that are relevant to our reading of the *Laozi*. First, despite being literate and aware of history, he thought—as Kongzi himself did—that when it comes to protocol, how it is *practiced* is more important than how it is *articulated*.[13] Or, as we might put it now, "the spirit of the law" is more important than "the letter of the law." Second, timeliness matters.[14] The question of whether one should involve oneself in community improvement when the current community leaders are pursuing strategies and goals that are incompatible with one's own was a key question for Kongzi. If Kongzi can be construed as advocating "strive for change from within," Laozi is here advocating "biding one's time until the moment is conducive." It is an interesting question that remains valid for us even today. Third, Laozi, like any fallibilist, is suspicious of overconfidence. One may be confident in what one knows, but this should always be tempered with the humility of knowing that there is still much that we do *not* know. This too is an issue that remains valid for us even today. In Sima Qian's narrative, Kongzi then goes on to compare Laozi to a dragon, remarking that he "cannot understand how he rides the winds and clouds up to Heaven" (不能知其乘風雲而上天). The narrative then continues:

> Laozi cultivated the Way and virtuosity, and his teachings used self-concealment and a low profile to do things. Having lived in the state of Zhou for a long while, he saw its decline, and consequently left. Arriving at the border, the border guard Yin Xi said, "Since you are going to into retirement, might I bother you to write a text for me?" So Laozi consequently wrote a text in two sections, articulating the meaning of the Way and virtuosity in just over five thousand words, and then departed. No one knows where he ended up.

> 老子脩道德，其學以自隱無名為務。居周久之，見周之衰，迺遂去。至關，關令尹 喜曰：「子將隱矣，彊為我著書？」於是老子迺著書上下篇，言道德之意五千餘言而去。莫知其所終。

---

13. "Protocol" (禮) is often translated as "ritual," but I prefer "protocol" because I find it applicable to a wider range of activities than is implied by the more formal English word "ritual." In fact, the Chinese word certainly has implications broader than either of these two options. I use "ritual" (儀) to translate a different Chinese word, one with a narrower semantic range, more formal and ceremonial, but it does not occur in the *Laozi*.

14. For passages on timeliness, see *Laozi* chapters 8, 9, 63, and 64.

8 | The Annotated *Laozi* 老子

Here we learn of a fourth item relevant to understanding the text: the importance of humility and keeping a low profile. This brief biography continues on with speculation about other names Laozi might have gone by, his possibly living to 160 or 200 years of age, and his lineage, but none of this matters to our understanding of the text.[15]

Early Chinese "Scholars texts,"[16] like the *Laozi*, often circulated—quite possibly in piecemeal form—for centuries without a formal **title**. Sima Qian, who died around 86 BCE, refers to "Laozi's words / sayings" (老子言) and "Laozi's text / writings / book" (老子書), but there was no shorthand way to denote titles, as we now do with italics. The *Laozi* was the title used by Liu Xiang, the royal librarian, before his death in 8 BCE, but Han Emperor Jing 漢景帝 (r. 157–141 BCE) is traditionally thought to have accorded the text the honorific title *Daodejing* 道德經 (The classic of the Way and virtuosity).[17] Wang Bi 王弼 (226–249 CE) called his commentary the *Daode zhenjing zhu* 道德真經注 (Commentary on the true classic of the Way and virtuosity), so the *Daodejing* title was presumably known by then.[18] So, which title—the *Laozi* or the *Daodejing*—is older? I cannot say with great confidence, but I've chosen to use the *Laozi*, for two reasons. One, Liu Xiang was a librarian, and had he thought that Han Emperor Jing's putative christening of the text as the *Daodejing* was "official," I think he would have used it. Also, Ban Gu, in his *Han shu* 漢書 (Han history; 92 CE), when listing a number of old books reportedly found sometime before 155 BCE, uses *Laozi* and not *Daodejing*.[19] Second, using *Laozi* reminds us to contextualize it with other

---

15. For the rest of Sima Qian's brief biography of Laozi, see William Nienhauser, ed., *The Grand Scribe's Records*, vol. 7 (Bloomington: Indiana University Press, 1994), 22–23.

16. That is, generally speaking, those whose author's names and eponymous titles end in *zi* (子).

17. That is, Jiao Hong 焦竑 (1540–1620), in his *Laozi Yi* 老子翼 (Supplement to the *Laozi*), said "the *Laozi* began to be called a 'classic' starting from the time of Han Emperor Jing" (老子之稱經，自漢景帝始也). This claim, made *a millennium and a half* after the fact, is not supported by the *Shiji* or *Hanshu*, but is partially supported by the Beijing University *Laozi* manuscript, obtained in 2009 and dated to ca. 100 BCE, insofar as this manuscript has titles for the two parts of the text, "Laozi Classic Part I" (老子上經) and "Laozi Classic Part II" (老子下經).

18. Or not. Victor Mair, in his translation of the Mawangdui *Laozi*, says that "the first explicit mention of the classic by this title" (i.e., the *Daodejing*) was "probably" by Wang Xizhi 王羲之 (321–379). Victor Mair, *Tao Te Ching* (New York: Bantam Books, 1990), 131.

19. See Ban Gu, *Han shu*, chapter 53.

Scholars texts, like the *Sunzi* 孫子, *Mozi* 墨子, *Zhuangzi* 莊子, *Mengzi* 孟子, *Guanzi* 管子, and *Xunzi* 荀子, among others. Such contextualization, which is certainly crucial to a historical understanding of the *Laozi*, and is probably also important to a philosophical understanding of it, is a little beyond the scope of the present translation.

Key Concepts

Before turning to the text, it may be helpful to familiarize ourselves with some important ideas in it, because the *Laozi* is a poetic, elliptical, and sly book. There are certainly more key concepts in the *Laozi* than the twenty articulated here, but I chose these as "key" and limited myself to twenty for reasons of space. I have divided the following list into cosmology and self-cultivation, with ten concepts apiece.

Cosmology

1. The Way and its metaphors: The word "way" (*dao* 道) is similar to the English word "way," insofar as it can refer to a literal path or road that one walks on, or to a metaphorical "way" of doing something like, say, playing the piano, or living your life. Though Chinese does not use an alphabet, and thus has no upper- or lowercase letters, when the "way" being referred to is the way of the entire cosmos, then I use the uppercase "Way." Further, classical Chinese has no definite or indefinite articles (i.e., no "the" or "a"), so these must be inferred for an English translation. Classical Chinese also has no singular or plural markers. Thus, scholars may disagree both about what *kind* of "way" is being referred to (cosmic or other) and also about how *many* "ways" are being referred to. The cosmic Way of the *Laozi* is not a thing made of matter, but is rather a principle.[1] The best analogy I know of is gravity: we can say that gravity "creates" things by being a fundamental

---

1. *Zhuangzi* chapter 16: "The Way is principle" (道，理也). Laozi's "Way" is not unlike Hindu *dharma*, and specifically its *rita dharma* (cosmic law); it is also similar to the early Greek idea of *logos* (principle of order, among other meanings).

12 | The Annotated *Laozi* 老子

force that "makes" things with mass be drawn to one another.[2] The verbs "creates" and "makes" in the previous sentence are in scare quotes because both imply, or can be taken to imply, intentionality, and intentionality implies consciousness, and gravity is not conscious. The same is true of the Way of Laozi: it can metaphorically be said to "create" the cosmos (see chs. 6, 21, 25, and 51), but it "acts" without intentionality: the Way is simply how things naturally evolve. But things do not "naturally evolve" in a vacuum: the laws of physics constrain and shape them. The Way of the *Laozi* points to the reality that the universe is, in fact, organized, rather than being an undifferentiated cloud or soup of random atoms or chemicals. The difference between a cosmos and chaos is the ordering principle for which Laozi had no real name, so he decided to simply call it the "Way" (ch. 25), which ultimately is just "the *way* things are."

The "Way" is, as it were, a "pen name" that Laozi applied to the natural order of the cosmos, but he also uses several poetic metaphors for it. These include:

> *the One* (chs. 10, 22, 39), which points to the fundamental unity of the cosmos;
>
> *root of Heaven and Earth* (ch. 6), for being the foundation of the cosmos;
>
> *ancestor of the myriad things* (ch. 4), for being the origin of the things between Heaven and Earth;
>
> *great semblance* (ch. 35; but also ch. 14 as "a semblance in nothingness"), as when inchoate things are on the cusp of becoming recognizable, so called because it is hard to see, and it heralds the birth of new things;
>
> *uncarved block (of wood)* (chs. 32, 37; but also used as a sagely goal in chs. 15, 19, 28, 57), a metaphor for rustic simplicity and innate potentiality;
>
> *mother* (chs. 20, 25, 52, 59), which denotes its productivity (as well as tenacity and protectiveness: consider how mothers protect their young, or how life comes back even after a devastating fire, or how plants grow up through the tiniest crack in concrete, thanks to "Mother" Earth);

---

2. This analogy is supported by the final sentence of chapter 32: "Metaphorically, the Way is in the world as creeks in valleys flow into rivers and oceans."

valley spirit (ch. 6), for depth, fecundity, and mystery;

water (chs. 8, 34, 78), which illustrates both flexibility and the willingness to humbly inhabit even the lowest places;

female (chs. 6, 10, 28, 55, 61), for fecundity (ch. 6), humble, adaptable flexibility (ch. 28), and effective, tranquil conciliation (ch. 61);

empty vessel (ch. 4), but a magical one, inasmuch as it never gets full;

supply wagon (ch. 26), because it gives us what we need; and

chief executioner (ch. 74), because it, ultimately, "decides" our fates.

2. Cosmogony: The *Laozi* has two cosmogonies, in chs. 21 and 51. Chapter 21 is a Yin interior cosmogony, while chapter 51 is Yang exterior. The first posits a five step creation: the Way, semblances, things, essences, and genuineness. The second has four steps: the Way, virtuosity, other things, and circumstances. But the text also has an *implicit* cosmogony, based on hints throughout the narrative, that is possible to reconstruct. This implicit cosmogony posits an abiding (though not necessarily eternal) material cosmos (i.e., Heaven and Earth and the myriad things in and between them) that began with a formlessness from which our formed cosmos spontaneously emerged (chs. 1, 40). We may further infer that not only does form arise from formlessness, but that it returns to formlessness and starts the cyclical process over, in an abiding (but not necessarily eternal) cycle (chs. 25, 40). Combining all this evidence results in a unified theory of creation that looks like this: In the beginning there was a gravity-like principle that we call the Way, as well as formless "material" that we call "physical energies" (see below). The Way first caused the "semblances" of things to arise: these are on the cusp of formlessness and form. These "semblances" evolved—guided by the gravity-like Way—into forms: specific types of things, like rocks and humans. These individual types of things are then shaped into individual things, individual rocks and humans, by two interior and two exterior processes. The exterior processes are "other things" (like other rocks or other humans) and "circumstances" (like where and when the rock or human evolves). The interior processes are "essence" (for non-living things, their structural development: think of the growth of crystals; and for living things, their ability to reproduce: one literal definition of "essence" is in fact "semen"), and "genuineness." This "genuineness" is an individual thing's individuality. It is what makes this piece of malachite different from that piece. One way to understand the entire purpose of the *Laozi* is to see the

14 | The Annotated *Laozi* 老子

text as encouragement for individual humans to realize their individuality, who they "genuinely" are.

3. Physical energies: *Qi* (氣) is that which everything is made of; we might think of it as "matter," if "matter" did not imply something inert and lumpen. *Qi*, translated here as "physical energies"—as both physical matter and the energy that moves it—in contrast, is dynamic, self-moving, and self-structuring: think of the water in clouds morphing into rain or snow or sleet, coming down, flowing in rivers, and evaporating back up into the clouds, in the continuous and ever-changing hydrologic cycle. Or think of the various (and changing) conditions of the "matter" in your breath, saliva, blood, muscles, cartilage, and bones. The term "physical energies" occurs in chapters 10, 42, and 55, and these showcase the term's flexibility and broad semantic parameters. In chapters 10 and 55, it refers to our individual bodies and energies, while in chapter 42, it refers to non-specific, cosmic physical substances and energies, close to the English words "matter" and "energy," as "that which constitutes and creates materiality," generally construed. I do not know of a single English word that conveys this "dynamic, ever-evolving, self-structuring, fundamental constituent," so "physical energies" will have to do for now.

4. Yin-Yang (陰陽): *Qi*, or physical energy, is often described as having two basic modalities, one active and one stable or receptive (the usual antonym to "active" is "passive," but this carries an unfortunate negative connotation), that might be conceived as analogous to the positive and negative charges of electricity, though a better analogy might be the spectrum of temperature from hot to cold.[3] Yin and Yang appear in the text only once, in chapter 42, but the dichotomy is implied in chapter 28 and, indeed, throughout the text. A Yin-Yang analytic is at work in cosmology, as the next key concept will show, and in anthropology, as the sixth key concept will show.

But I think the most trenchant use of the Yin-Yang idea manifests in all of the key concepts for self-cultivation detailed here. For example, unlearning, introspection, non-contrivance, contentment are all certainly good bits of advice, but implicit in each of them is their opposite: after unlearning, there must be learning; after introspection, there must be action;

---

3. Sometimes the either-or of positive-negative will work better, as with life-death; but often there are a range of conditions that may be situated along a spectrum between two poles, as with contrived-uncontrived action.

non-contrivance is ideal for one's personal life, but contrivance is necessary for one's social and professional life; a certain degree of contentment is certainly necessary for happiness, but there are times when discontent will be crucial for beneficial change. In a world of clear Yang-specific norms and rules, there will be times—sometimes very *decisive* times—where fuzzy Yin contingency must contravene them. Recognizing this truth, to me, is the genius of Yin-Yang thinking.

5. Heaven-Earth (天地): Cosmologically, what we now call the "universe" or the "cosmos" was conceived as a Heaven-Earth dyad, with Heaven being Yang active (think of the constant movement of the sun, moon, stars, meteors, clouds, etc.) and Earth being Yin receptive. The Yin-receptive proclivity of physical energy resonates with the image of "Mother Earth," receptive to the thunder, lightning, and rain of Heaven. It is patient, enduring, and fecund, and thereby has its own kind of strength (just not the showy, Yang-Heavenly kind, which features storms and eclipses). The "mutual union of Heaven and Earth" in chapter 32 gives us a foundational (and metaphorically conjugal) image for cosmic genesis. Thus, instead of a single (usually male) deity commanding the cosmos into existence, here we have Heaven and Earth as our ultimate parents, and procreation as the means, in a cosmogony that extends to our own existence. That is, whereas the most popular religions on our planet posit an immortal creator-god that said, "Let it be," and then it was, early China has an abiding *qi*-substance, or "physical energy," with shifting Yin-Yang states of being (or, rather, "becoming"), causing a cyclical formless-form dynamic, and these cosmic interactions, from the point of view of those of us on Earth, appear to us through the Heaven-Earth dyad.[4]

Many centuries later, Shinto would describe the same dynamic in its creation story involving the sexual union of Izanagi and Izanami, but despite the imagery of chapter 32, I don't think the primary cosmological image for Laozi is a conjugal Heaven and Earth. That union is certainly

---

4. A thousand and more years later, Zhang Zai 張載 (1020–1077) would write his "Western Inscription" (西銘) that says: "Heaven is my father and Earth is my mother, and even such a small creature as I finds an intimate place in their midst. Therefore that which extends throughout the universe I regard as my body and that which directs the universe I consider as my nature. All people are my brothers and sisters, and all things are my companions. . . . In life I follow and serve (Heaven and Earth), and in death I will be at peace" (乾稱父，坤稱母；予茲藐焉，乃混然中處。故天地之塞，吾其體；天地之帥，吾其性。民，吾同胞；物，吾與也. . . . 存吾順事，沒吾寧也).

16 | The Annotated *Laozi* 老子

foundational, but it resides in the background, like some sleeping dragon: important, but mostly out of sight when reading this text. Rather, it is the feeling and perception of nameless mystery that the *Laozi* foregrounds (and, indeed, starts out with in chapter 1): the mystery that the child (and the childlike, though not the childish) feels when turning over rocks in the backyard, or discovering tadpoles in the nearby creek, or waving back to anemones in a tidepool, or finding crystals in a cave. Nevertheless, while the awe of encountering mysterious things, events, and ideas may permeate the text, the Heaven-Earth dyad remains the most salient and (relatively) concrete image for global creation.

6. *Hun-po* 魂魄 (souls): The ontological Yin-Yang dyad is reflected in the cosmological Heaven-Earth dyad, but also in the anthropological Yang-ethereal *hun* soul–Yin-corporeal *po* soul dyad. (Yes, early Chinese texts posit that we have *two* souls.) Only the latter appears in the *Laozi*, and only in chapter 10, but we might presume that the author and their audience were aware of the former. Though this text does not elaborate on these souls, from other early texts we may infer that the Yin-corporeal soul correlates with the body while the Yang-ethereal soul correlates with the creative, cognitive aspects of the mind. These souls are like "life forces" for body and mind, and though they may persist for a time after death, they are not like the deathless, "eternal" souls that some religions posit. Eventually, they, like the body, will decompose and "evaporate."

7. Essence (精) and spirit/ousness (神): If spontaneously moving physical energy can be conceived as a "dance" between its more active and more stable modalities, the impetus for this metaphorical dance, what we might call its "creative edge," is called "essence" (精). This essence appears in only two chapters, once cosmologically and once anthropologically. The first part of chapter 21 is a description of the Way: it is, like a hazy, prescientific theory of gravity, "obscure and hidden," but inasmuch as there must be *some* principle of order in an obviously ordered cosmos, this ostensible Way is, clearly, efficacious. Thus, though "obscure and hidden, yet within it are essences." The "within" is a spatial metaphor, since the Way, again, like gravity, has no "inside" or "outside." If the cosmic Way is like universal gravity, then specific essences are the mysterious causes of change: from whatever it is that "causes" the growth of inanimate crystals to whatever it is that "impels" animate cells to reproduce. The Way acts on, for example, all rocks, but its essences are seen to be at work in the moving luminescence

Key Concepts | 17

of opals and the flow of volcanic lava. Thus, the Way's creativity (again, spontaneous, not intentional) is conceived as the "essence" of general physical energy. The "essence" of anthropological creativity appears in chapter 55 as "essentialness." Here it is in the growth and diversification of biological constituents where the Way is manifesting its creativity.

As "essence" is the "creative edge" of both the cosmos and humans, so "spirit/ousness"[5] (神) is the creative edge of the *conscious* aspects of both the cosmos and humans. In the cosmos, that means literal spirits, as in chapter 39. As unseen, intentional agents, the idea of spirits is ripe for use as a metaphor. The "valley spirit" in chapter 6 might be a literal spirit, but I think it more likely a metaphor for humility (because valleys are low-lying) and fecundity (because valleys often have streams or rivers running through them that support vegetation and because spirits are creative). The "spiritous vessel" in chapter 29 could likewise be construed literally or met-aphorically, either as vessels that literal spirits might use, or as a metaphor for being cleverly and delicately wrought. But the "spirited" in chapter 60 is clearly an adjective that in other early Chinese Scholars texts would denote cognitive creativity, and here denotes a nefarious kind of cognitive creativity (hence my translation as "spirited"—like a "spirited" horse—rather than "spiritous"). That the implications of spiritousness were not clear-cut (much as the implications of "spirituality" in the modern world are not at all clear-cut) in chapter 60 is revealed by how the second, third, and fourth sentences of that chapter tentatively unfold.

8. Yin (陰) **preference** and **formlessness** (無): Though Yin-Yang harmony is the goal, the *Laozi* displays a slight, and perhaps counterintuitive, preference for Yin over Yang. It might be counterintuitive because it is possible (though not certain) that the "way of (Yang) Heaven" is, in fact, shorthand for the "Way" and what could be better than that?[6] But a slight preference for Yin is nevertheless unmistakable. What I am calling a "preference" may simply be the observation that, in the realm of living things, Yang activity, to be efficient, often needs to be preceded by Yin rest. Think of sleeping before

---

5. I use this peculiar locution to denote that the word functions as both a noun ("spirit" and "spiritousness") and as an adjective ("spiritous").

6. Just as gravity is conceived as a cosmic or universal principle, rather than a specifically "earthly" principle, so the "Heavenly way" (天道) or "way of Heaven" (天之道) appears in chapters 9, 47, 73, 77, 79, and 81, but the locution of an "Earthly way" is never used.

18 | The Annotated *Laozi* 老子

waking, or thinking before acting (or planning before doing). Thus, this concept could just be a logical axiom. But there is more to this preference, insofar as the *Laozi* sees Yin flexibility as more effective, in the long run, than Yang "stiff" or "rigid" inflexibility. Hence the use of the "mother" and "female" metaphors for the Way, noted earlier. It would be overstating the case to say that the *Laozi* prefers females to males, but it would be accurate to say that it prefers a stereotypical female "way" of patient flexibility to a stereotypical male "way" of impatient inflexibility, of quiet thoughtfulness over loud bluster. Early Chinese society, like most cultures worldwide, was certainly patriarchal, which adds to the counterintuitiveness—but also to the appeal, even today—of the *Laozi*'s slight Yin preference.

This Yin preference is evident in a number of self-cultivation concepts that we will look at shortly: of relaxed non-contrivance over fretful contrivance, of doubt-embracing fallibilism over overconfident certainty, of humble selflessness over arrogant self-promotion, and of quiet introspection—if not "over," then at least "prior to"—overt action. But it is also evident in the ontological priority of formlessness before form. This, again, may just be a logical inference rather than a conscious preference, insofar as the implied cosmogony posits form spontaneously and naturally evolving out of formlessness (chs. 1, 40). Formlessness, however, is a tricky concept, insofar as we live in a world of concrete forms, and this slipperiness is seen in the variety of words used to convey it. Ontological "formlessness" (無) appears in chapters 1, 2, and 40, but the same Chinese word is also the first half of the adjective-noun phrase "nothingness" (無物) in chapter 14, and I translate the same word (i.e., 無), when applied to the empty spaces in objects like cups and doors, as "openness" in chapter 11 and, when applied to minds, as "open-mindedness" (無心) in chapter 49.[7]

We have spoken of formlessness, nothingness, emptiness, and openness and, in early Chinese just as in modern English, there is more than one word used to convey these ideas. Hence, I use "open-mindedness" for *wuxin* 無心 in chapter 49, but I take this as functionally equivalent to "openness" for *xu* 虛 in chapter 16. Similarly, the idea of formlessness or "nothingness" is implied both by metaphors like the "valley spirit" noted

---

7. The "open" of the English word "open-mindedness" is a spatial metaphor; "empty" is another spatial metaphor, but being "empty-minded" would carry a negative connotation in English that prohibits its use in translation.

earlier, and conveyed by other, synonymous or nearly synonymous words like the "empty" (虛) bellows in chapter 5, the implied emptiness of the "valley" and "gate" metaphors in chapter 6, the "empty" (窪) of "empty then full" in chapter 22, the "empty" (寥) of the "quiet and empty" in chapter 25, and the "empty" (沖) that may characterize "great fullness" in chapter 45. Further, the images of the mother and the female, to the degree that they are metaphors for fecundity, rely upon the (unstated) capacity of an "empty" (but receptive) womb. Clearly, formlessness / nothingness / emptiness / openness is a fundamental trope in the *Laozi*, and this condition, literal or metaphorical, can be taken as evidence for a preference for Yin, just as the author makes use of mother and female metaphors somewhat more often than father (ch. 42) or male (ch. 55) metaphors. When chapter 28 says, "Know the male, but preserve the female," both knowing and preserving are important activities, but the latter is slightly *more* important.

9. The myriad things (萬物): This is simply a term for all the things that exist within the Heaven-Earth dyad. Humans are one of them. The term appears in too many chapters to list here (but they are listed in the index).

10. Virtuosity (德): The modern Chinese word for "ethics" is *daode* 道德, which brings together two ancient Chinese concepts: the macro and the micro, the cosmic Way and the individual way, the latter of which is translated here as individual "virtuosity." This individual way applies to all of the myriad things, both as particular species and as individuals within communities. "Virtuosity" was chosen for translation in order to bring to mind two related words: the practical skillfulness of a "virtuoso" and the "virtues" of ethically good people. Both technical virtuosos and ethically virtuous people often manifest a charisma that we mere mortals might characterize as "mysterious." In the *Laozi*, the term appears in fifteen chapters, and can refer to an aspirational state (or states) that all humans might seek, including the expansive "mysterious virtuosity" (玄德) in chapter 10, the focused "pervasive virtuosity" (孔德) in chapter 21, the slight Yin preference of "abiding virtuosity" (恆德) in chapter 28, and the practical "ingrained virtuosity" (積德) in chapter 59. There is "lofty virtuosity" (上德) and "lowly virtuosity" (下德) in chapter 38, and people "with virtuosity" (有德) and "without virtuosity" (無德) in chapter 79. Chapter 54 notes that the person (身), the family (家), the community (鄉), the state (邦), and the world (天下) each have their own virtuosities, or ideal ways

20 | The Annotated *Laozi* 老子

of functioning.[8] Ghosts are said to have virtuosity in chapter 60. We are asked to "requite resentment with virtuosity" (報怨以德) in chapter 79. The word can also be used to characterize specific virtues, as in the "virtuous competence" (德善) and "virtuous trustworthiness" (德信) in chapter 49,[9] as well as "the virtuosity of non-contentiousness" (不爭之德) in chapter 68. The close connection between the Way and virtuosity is described in chapters 23, 51, 55, and 65. All these kinds of virtuosities suggest a variety of ways of optimally functioning in the world, from something as specific as your own individual person, through virtuosities that all humans might aspire to, to the virtuosity of the cosmic Way itself. Some of the specifics of these human virtuosities are articulated in the following ten concepts.

Self-Cultivation

The aspirational goal(s) articulated in the *Laozi* are for us to become (or aim to become) sages (聖) who "accord with" (同於; ch. 23) the Way[10]—the natural principle(s) of Heaven and Earth—and thereby gain competence (善) in our uncontrived actions. One piece of self-cultivation advice that the author gives us to realize this goal we have already seen in the appreciation given to the formless and empty and open aspects of our physical world. Other bits of advice include the following.

11. Language skepticism: In contradistinction to the trust that religious people of a literal bent with ostensibly infallible scriptures place in the words of those texts, the *Laozi* begins by casting doubt on the reliability of language (ch. 1: "a name that can be [fully] descriptive is not an abiding name"). Part of this may be due to the underlying assumption that everything in the cosmos

---

8. These five might bring to mind the four *dharma*s of Hinduism: the individual way (*svadharma*), the way of those at a particular stage in life (*ashrama dharma*), the way of one's caste (*varna dharma*), and the cosmic way (*rita dharma*).

9. These might also have been translated as "virtuoso-level competence" and "virtuoso-level trustworthiness."

10. Several other verbs are used to characterize our ideal relationship with the Way: we are to "grasp" (執; ch. 14), "protect" (保; ch. 15), "follow" (從; ch. 21), "pursue activities with" (從事於; ch. 23), be "with" (在; ch. 24), "have" or "be with" (有; chs. 24, 31, 77), "comply with" (法; ch. 25), "use" (以; chs. 30, 60, 65), "know" (知; ch. 47), "pursue" (為; ch. 48), and (metaphorically) "walk" (行; ch. 53) it, as well as not "abandon" (癈; ch. 18), "lose" (失; ch. 38), or be "without" (無; ch. 46) it.

Key Concepts | 21

is in flux, as well as that language itself inevitably changes over time (as it also does across space). This skepticism is certainly clear with respect to the "Way" being something of a temporary placeholder, akin to a writer's "pen name" (chs. 1, 14, 25, 41).[11] Similarly, in chapters 22 and 36, the logical relativity of linguistic adjectives is recast with a focus on probable change: sometimes "empty" things are made "full." It also is implied in chapter 2, where the relativity of adjectives (like "long and short") is highlighted, and in chapter 12, where the limitations of conventional descriptors for colors, sounds, and flavors is lamented. This skepticism is probably connected to the feeling of being "hazy" and ostensibly "stupid" that the author feels in chapter 20. Further, we are reminded that sages favor "wordless teaching" over authoring texts (chs. 2, 43). And there is the claim that "to rarely speak is natural" (ch. 23). Chapters 41, 45, 58, and 67 remind us that things are not always as they appear, and this insight, too, implies the provisional status of the language used to describe those things.

Another aspect of Laozi's "language skepticism" questions specific words or specific kinds of words. Examples of these begin in chapter 2, with "beautiful" and "competent" interrogated for their (potential) imprecision, and more are adduced throughout the text. Thus, when chapter 32 says "once there were names, there also should have been a knowing when to stop," I don't think the author was referring to "names" like "blue" or "chair," but rather to words like "beautiful" and "competent," the definitions of which will always, to some extent, lie in the eye of the beholder. "Skepticism" may be a loaded term for those with a background in philosophy, but I use it here only in its plain, everyday sense of highlighting the prudence of caution and not assuming that words mean the same thing for all people in all places at all times. The *Laozi* reminds us of such caution in its final chapter, which opens with: "Trustworthy words are not (always) beautiful, and beautiful words are not (always) trustworthy."

12. Fallibilism: The underlying attitude of fallibilism in the *Laozi* may be the single most important piece of advice in the entire text. There is no technical term for "fallibilism" in classical Chinese and, indeed, the English word does not hold much currency among English speakers. As

---

11. The reticence to assign a permanent name to what we (still) refer to as the "Way" should not, however, be taken to imply that there is *nothing* that can be said about it, as some people construe the first half of the first sentence of chapter 1. If that were true, then the author could not have continued on to write another eighty chapters on it.

22 | The Annotated *Laozi* 老子

with "skepticism," I use "fallibilism" here not in any technical, academic sense, but rather to describe the attitude that underlies the saying "Don't believe everything you think." That is, be aware that no human has ever known *all* the facts about a given situation, and that new information is always being discovered. If you are an expert in something, by all means, be confident in your expertise (if it is truly warranted), just also keep in mind that tomorrow may bring new evidence that may slightly alter, or even completely change, it.[12] Though the term "fallibilism" was coined only in the late nineteenth century (by Charles Peirce), the idea that we could be wrong about things we think we know is in the ca. 400 BCE *Laozi*. This attitude is revealed in a number of ways.

One way is the language skepticism described previously: if we cannot be certain that our language is dependable, then we cannot be certain that the claims we make, in language, about the world, are infallible. Another indication is the text's explicit and repeated endorsements of humility (chs. 22, 24, 28, 29, 30, 61) and caution (chs. 9, 13, 15, 50, 60, 73). A third implication is in the flexibility and open-mindedness to be discussed later. It also may well be related to the use of the word "mystery" (玄; chs. 1, 6, 10, 15, 51, 56, 65), insofar as this word is employed to describe things that we do not yet know, as well as those things we may never know. But the most trenchant evidence for fallibilism is in the opening words of chapter 71, "To know when you do not know is best, and to not know but think that you *do* know is a kind of sickness."[13]

13. Non-anthropocentrism and ethics: Anthropocentrism is the idea that humans are the most valuable entities in the universe, that we *ánthrōpos* (Greek: "humans") are somehow at the center of the cosmos. Anthropo-

---

12. David Deutsch, in his *The Beginning of Infinity* (New York: Penguin Books, 2011), says that fallibilism is basic to science, and says, "Fallibilists expect even their best and most fundamental explanations to contain misconceptions in addition to truth, and so they are predisposed to try to change them for the better. . . . The logic of fallibilism is that one not only seeks to correct the misconceptions of the past, but hopes in the future to find and change mistaken ideas that no one today questions or finds problematic" (9).

13. This sentence seems to summarize what is now known as the "Dunning-Kruger effect" formulated in 1999. This effect was studied by the social psychologists David Dunning and Justin Kruger, and is a cognitive bias whereby humans tend to have greater confidence in topics about which they know little and, conversely, also describes how our confidence actually fades the more one learns about said topic (i.e., the more you know, the more you know that you don't know).

Key Concepts | 23

centrism is implied, for example, in the "Genesis" creation story, with the creation of humans being the last, and implicitly best, of all things: the "pinnacle" of creation. The *Laozi* does not explicitly argue against such anthropocentrism, but it also does not assume or imply it. The Way is the way of everything—all the "myriad things"—not just humans (chs. 34, 51). The cosmogonies described earlier are notable for not even mentioning humans. Aspirational figures include the sage, who is certainly human but, unlike in other early Chinese texts, here there are no specific, named, historical aspirational figures. Rather, we find aspirational "figures" in the myriad things themselves (chs. 34, 51), as well as in Heaven and Earth (chs. 5, 23); valleys (chs. 6, 15, 28, 41); water (chs. 8, 78), including mountain streams (ch. 28), rivers and oceans (chs. 32, 66), and river deltas (ch. 61); (tree) roots (chs. 16, 39); plants and trees (ch. 76); and even bows (ch. 77).[14]

A non-anthropocentric worldview without deities invites the question of how to derive one's ethics. If not from divine entities, or "prophets" working on behalf of divine entities, or specific authoritative individuals, where should readers of the *Laozi* turn for ethical advice? I am a sinologist and not a professional ethicist, but I nevertheless see eight ways in which humans derive ethics, and these eight paradigms fit into three categories: individual rules, community rules, and non-human rules. The "individual rules" category has only one paradigm: (1) follow your conscience (aka natural law). This is often a good rule, and one that Laozi espouses too, unless one is a psychopath or sociopath, in which case the rest of the community might beg you to *not* follow your conscience. The "community rules" category contains four paradigms: (2) majority rules (aka majoritarianism), which sounds fair but leaves individuals open to the "tyranny of the majority"; (3) ethical pluralism, which attempts, with varying degrees of success, to embrace a variety of differing cultural norms, along with some legal mandates that everyone must accept; (4) outcome-based rules, like Kant's categorical imperative or Bentham's utilitarianism; and (5) amoralism, which (gingerly) replaces morals with love and law (the former for family and the latter for strangers).[15] The "non-human rules" category has three paradigms. The most well known is (6) divine command, whereby a deity (or its prophet or book) commands

---

14. Counterevidence to this claim is in the aspirational figures of mothers and females, noted earlier in the "metaphors of the Way" paragraph, as well as in infants (chs. 10, 28, 55), noted for their flexibility and reliance on the "mother."

15. This kind of amoralism is described and defended by Hans-Georg Moeller in his *The Moral Fool: A Case for Amorality* (New York: Columbia University Press, 2009).

24 | The Annotated *Laozi* 老子

us to do certain things (e.g., the "Ten Commandments"); (7) ancient ethical realism, whereby we are to derive our ethics, predicated on the prima facie goals of social harmony and individual well-being, on nature;[16] and (8) modern ethical realism, whereby we are to derive our ethics, predicated on the prima facie goal of "well-being," on science.[17]

As I read it, the *Laozi* implicitly espouses the first, "follow your conscience," the third, "ethical pluralism," the fifth, "amoralism" (*if* we assume that "morality," by definition, includes a degree of outrage and judgmentalism), and last, "ancient ethical realism," with ethics derived from certain, specific aspects of nature. (For example, we should be trustworthy, just as Heaven's seasons reliably come and go, and we should be competently productive, just as Earth competently produces all flora and, by extension, all fauna.) This latter, ethical realism, is in a sense the most fundamental, insofar as our exemplars precede the existence of humans. It is also by definition non-anthropocentric, insofar as we are to look not to any human authority or anthropomorphic deity, but to the mute cosmos itself, for our ethics.[18]

Fallibilism operates within ethical realism by maintaining an attitude of "let's see what works and change our rules as necessary." The natural world is both a harmonious ecosystem *and* "red in tooth and claw," and though activities associated with the latter may perhaps be easily dismissed as not conducive to social harmony, there are many activities associated with the

---

16. Mark Lewis does not use the phrase "ethical realism," but he does note a reciprocity between "the natural world" and "the human world" in his discussion of the *Odes* and *Changes* classics: "This [implicit reciprocity] suggests that the idea of a correspondence between the natural and human realms emerged out of the ancient social and religious milieu in which the phenomena of the natural world were scrutinized and recorded as guides to human actions." See his *Writing and Authority in Early China* (Albany: State University of New York Press, 1999), 263.

17. This kind of modern ethical realism is described and defended by Sam Harris in his *The Moral Landscape: How Science Can Determine Human Values* (New York: Free Press, 2010).

18. Ethical realism is a niche academic pursuit, insofar as "Hume's guillotine"—the claim that no ethical "oughts" can be derived from any thing that empirically "is"—is thought by many professional ethicists to be ironclad. Harris (see previous note) argues against this, saying that there can be no coherent ethics that do *not* include human well-being, and therefore striving for well-being is not something we "ought" to do, but something that we cannot *not* do (with, perhaps, exceptions for psychopaths and sociopaths). In any case, whether or not the *Laozi*'s implicit a priori value of the "flourishing" of the myriad things (including harmonious human societies and the well-being of individuals) escapes "Hume's guillotine," it is too far outside my field of expertise to speculate further.

former that we humans should consider. Fallibilism is the engine of the process that considers which things to emulate, under what circumstances, and when to change our collective minds about old practices that didn't work out.

In any case, a non-anthropocentric worldview does not deny the importance of human action. Chapter 37 notes that if humans in positions of power would abide by the Way, then "the myriad things would develop themselves." This ultimately implies a "hands-off" approach to an evolving environment, but it also implies that rulers who do *not* abide by the Way will impede the development of those myriad things. And chapter 39 adds that if those same people in positions of power were to abide by the Way, then the world would be "made . . . correct." A thing that is "correct" (正) is a thing that has successfully realized its virtuosity. Human values, wherever they are derived from, certainly have consequences for all of the myriad things.

But as powerful as humans are in the environmental scheme of things, the *Laozi* contrasts the "way of Heaven" with the "way of humans" (ch. 77), and the latter is characterized as decidedly unjust (and biased and vain and probably selfish). The way of Heaven and Earth is characterized as impartial (ch. 5), but it (or rather, the way of Heaven) nevertheless naturally "seeks" equilibrium, in that it "reduces excess and increases what is insufficient" (ch. 77). Further, though "it has no favorites," it "abides with competent people" (ch. 79) and "benefits but does not harm" (ch. 81). Thus, this Way may be impartial, but it nevertheless has certain "inclinations," just as we might say that gravity—or any natural principle, or "law of nature"—is impartial, but it still describes certain proclivities. That the law of gravity "dictates" that things with greater masses will experience greater gravitational pull may be construed as somehow "unjust" with regard to things with lesser masses, does not change the fact of the principle.[19]

14. Unlearning: *Laozi* chapter 64 contains the typically poetic (and ostensibly contradictory) advice to "learn to not learn." Similarly, chapter 20 opens with "Relinquish . . . learning." And chapter 48 opens with the claim, "Those who pursue . . . learning increase every day, while those who pursue the Way reduce every day." Some interpreters of the *Laozi* take such statements to mean that

---

19. Another analogy may be found in the dynamics of animal populations. Evolution is "impartial," and yet typical predators (e.g., wolves) have fewer offspring than their prey (e.g., rabbits). But this is not because evolution, or nature, somehow "favors" rabbits (assuming that more offspring is "better" than fewer).

26 | The Annotated *Laozi* 老子

the author is advising rulers to keep their citizens stupid, because this will make them easier to govern and control. I side with those who think that such claims, in the context of the book as a whole, are implicitly only against certain *kinds* of learning. Specifically, the *Laozi* is against *contrived* learning (and thinking and acting); hence my understanding of these three passages as "learn to not learn (contrivedly)," "relinquish (contrived) learning," and "those who pursue (contrived) learning." (I discuss "non-contrivance" later.) By the same logic, contrived *virtues* are criticized in chapters 5, 18, 19, and 38.[20] Likewise, contrived *mental categories* are disparaged in chapters 2, 3, 10, and 12; the advice to "think outside the box" is a modern, idiomatic, English metaphor, but the *Laozi* clearly implies it.

One reason to engage in "unlearning" is the *Laozi*'s contention that things are not always as they seem (chs. 41, 45, 58, 67).[21] For example, chapter 41 says "great purity may (sometimes) seem disgraceful." For a hypothetical illustration of this, consider the following scenario: let us say that a particular culture has a norm whereby "men should not touch women (whom they do not know)," and that following this norm is considered a matter of "great purity." Without an articulated list of exceptions, what should be said of the man who rescues a drowning woman (whom they do not know)? A literalist might call such a man "disgraceful" for breaking the rule, but a more flexible reading of the norm would say he did the right thing.[22] Hence, things are not always as they seem. In fact, as we saw earlier, the final chapter revisits this theme, opening with "Trustworthy words are not (always) beautiful, and beautiful words are not (always) trustworthy."

Reading between the lines, and gathering the various strands of evidence in the previous two paragraphs, I construe the *Laozi*'s advice for us to "unlearn" as a specific (albeit implicit) suggestion: when we "come of age," and become adults, we should cast a critical eye upon all that we

---

20. By "By the same logic," I mean that the claim "learn to not learn" is a simple contradiction. Similarly, the author cannot be against *all* virtuosity (as implied by reading the opening statements of chapters 18–19 without my added parentheticals), because chapter 51 says, "all the myriad things venerate the Way and value virtuosity," and other chapters are also "pro-virtuosity." For one specific example, "filiality" (孝) is bad in chapter 18 but good in chapter 19. So either the author is contradicting themselves or, as I claim, they are only against *certain kinds* of learning and virtuosities (and actions and categories, etc.).

21. This claim, or observation, could also be used to support the advice for fallibilism.

22. This illustration comes from another early Chinese text, *Mengzi* 4A17, which advises us to "weigh the circumstances" (權) when applying the norms of virtue.

Key Concepts | 27

have uncritically absorbed while growing up, and make conscious decisions about which (familial and cultural) norms to keep, and which to reject.[23] Daoist "unlearning," then, may be said to underlie the attitude behind the slogan "Question authority."[24]

15. Introspection: The ontological priority of formlessness, and the *Laozi*'s slight Yin preference, manifest themselves in the advice for psychological introspection. Introspection is hinted at with the "root" metaphor (chs. 6, 16, 26, 39, 59), the "valley" metaphor (chs. 6, 15, 28, 41), the "(precious) jade" that sages hide within their clothes metaphor (ch. 70), and the spatial metaphor of "In the mind, competence lies in *depth*" (ch. 8). Inwardness can also be seen in the "know thyself" advice of chapter 33, as well as the (poetically hyperbolic) "The farther one goes, the less one knows" of chapter 47. The prevalence of emotional tranquility in the text (chs. 15, 16, 20, 26, 37, 45, 57, 61) may also be construed as hinting at introspection, insofar as the former is (often) requisite for the latter. The clearest evidence, however, is seen in the chapter 5 advice to "preserve what is within," as well as in the chapter 1 advice to "abide in formlessness." Nevertheless, the most poetically compelling evidence comes from a line that is repeated twice in the *Laozi*: "blunt the sharpness, untangle the knots, soften the glare" (chs. 4, 56). This very much sounds like settling down to look within.

16. Non-contrivance (無為): Non-contrivance is almost certainly the most well-known piece of self-cultivation advice in the *Laozi*.[25] It describes the state of acting genuinely, unselfconsciously, or, as we might say, "from the heart," as opposed to doing something self-consciously, because others expect you to, or because you are coerced. It explicitly appears in chapters 2, 3,

---

23. From such a program of "unlearning" (and subsequent "relearning" as critical-thinking adults), one can easily extrapolate a support for individualism within the broader community. I note this because Daoist individualism is often contrasted with Ruist (Confucian) hierarchy and regard for the community over the individual.

24. Ruism (Confucianism), on the other hand, would support the competing slogan "Question authority (and write down the answers)." These two positions, we might note, while diametric, are not thereby incompatible.

25. Often unfortunately (and inaccurately) translated as "inaction," this word, pronounced *wu wei* in Chinese, is the subject of two quite different books by Edward Slingerland: *Effortless Action: Wu-wei as Conceptual Metaphor in Early China* (New York: Oxford University Press, 2003), and *Trying Not to Try: Ancient China, Modern Science, and the Power of Spontaneity* (New York: Broadway Books, 2014).

28 | The Annotated *Laozi* 老子

10, 37, 38, 43, 48, 57, 63, and 64 but, as I read the text, it is implied in many more chapters than these ten. In the *Laozi*, non-contrivance is explicitly linked with the relativity of perspective (chs. 2, 3) or mental flexibility (chs. 43, 48, 57, 64), but the notion that this state of mind is a result of *practice* is most clear in chapters 48 (where one must consciously decrease contrivances before "one arrives at non-contrivance") and 54 (implied via the advice to "cultivate" the Way), but I think it is implied throughout the text. (The "practice makes perfect" approach to non-contrivance is clearer in the *Zhuangzi*, with two notable stories of craftspeople honing their skills over many years.) Non-contrivance is, like sagacity and competence, an aspirational goal, but like all the other pieces of self-cultivation advice noted here, it is not an all-or-nothing achievement, and is rather a matter of degree.

As central as non-contrivance is to the *Laozi*, it is nevertheless a rule of thumb, and not an immutable law never to be contravened. No one likes to force a smile, or to feel compelled to use blathering jargon, or to abide by myriad social conventions . . . but sometimes we must, if we want to belong to a variety of social groups (including one's own family).[26] As with the rule of thumb for men to not touch women that they do not know, with exceptions for things like saving drowning women, so the rule of thumb to be uncontrived is a good one, with certain exceptions that only the individual will be able to decide upon.

Though "non-contrivance" is the most famous instance of this "negative" locution (i.e., non- or without-X: 無-X), the author employs several others. These are, unfortunately, not always easily identifiable in the translation, though they are obvious in the Chinese. They include "without (contrived) knowledge" (無知), "without (contrived) desires" (無欲), "selfless" or "without (a contrived) self" (無私), "nameless" or "without (contrived) names" (無名), "without (contrived) activities" (無事), and "open-minded" or "without (a contrived) mind" (無心).

17. Flexibility (柔, 弱):[27] Mental flexibility is implied by the pervasive use of water metaphors in the *Laozi*, as water is a paragon of flexibility (ch.

---

26. A few centuries later, the early Chinese scholar Xunzi 荀子 would make this case most persuasively.

27. I translate two Chinese graphs as "flexible," except when they occur together, in which case I translate *rou* 柔 as "flexible" and *ruan* 弱 as "supple." One or both of these appear in chapters 3 (弱), 10 (柔), 36 (柔弱), 40 (弱), 43 (柔), 52 (弱), 55 (弱柔), 76 (柔弱), and 78 (柔弱).

Key Concepts | 29

78: "Nothing in the world is more flexible and supple than water"). In fact, the concepts of language skepticism, fallibilism, non-anthropocentrism, and unlearning all assume (and require) a considerable degree of mental flexibility. Flexibility is specifically recommended for the will (ch. 3) and implicitly for the mind (ch. 10), but perhaps the most trenchant claim is that "flexibility is the utility of the Way" (ch. 40), implying that it is simply a useful attitude to have. If, as noted two paragraphs earlier, these "key concepts" involve a balancing of competing proclivities to appropriately fit a variety of situations, then flexibility is precisely the virtue of being able to make those choices.

Ethically speaking, many people recoil at the thought of being "ethically flexible," but I have never met anyone who objected to the ethical flexibility in the aforementioned story of the man who saved a drowning woman. It is easy to say "thou shalt not steal" or "thou shalt not kill," but I am confident that everyone who abides by these rules is, in fact, flexible in their application (or, at least, could be, in theory). But even if one rejects flexibility in ethics, it seems incontestable that patient adaptability is an effective strategy for navigating the multifarious vicissitudes of life.

18. Simplicity (樸): The penultimate chapter of the *Laozi* paints a picture of a simple life. For some, such a picture is a nostalgic reminiscence of a past, bucolic age where simplicity was a prized virtue. The Chinese word for "simplicity" in the *Laozi* derives from the rustic image of an "uncarved block of wood."[28] But the *idea* (and ideal) of simplicity is implicated in several other suggestions in the text. We may infer it, for example, in the suggestions (sometimes only implied) to discard "excess" (chs. 29, 44, 50, 53, 77) and "ostentatiousness" (chs. 22, 24, 35, 58, 72). We may also connect it to the goal of "frugality" (chs. 59, 67) and the chapter 81 claim that "Sages do not accumulate, since the more they do for others, the greater their gain." Excessive or contrived desire is also problematized in this book, with chapter 64 saying (again, playing with ostensible contradiction) that "sages desire to not desire (contrivedly)." Chapter 19 concludes with a fairly concise summary of much of the *Laozi*: "manifest purity, embrace simplicity, reduce selfishness, and decrease (contrived) desires."

---

28. Simplicity is the most commonly derived meaning from this image (chs. 19, 32, 37, 57), but two other meanings are "solidity" (ch. 15) and "potentiality" (ch. 28), both of which are intuitively derivable from it.

30 | The Annotated *Laozi* 老子

19. Contentment (知足): Contentment is also tangentially related to simplicity. In the (hyperbolic) "good ol' days" scene depicted in chapter 80, the people "have boats and vehicles" but "no one will ride them," not because they are incurious, but because they are so content with their lives as they are. Contentment is also implicit in the "belly" (which is easily filled) versus "eye" (which, for some, is always looking around for more) comparison in chapter 12. Contentment is adduced as an explicit goal in chapters 33, 44, and 46, with the latter claiming, "no calamity is sadder than (always) wanting more; no misfortune is greater than not knowing contentment."

But contentment, as we noted earlier with non-contrivance, raises an enduring problem that nearly everyone, at some time in their life, must negotiate. The problem arises from conflating contentment with indifference and inertia. If one is "fully" content, then why put energy into effecting change? Ideal contentment, then, implies a (Yin-Yang) balance. This balance has both an inner and an outer aspect. The inner aspect is seen in that old chestnut, the "work-life balance." In a society, or even just a situation, where success requires excess, one's work-life balance may be an ongoing, lifelong consideration. The outer aspect might be articulated as a "flexibility versus fortitude" balance, thereby implicating the aforementioned advice to be flexible in our interactions with others. Certainly, it is often good to be flexible: such an attitude reduces stubbornness and friction and increases creativity and harmony. On the other hand, too much flexibility results in spinelessness: sometimes one should stand up for what (one thinks) is right. This delicate problem is hinted at in chapter 44, which concludes that we should "know (when and where) to stop and do not fall into danger," implying that we should be flexible until the point of "danger." But the risk assessment of danger varies from person to person. And this advice does not take into account the decision of when we should show fortitude on behalf of *other people*. The problem(s) involved with contentment remains as interesting as ever.

20. Non-contentiousness (不爭): Non-contentiousness might also be implicated in the "flexibility versus fortitude" problem in the previous paragraph, and insofar as "contention" implies violence, it accords with the "do not fall into danger" advice of chapter 44. Exactly when violence is justified is another interesting, enduring problem, but it is not a question addressed in the *Laozi*. This text is certainly not pacifist, insofar as weapons are construed as necessary (chs. 57, 69, 80), albeit unfortunate (chs. 30, 31, 50). Non-contentiousness, rather, is more a strategy for self-cultivation than a

Key Concepts | 31

political (or military) maxim. It shows up as early as chapter 3, is used to describe the quintessential Daoist metaphor of water (ch. 8), is predicated of "the way of Heaven" (ch. 73), and is the last word of the entire text: "the way of sages acts but is not contentious."

All ten of these key concepts in self-cultivation might be stated in Yin-Yang form, and thereby all might be considered paradoxes, as claims that might appear self-contradictory but that actually express a truth that requires balancing. We should be skeptical of language, but not to the point where we think all words are meaningless. We should maintain an attitude of fallibilism, but not to the point of thinking there is no such thing as truth. We should be non-anthropocentric, but not to the point where human life is considered unimportant. We should unlearn, but not to the point where we do not relearn things with critical thinking. We should practice introspection, but not to the point where we cannot support ourselves or contribute to society. We should aim for non-contrivance, but not to the point where we cannot muster a contrived smile for a coworker we dislike. We should be flexible, but not spineless. We should aim for a simple life, but without shrinking from all technology (or complexity). We should be content with our lives, but not to the point where we don't care about improving our lives or our communities. We should practice non-contentiousness, except when fighting (literally or metaphorically) is the right thing to do. These ten pieces of advice proffered in the *Laozi* (though there are many more) are all balancing acts contingent upon time, place, and person. Choosing how to implement such advice necessarily entails following our own consciences, but doing so within a pluralist community that tolerates a variety of social expectations, while also contextualizing ourselves and our communities within the wider natural systems of Heaven and Earth.

Translator's Note

The translation is italicized; everything that is not italicized—the key ideas, notes, and explanations—are the words of the translator. Parenthetical words in the translation were added by the translator as implied by context.

As a sinologist, my reading of the *Laozi* focuses on a close and careful reading of the text. But, in addition to this translation being more philosophical than historical, as noted in the introduction, I do make considerable use of two interpretive devices that are more often implied than explicitly stated. One is a **"Yin-Yang analysis"** that I think implicitly underlies many situations described in the text, from cosmology to psychology to ethics. This is reflected in the last paragraph of the "key concepts" section, and will be made clear over the course of reading my chapter explanations in the translation. The other is my resolving textual contradictions by inferring that the author has an **implied "contrived"** in many claims. The author in several chapters derides ostensibly good activities like doing (為), having activities (事), learning (學), and knowing (知), as well as common virtuosities like goodness (仁), propriety (義), and filiality (孝). But in all these cases and more, it is clear that they are deriding only the *contrivance* that may infect an uninspired and merely performative version of all these activities and virtuosities. This is made apparent in my additions of a parenthetical "(contrived)" to several of the chapter translations. Both "Yin-Yang" and "non-contrivance" were noted in the "key concepts."

I often use these interpretive devices even while noting that they seldom appear explicitly in the text. "Yin" and "Yang" appear only in chapter 42, and "contrivance" (偽) appears in its most unambiguous form only in chapter 19. Thus, the relative paucity of these words in the text might make one think that I overemphasize their implicit importance. All I can say in reply is that a Yin-Yang analysis often makes good sense to me, and brings

33

34 | The Annotated *Laozi* 老子

out otherwise-hidden ideas, and that without an implied "contrivance," the text would often be self-contradictory. This internal contradiction can be seen both logically and rhetorically. Take, for example, chapter 3, the first chapter in which I claim "contrived" is implied. If it were not implied, then we may read Laozi as saying that we should never "celebrate worthies," never "value difficult-to-attain goods," and never "display that which is desirable." If this were the case, then a good Daoist could not, logically, "celebrate" Laozi or Zhuangzi or anyone they thought "worthy"; could not "value" a nice piece of jade (explicitly valued, even if metaphorically, in chapter 70) or, say, a nice antique from your grandparents; and could never "display" that nice jade or antique. I do not think this is Laozi's message, hence the parenthetical "contrived" is necessary. Rhetorically, chapter 3 tells us to be "without (contrived) knowledge" and "without (contrived) desire." Removing the parenthetical means that the author is saying we should have no knowledge or desire. But this cannot be the case, because elsewhere in the text, knowledge and desire are explicitly things that we should have. Chapter 14 says we should "*know* the ancient beginnings," chapter 16 says we should "*know* how to abide," chapter 28 says we should "*know* the male," and so on. The same is true with "desire," which can also be translated as "want." Chapter 61 says that great states "*want* to unite (with smaller states) to nurture the people," and chapter 66 says sages can "*want* [i.e., *desire*] to lead people." Thus, an understanding of, or a translation of, this text that does not take such logical or rhetorical implications into account will result in incomprehensible claims such as "the Daoist sage has no knowledge" and, when asked what this might mean, such an understanding can only reply that the *Laozi* is "mystical" or "beyond our understanding" (if we are not, ourselves, sages). All of which is to say that, to read the *Laozi*, one must read between the lines.

If you cannot read Chinese, you will probably want to skip the rest of this translator's note.

I noted in the key concept of "non-contrivance" that "non-contrivance" (無為) appears in ten chapters. All instances of *wu-wei* 無為 mean "non-contrivance" (or "uncontrived") without exception. (It appears twelve times in those ten chapters.) A more difficult question is: In addition to the twelve instances of *wei* 為 in the phrase *wu-wei* 無為, which of the ninety-eight other instances of *wei* 為 should (also) be read as "contrive"? *Wei* 為 is a common word (hence the 110 appearances) and has several meanings, including "as" and "act" (ch. 2), "become" (ch. 3), "play the role

Translator's Note | 35

of" (ch. 10), "make" (ch. 11), and "are for" (ch. 12).[1] Nevertheless, I think the answer is eleven times in six chapters.[2] They are:

Chapter 3: "And cause those (contrivedly) 'knowledgeable people' to not be presumptuous and not *be contrived*. Be uncontrived, then nothing will be disorganized" (使夫「知者」不敢不為。為無為則無不治). Alternatively, "to not be presumptuous and not be contrived" (不敢不為) could be "to not be presumptuous and not act (contrivedly)." But Occam's razor suggests the former (even though English grammar necessitates the "be").

Chapter 29: "Those who want to gain (leadership of) the world and *be contrived* with it: we see their lack of success. The world is (like) a 'spiritous vessel' and cannot *be contrived*. Those who *are contrived* will fail in it; those who are attached will lose it" (將欲取天下而為之：吾見其不得已。天下「神器」，不可為也。為者敗之，執者失之). Alternatively, "be contrived with it" (為之) could be "act (contrivedly) upon it," "cannot be contrived" (不可為) could be "cannot be (contrivedly) acted upon," and "Those who are contrived will fail in it" (為者敗之) could be "Those who act (contrivedly with it) will fail in it." I went with Occam's razor again.

Chapter 38: "People of lofty virtuosity may be uncontrived, but they may lack the means of practicing it; people of lofty goodness may *contrive it*, but they (too) may lack the means of practicing it; (meanwhile,) people of lofty propriety may *contrive it*, but they have the means of practicing it; and people of lofty protocol may *contrive it*, but if no one responds to

---

1. For *wei* 為 as "contrive," see Paul Kroll, *A Student's Dictionary of Classical and Medieval Chinese*, revised edition (Leiden: Brill, 2017), 472. A graphically and semantically similar word to *wei* 為 (do, contrive) is *wei* 偽 (contrived, fabricated), which appears only in chapter 19.

2. One potential example that I find interesting, but that I did not include in my eleven, is in chapter 2. I have: "When everyone in the world 'knows' the beautiful as beautiful, this is just ugly; and when everyone 'knows' the competent as competent, this is just incompetent" (天下皆知美之為美，斯惡已；皆知善之為善，斯不善已). But I wonder if it shouldn't be: "When everyone in the world knows (only) the contrived beauty of beauty [i.e., the subset of "contrived beauty" within the larger category of "beauty" more broadly construed], this is just ugly; and when everyone knows (only) the contrived competence of competence [i.e., the subset of "contrived competence" within the larger category of "competence" more broadly construed], this is just incompetent."

36 | The Annotated *Laozi* 老子

them, then they roll up their sleeves and coerce them." (上德無為而無以為，上仁為之而無以為，上義為之而有以為，上禮為之而莫之應，則攘臂而扔之。) One might ask why I say "lack the means of practicing it" (無以為), when I might have said "do nothing by contrivance." But "People of lofty virtuosity may be uncontrived but / and do nothing by contrivance" would be tautological.

Chapter 47: "This is why sages can know without traveling, can be percipient without inspecting things, and can be complete without *contrivance*" (是以聖人不行而知，不見而明，不為而成). Of my eleven examples, this one gives me the most pause. I know that the author is being hyperbolic about the "without traveling" and "without inspecting" (I am confident that Laozi does want us to travel places and inspect things), and it is tempting to continue the hyperbole with a final "without acting." I do think he is using "without acting / contrivance" (不為) as a double entendre; that is, I think it means both, simultaneously. But I also think the primary goal of this chapter is to say Yang activity is insufficient, and particularly the Yang activity of having ill-considered—and contrived—theories about the world, that we then (unwisely) act upon.

Chapter 64: A phrase from chapter 29 reappears here, except in chapter 29 the context implies that the "it" in both cases refers to the preceding "world," whereas in chapter 64 there is no preceding subject, so the "it" in both cases refers to whatever one contrives or becomes attached to, thus: "Those who *are contrived* will fail in it; those who are attached will lose it" (為者敗之，執者失之).

Chapter 75: "The difficulty in organizing the people is due to their leaders being *contrived*. . . . Only those who do not live *contrivedly* are more worthy than those who value life" (百姓之難治，以其上之有為. . . . 夫唯無以生為者，是賢於貴生).

Two final notes. First, ancient Chinese texts were usually not punctuated, and the punctuation that follows is mine. Second, the abbreviations in the notes refer to exemplars noted in the appendix. They include Guodian (GD), Mawangdui (MWD), Beida (BD), Yan Zun (YZ), Wang Bi (WB), Xiang'er (XE), Heshang Gong (HSG), Fu Yi (FY), Xuan Zong (XZ), Fan Yingyuan (FYY), and Daozang (DZ). If variations among exemplars do not interest you, just ignore them.

The Annotated *Laozi*
Translation and Explanation

Chapter 1

Key Ideas

The abstract and sublime Way; language limitations; formless-form cosmology; introspective-extrospective psychology.

道可道非恆道；名可名非恆名。
「無」，名天地之始；「有」，名萬物之母。
故恆無，欲以觀其妙；恆有，欲以觀其徼。
此兩者，同出而異名。同謂之「玄」；玄之又玄：衆妙之門。

The way that can be (fully) conveyed is not the abiding Way; a name that can be (fully) descriptive is not an abiding name.

"Formlessness" is the name of the beginning of Heaven and Earth;[1] "form" is the name of the mother of the myriad things.[2]

---

1. MWD A, B, BD have "the myriad things" (萬物) instead of "Heaven and Earth" (天地).

2. There is considerable debate about this sentence (as well as the next). In a nutshell, it is possible to read "'Formlessness' is the name of" (無名) as "The nameless is" and "'form' is the name of" (有名) as "the named is" because *wu* 無 (formlessness, without) and *you* 有 (form, with) can function either as the nouns "formlessness" and "form" or as modifiers meaning "without" (as "name*less*," literally "without name") and "with" (as "named," literally "with name"). (This is easier than it sounds: if you can read the Chinese, simply move the two commas one place to the right.) I read this line and the next as articulating cosmic and psychological aspects of a formlessness-form cycle, whereas others read them as describing a nameless-named dichotomy and a desireless-desire dynamic, respectively. For a technical explanation of this reading of this sentence and, indeed, this entire chapter, see Anthony Yu, "Reading the *Daodejing*: Ethics and Politics of Rhetoric," *Chinese Literature: Essays, Articles, Reviews* 25 (December 2003): 165–87.

40 | The Annotated *Laozi* 老子

*Thus, if you abide in formlessness, you may thereby observe
its wonders; and if you abide in form, you may thereby observe its
manifestations.[3]*

*These two appear together but have different names. This
togetherness, we call it "mysterious"; mystery and more mystery: the
gateway to many wonders.*

Chapter 1 Explanation

The opening sentence establishes the main topic of this book—"the abiding
Way"—and cautions the reader that this book will not be an exhaustive
treatise on it. "The way that can be (fully) conveyed is not the abiding Way"
implies (at least) three things: (1) A fundamental distrust of language, because
language changes over both space and time.[4] In this sense, the Way cannot

---

3. The term *yu* 欲 (may, would, desire) means "may" here, similar to its use in chapter
36 (see chapter 36, note 1). Here, too, "If you abide in formlessness, you *would* thereby"
also works. The two excavated MWD exemplars, however, add two graphs that can
function as commas (i.e., 也), and they appear one space to the right of where I have
the commas, which changes the grammar, and therefore the meaning, from "if you abide
in formlessness, you *may* thereby" to "if you abide without *desire*, you will thereby" and
from "and if you abide in form, you *may* thereby" to "if you abide with *desire*, you will
thereby." So the question is: Should we follow the ca. 168 BCE MWD texts and deal
with the logical contradiction of "abide without desire" yet also "abide with desire," or
should we assume, on the grounds of internal coherence, that these early scribes misun-
derstood (and thereby mis-transcribed) the text? I choose the latter (with Chen Guying
and Anthony Yu), but some scholars choose the former. (And, though the MWD texts
do not add "commas" in the previous sentence, some scholars nevertheless punctuate
it similarly, giving us the "nameless" [無名] and the "named" [有名], which rhetorically
correlate with "without desire" [無欲] and "with desire" [有欲].)

4. In addition to changing "over both space and time," we should add the differences
allowed in the semantic parameters of a particular word even at one place in one time.
We see this precisely in the debates on how to read the next two sentences (see the
previous two notes). Two more examples are knowledge (知) and delight (樂). It is uncontroversial to claim that the (objective) knowledge that "the sky is blue" is qualitatively
different from the (subjective) knowledge that "I am sad." More to the point in this
text, however, is the difference between the (contrived) "knowledge" of so-called beauty
and competence in chapter 2 (echoed in chapters 3 and 10) and the more (theoretical)
knowledge of chapters 4 (Can we know if the Way has parents?) and 14 (Do you know
the ancient beginnings?). For delight, is the "delight" that some take in killing humans
(ch. 31) the same as the "delight" people take in their customs (ch. 80)? Or are these

Chapter 1 | 41

be "(fully) conveyed," or described, because language is not up to the task because it is too indefinite. (2) The Way—while it "stands alone and does not change" (ch. 25), is "vague and elusive" (chs. 14 and 21) and therefore difficult to fully convey—is something we can (tentatively) *apprehend*, but not (fully) *comprehend*. In this sense, the Way is too abstract to be "fully" described, just as most of us (non-physicists) cannot "fully describe" gravity. (3) Individuals will harmonize with the abiding Way differently, depending on their individual destinies (implied more pointedly by the "uncontrived activities" in the next chapter and throughout the *Laozi*, because "contrived" action is usually action, sanctioned by tradition, that is uniform across a community or culture, whereas fulfilling individual potential is more idiosyncratic). That is, the normative aspect of "the abiding Way" will probably differ, to a degree, among those humans who try to follow it. Hence, to emphasize this third point, we might understand the phrase as: "A (normative) way that can be (fully) conveyed (from one particular Daoist to another, as universally applicable) is not (exhaustive of all the time- and place-specific nuances of instantiating) the abiding Way."

"A name that can be (fully) descriptive is not an abiding name" reiterates this fundamental distrust of language more specifically, just in case the first point of the preceding paragraph was obscured by the following two points. We could also connect the two parts of this sentence more clearly, thus: "The way that can be (fully) conveyed is not the abiding Way *because* names (for things) that are (fully) descriptive are not abiding names." There are two ways to construe this distrust of "names." One is to distrust language in general, because "names" can be slippery and they do change. The second is to question the universality of certain specific "names." We see this already in chapter 2, with its interrogation of "beauty" and "competence," but the list of suspect "names" will grow, and the author (and I) will return to the subject in chapter 32. It is a bold move to begin a book consisting entirely of words—that is, "names" for things and actions—by telling the reader to be skeptical of words.

" 'Formlessness' is the name of the beginning of Heaven and Earth; 'form' is the name of the mother of the myriad things" implies a cosmogony: in

---

actually different emotions? This fundamental distrust of language makes an interesting contrast with religious conservatives who are certain of an unchanging literal reading of their scriptures. On the other hand, this Daoist language skepticism may be neatly exemplified by, for example, the historical shift in the number of Christians and Muslims who believe in a literal six-day creation story to those who take that story metaphorically.

42 | The Annotated *Laozi* 老子

the beginning there was a formless, undifferentiated mass of physical energy, which then spontaneously separated, via Yin-Yang proclivities, into Heaven and Earth and the myriad things (and will, or may, someday spontaneously revert back into formless physical energy). The "mother" metaphor occurs again in chapters 20, 25, 52, and 59.[5]

"Thus, if you abide in formlessness, you may thereby [i.e., with formlessness] observe its [i.e., the Way's] mysteries; and if you abide in form, you may thereby [i.e., with form] observe its [i.e., the Way's] manifestations" extends cosmology into psychology. Just as the cosmos is an interplay of form and formlessness, and just as human biology includes an alternation of wakefulness and sleep, so human psychology can and should shift from an introspective, ratiocination-suspending "abiding in formlessness" mode, whereby we may be more receptive to creative insight and ideas, to our usual "abiding in form" mode, whereby we may perceive (and, not coincidentally, name) the differentiated things of the world: the "manifestations" of what was once formless.

Thus, there are two examples of ethical realism in the first and third sentences. If we take the Way as a natural principle (or as the sum of all natural principles), and if we assume that the Way is something we humans should emulate, then "The way that can be (fully) conveyed is not the abiding Way" implies that we, too, should not be "fully conveyable," which is to say, fully describable. That is, we should not define ourselves into a corner, should not put ourselves into a box (to mix metaphors), but should allow ourselves to keep "becoming" who we are, and will be, without the constraints of a pigeonholed and unchanging "identity." (Thus, I think the opening phrase of the *Laozi* actually implies *four* things.) And if we accept, even metaphorically, a "formless-form" ontology, then we can emulate that by "abiding in" both the forms of everyday life and the formlessness of introspection.

"These two [i.e., formlessness and form] appear together but have different names" says that the two states of physical energy, also known as

---

5. In chapters 20 and 25, it seems to be a straightforward metaphor for the Way, and in chapter 59, I suspect it is too. I think this is also the case in chapter 52, but there the "beginning" and the "mother" are conflated. Here they are functionally separated, but as the final sentence makes clear, they are also ontologically "together." Thus, at first glance, the Way-as-mother may appear to correlate only with form, but looking ahead to the end of this chapter, and to chapter 52, we can see that it is also implicated in the formless Way-as-the-beginning.

Yin-Yang states (Yin formless and Yang form), are two sides of one coin: not two separate *things*, but two distinct *states* of physical energy.

"This togetherness, we call it 'mysterious'; mystery and more mystery: the gateway to many wonders": the "togetherness" indicates both the fundamental changeability and back-and-forthness—and, simultaneously, the *unity*—of the cosmos, the seasons, the life cycles of living things, the sleep-waking cycle of those animals that have it, and the introspective-extrospective (i.e., externally engaged) cycle that Daoism recommends. This unity is why one of the alternative names of the Way is "the One," which we will meet in chapter 10.

The cosmic aspect of this "mystery" describes cosmic inscrutability (Do *you* understand quantum physics?), while the psychological aspect of this "mystery" describes the process of self-discovery that commences when the formless-form cycle of self-cultivation begins, insofar as self-cultivation necessarily includes both introspection and action in the world. This "mystery" also foreshadows some uncertainties that are to follow, namely: when and how often one should "abide in" introspection versus activity; when and how often one should be flexible versus holding fast in fortitude to one's ideals; and, for those who use books like this one in their self-cultivation, when one should read things literally versus metaphorically. A further implication of the word "mystery" that informs all its uses throughout the text is a poetic understatedness, an inscrutability that returns the reader to the opening sentence. Finally, this "mystery" suggests the forward-looking, doubt-embracing attitude of fallibilism. Here, the "togetherness" implicates the knowing what we know (i.e., form) and the knowing that there will always be that which we do not know (i.e., formlessness); it blends confidence and humility in the forward-looking attitude and creativity of fallibilism. This observation and subsequent attitude lead naturally to the next chapter.

Chapter 2

Key Ideas

Relativity of beauty, competence (et al.); sages practice non-contrivance, wordless teaching, acceptance (et al.).

> 天下皆「知」美之為美，斯惡已；皆「知」善之為善，斯不善
> 已。
> 故：有無相生，難易相成，長短相形，高下相盈，音聲相和，
> 先後相隨。
> 是以聖人居無為之事，行不言之教：萬物作而弗辭。「為而弗
> 恃，成功而弗居」。夫唯弗居：是以弗去。

When everyone in the world "knows" the beautiful as beautiful, this is just ugly; and when everyone "knows" the competent as competent, this is just incompetent.[1]

Thus, form and formlessness produce each other; difficult and easy complete each other; long and short construct each other; above and below fulfill each other;[2] note and chorus harmonize with each other; before and after follow each other.

---

1. As noted in the "translator's note," there is ambiguity in the word translated as "as" (為); it can also function as the verb "strive to be" (or even "contrive to be"), in which case this sentence would read: "Everyone in the world knows that when the beautiful strive to be beautiful, that this is just ugly." I have decided instead to locate the problem in "knowing," but I could be wrong. "Competence" (善) might also be translated as "excellence" or "skillfulness."

2. HSG has two different graphs in these two middle phrases (較 for 形 and 傾 for 盈), rendering these phrases "long and short *complement* each other, above and below *incline toward* each other."

44

This is why sages are occupied with uncontrived activities and practice wordless teaching:[3] *the myriad things arise, but (sages) do not deny them. (Sages) "act, but without expectation;*[4] *and complete tasks, but without dwelling (on them)."*[5] *Simply not dwelling (on such things): by this they are not dismissed.*[6]

Chapter 2 Explanation

This chapter advises the "unlearning" of contrived social norms and the inclusive acceptance of difference. This "unlearning" is an instantiation of the "formless" open-mindedness of the first chapter, whereby we are asked to (tentatively, humbly, non-contentiously) "form" our own opinions on things like beauty and competence.

"When everyone in the world 'knows' the beautiful as beautiful: this [contrived 'knowledge'] is just ugly." One of the beauties of beauty is that it is in the eye of the beholder: no one wants to be told what is and is not to be found aesthetically beautiful. (Although, interestingly, plenty of people apparently *do* want to be told what is and is not fashionable.) Thus, "the beautiful" refers to that subset of "beautiful" that is currently in vogue

---

3. Chapter 43 also mentions "wordless teachings," as does *Zhuangzi* chapter 22.

4. GD A and MWD A have "expectation, will" (志); MWD B and BD have "expectation, wait upon" (恃), while HSG and DZ have "expectation, count on, rely on" (恃). I think all three of these would have the same implication: sages go about their business without (contrived, socially imposed) expectations, and thus they do not "impose their will on," "wait upon," or "rely upon" what others think, nor do they expect their own (past) actions to define them.

5. The phrase "act, but without expectation" (為而弗恃) is also in chapters 10, 51, and 77 (though in chapter 10 it is not in the MWD A, B or BD exemplars). The "complete tasks, but without dwelling (on them)" (成功而弗居) is also in chapter 77. HSG and some later exemplars have a third phrase in this sentence: after "reject them" and before "act," it has "produce, but without possessiveness" (生而弗有), a phrase that appears in chapters 10 and 51. (HSG uses 不 rather than 弗, but 弗 is the older locution, which I retain both here and in the other chapters mentioned in this note as an intentional archaism.) I don't include it because the four earliest exemplars—GD A; MWD A, B; BD—do not have it.

6. Dwelling on things can inhibit getting them done. This is not to say we shouldn't think about things before doing them, but rather that we shouldn't cloud our minds with excessive competition with others—denying them or worrying about their expectations—otherwise, we'll either never finish or will give up before completion.

46 | The Annotated *Laozi* 老子

in one's community. We might thereby interpret this sentence as "When everyone in the world (presumes that they) 'know' (that prevalent ideas about what defines) the beautiful (actually exhaust what counts) as beautiful (for everyone): (then) this (contrived 'knowledge') is just ugly (because it forces ideas of beauty—even if those ideas are confirmed by the majority—on those whose ideas do not conform to those ideas)."

"When everyone in the world 'knows' the competent as competent: this [contrived 'knowledge'] is just incompetent." As in the previous paragraph, here we all have different skills, and different destinies (i.e., latent and cultivated potentialities) in which to utilize our different skills. Success can be measured in several different ways, and the ways that "everyone in the world 'knows' " may not be the ways we personally value. This opening sentence is the first example of "ethical pluralism" (described in the "key concepts" section on non-anthropocentrism and ethics), because it asks us to accept a variety of definitions of "beauty" and "competence."

"Thus, form and formlessness produce each other." It says "Thus" because the text contrasts the claim that beauty and competence are relative with the following claim that *many* such adjectives in fact exist on a sliding scale.[7] It is often not the case that an object is judged either beautiful or ugly, but rather we can appreciate a *spectrum* of beauty. Similarly, all things are in a constant state of flux—coming to be and passing away—and thus simultaneously are involved with both form *and* formlessness. The six phrases of this second paragraph are adduced to make the point that judging something to be one or the other is in fact always a matter of relativity, and that framing such assessments as "either-or" choices is often a false dichotomy. Extrapolating from them to ourselves, we are thereby perhaps better described as "human becomings" rather than "human beings."

"This is why sages are occupied with uncontrived activities and practice wordless teaching." This is the first appearance of this text's aspirational figure of the "sage" and the first appearance of the fundamental Daoist tenet of non-contrivance. It also introduces the well-known Daoist trope of teaching by doing—by setting an example—rather than by words. This resonates superbly with the distrust of language in the previous chapter. The "This is why" points to the fact that in a world of flux, the best approach is one of flexibility: we should reject rigid traditionalism and epistemological certainty in favor of what Charles Peirce called "fallibilism"; we should always be open to new evidence and its effect on our theories and knowledge rather

---

7. However, the GD A and MWD A, B exemplars do not have this "Thus" (故).

Chapter 2 | 47

than presuming to know "eternal truths" or contriving to be someone that others (or even ourselves) think we *should* be.[8]

"The myriad things arise, but (sages) do not deny them." Understanding that the things mentioned in the second paragraph (form and formlessness, et al.) are relative allows the sage to be uncontrived and to not be fussy about (fully) articulating their teachings; it also facilitates their acceptance of the myriad things, no matter what sort of adjective (e.g., beautiful, ugly, competent, incompetent) one might choose to describe them.

Similarly, "(Sages) 'act, but without expectation; and complete tasks, but without dwelling (on them).' " These two phrases are in quotation marks because they seem to be stock phrases that appear elsewhere in the text. To "act, but without expectation" means that they interact with the myriad things without presuppositions about how those things "should" be, *and* that they do not expect other people to assess their actions (as, e.g., beautiful or competent, difficult or easy) as they themselves might. That they do not dwell on their completed tasks denotes a corollary to non-contrivance: not living in the past. This mark of the sage will be described, in other words, as "the way of Heaven" in chapter 9.

"Simply not dwelling (on such things): by this they are not dismissed." That is, because sages do not dwell on their completed tasks—both within their own minds and in their speaking to others about said tasks—they are not perceived as self-centered or self-aggrandizing. But I think the implied "such things" actually includes more than just the tasks that sages complete, and in fact refers to everything described in this chapter: because sages understand the relativity of many human judgments (as beautiful, competent, and the rest), they can inhabit a life characterized by uncontrived activities, wordless teachings, and a proclivity to not deny things. That is, this final sentence tells us that sages are accepted *by* the people because they are accepting *of* the people. The "mystery" of the first chapter, then, is reflected in both the relativity and non-exclusion of this chapter, and these two latter themes are continued in the next chapter, which opens by warning us that though sages may be accepted by the people, we should not thereby cast them as heroes to be worshipped.

---

8. To those who might object that I am presenting "fallibilism" itself as an "eternal truth," I can only reply that the "I think X is the case, but I could be wrong" formulation of fallibilism is more a useful subjective *attitude* to have rather than an allegedly true *claim* about the objective world. Also, a thoroughgoing fallibilist would presumably be the first to admit that fallibilism itself could be wrong.

Chapter 3

Key Ideas

Relativity of worthiness, valuables, desire; sages open minds, fill bellies, and organize without (contrived) knowledge.

不尚賢，使民不爭；不貴難得之貨，使民不為盜；不見可欲，
使民心不亂。

是以聖人之治：虛其心，實其腹；弱其志，強其骨。恆使民無知
無欲，使夫「知者」不敢不為。為無為則無不治。

Do not celebrate worthies (contrivedly),[1] and people will thereby not become contentious. Do not value difficult-to-obtain goods (contrivedly),[2] and people will thereby not become thieves. Do not display that which is desirable (contrivedly), and people's minds will thereby not become disordered.

This is how sages organize: open the mind, (but also) fill the belly; make flexible the will, (but also) strengthen the bones. They abidingly cause the people to be without (contrived) knowledge and without (contrived) desire, and cause those (contrivedly) "knowledgeable people" to not be presumptuous and not be contrived. Be uncontrived, then nothing will be disorganized.[3]

---

1. "Celebrating worthies" (尚賢) is the title of *Mozi* chapters 8–10, and is one of that author's key policies.

2. The phrase "difficult-to-obtain goods" (難得之貨) appears again in chapters 12 and 64.

3. The three earliest exemplars of these last two sentences are shorter, with one sentence instead of two. MWD B, BD, and XE all have "not be presumptuous and not be contrived" (MWD B, BD: 不敢弗為; XE: 不敢不為), while later exemplars drop the second

48

Chapter 3 Explanation

"Do not celebrate worthies (contrivedly), and people will thereby not become contentious" might be a criticism of Mozi 墨子, who titled three of the chapters of his eponymous book "Celebrating Worthies" (parts 1, 2, and 3), or, depending on how you date the *Laozi*, Mozi (also ca. 400 BCE?) might have been criticizing Laozi. Mozi wanted more social conformity as a recipe for social harmony. Laozi is much more of an individualist than Mozi, and here he can be read as cautioning us about two things. First, we should not "celebrate" a particular, *contrived* idea of what a "worthy person"[4] is supposed to be, which is a direct continuation of the theme of the previous chapter. But here, rather than saying that such distinctions are "ugly" or "incompetent," or implying that they might lead to some people being "denied," the problem is developed as leading to disharmonious social "contentiousness."

We might also make a second inference here. Even if we all were to agree on what constitutes a "worthy person" (which is unlikely, but possible), we should not "celebrate" them in a perfunctory way. Which is to say, to automatically celebrate a "worthy person" who has "checked all the boxes" of what we have agreed it means to be a worthy person: this would be to take a qualitative attribute ("worthy") and turn it into a quantitative matter (i.e., the quantity of "checked boxes").[5] Such perfunctory behavior would itself be another form of contrivance.

By the same logic, "Do not value difficult-to-obtain goods (contrivedly), and people will thereby not become thieves. Do not display that which is desirable (contrivedly), and people's minds will thereby not become disordered." The double-negative sounds better in Chinese, but the observation is clear. As discussed earlier, we can analyze these two sentences in two ways: just because something is "difficult to obtain" or "desirable" to many people, that does not necessarily mean that all of us will value or will want to own such things. For example, diamonds and gold are relatively "difficult to obtain," and certainly many people throughout history have found them "desirable," but some of us might not find them particularly attractive, and

---

negative, which might then be read as "not be presumptuously contrived" or "not presume to be contrived" (不敢為也), a locution found at the end of chapter 64.

4. We probably may conflate "worthies" here with the "sages" in the previous chapter.

5. This is an example of what is now known as Goodhart's law: "When a measure becomes a target, it ceases to be a good measure."

50 | The Annotated *Laozi* 老子

might further suspect that their "value" is not inherent but is something of a historical accident. That is, their "value" may be "contrived" (by, for example, the jewelry industry). And second, even if we were to agree on what constitutes "difficult to obtain" and "desirable," that does not mean that these qualities can be quantified, and thereby handled uniformly or perfunctorily.[6] Maybe you want to display your grandparents' "valuable" porcelain plates (per your parents' wishes) and maybe you'd rather keep them in a box. It's your call.

Returning to the aspirational figure of the sage: if such a one were in charge,[7] the following is what they would do, in two parts. First: "open the mind, (but also) fill the belly; make flexible the will, (but also) strengthen the bones." Some scholars translate "open" (虛) as "empty" and construe this to mean that the Daoist sage-ruler wants to "dumb down" the populace so that they become simple-minded and, thereby, happy and content. But this sentence actually toggles between advising us to be open-minded about the varieties of worthiness and the values of material possessions (just as we were told to do with beauty and competence in the previous chapter)—that is, issues of the mind and will—while keeping an eye on the fundamentals of food and health, matters of the belly and bones. This sentence is saying: be open-minded, but not so much that your brain falls out. It concludes by giving two specific examples of what it means to be "open-minded": "abidingly cause the people to be without (contrived) knowledge [of confining mental categories] and without (contrived) desire [for arbitrary, socially prized possessions]." Without the parenthetical annotations we are left with the problematic and incorrect idea that sages want us to be without *any* knowledge and without *any* desires. Such a "sage" is entirely alien to early China.

Second: "cause those (contrivedly) 'knowledgeable people' to not be presumptuous and not be contrived." The text does not describe just how sages would go about persuading these "knowledgeable people" to not celebrate certain kinds of worthiness and certain kinds of material goods, but

---

6. One might argue that "difficult to obtain" is in fact quantifiable, but consider again the case of diamonds: are they "difficult to obtain" because there are so few of them in the earth, or because they have been hoarded by diamond merchants who want to maintain high prices?

7. I translate *zhi* 治 (organize, put in order, govern) as "organize" in the nine *Laozi* chapters in which it appears, but other readers may want to infer a more overtly political tone, in which the sage is construed as a sage-ruler.

Chapter 3 | 51

presumably they would try to persuade them with texts like this one. The supposedly "knowledgeable people" (知者) in this chapter are connected to the contrived "knowing" (知) in the previous chapter but, as we might expect from such a generic descriptor (and from a language skeptic), the same phrase is used with a positive connotation in chapter 56 (where it is translated as "those who know").[8] The author's critique of "presumptuousness" (敢) continues in chapters 30, 64, 67, 69, 73, and 74.

The chapter ends: "Be uncontrived, then nothing will be disorganized." Recommending that humans behave in an uncontrived manner seems to assume that we have at least a benign, if not a good, human nature, assuming the author was not a proto-existentialist and did not believe that humans even have natures. In fact, this text does not use the word "(human) nature" (性), though it would become central to early Chinese intellectual history in the following centuries. Nevertheless, in this text, being uncontrived is clearly the goal, and such non-contrivance follows from open-mindedness, an attitude exemplified by the first image of the next chapter.

---

8. The phrase appears a third and final time in chapter 81, translated as "those who know," but with a slight negative connotation.

Chapter 4

Key Ideas

The Way is "empty" but always useful; it is ancient and calms the myriad things; it seems to precede the Progenitor.

道沖，而用之或不盈。淵兮似萬物之宗。
挫其銳，解其紛，和其光，同其塵。
湛兮似或存，吾不知誰之子。象帝之先。

The Way is like an empty vessel,[1] yet using it seems to not fill it. Deep, it seems to be the ancestor of the myriad things.

It blunts their sharpness; untangles their knots; softens their glare; merges with their dust.[2] Unfathomable, it seems as if it

---

1. The second graph, *chong* 沖, primarily means "to gush forth," but the rest of the sentence makes clear that in this case it should be read as *zhong* 盅, an empty vessel, which is the graph used in the FY exemplar. It would not make much sense to say that one could "use" this "gushing forth" yet "not fill it." Both "gush forth" and "empty" are definitions for *chong* 沖 in Kroll, *A Student's Dictionary of Classical and Medieval Chinese*, 53, though "empty vessel" is not; some scholars say they are graphic variants. This word appears with the "empty" meaning in chapter 45 and also appears with its primary meaning in chapter 42, there translated as "blend." Note the poetic resonance between cosmic "formlessness" (無) in chapter 1 with spatial / practical "emptiness" in chapters 4 (沖), 5 (虛), 6 (implied by the valley [谷] and gate [門]), 11 (無), 22 (窪), and 45 (沖).

2. Chapters 52 and 56 have similar descriptions of introspection, but there *we* are the subject of these verbs and here it presumably is the Way. Or so the context implies, as the Way is the subject of the sentences before and after this one.

52

Chapter 4 | 53

persists, but we[3] know not whose child it may be. It seems to have preceded the Progenitor.[4]

Chapter 4 Explanation

"The Way is like an empty vessel, yet using it seems to not fill it." The Way was associated with both form and formlessness in chapter 1, but Laozi's slight Yin preference shows itself in this metaphor, where the Way is compared to an empty vessel, but a magical one that can never be filled, sort of like the inverse of the mythical "horn of plenty" that is always full no matter how much one takes from it.

"Deep, it seems to be the ancestor of the myriad things." Here, "deep" (淵), as in a place where water is deep, is an image for something both fluid and distant, something that, as we will see later, is "vague and elusive." The "seems to" (或, 似) in this sentence and the previous sentence both reiterate

---

3. There are two words in early Chinese that can be translated as "I" or "we" (i.e., *wu* 吾 and *wo* 我), and they are mostly interchangeable. But this raises the question: If they are truly synonymous, why have two words? I have examined all the cases in the *Laozi* in which these words appear and have decided to translate them all as "we." (吾 is used in fifteen chapters and 我 appears in seven; they are both used in chapters 57 and 70.) Translating them all as "I" might imply that Laozi thought that only he could be a proper Daoist, which would run counter to the advice to be humble that runs throughout the text (and which is explicitly undermined by the "few" in the final sentence in chapter 43 and the multiple references to plural "sages"). Translating them differently (吾 as "I" and 我 as "we" would work better than the reverse) is possible, but it would still retain the problem of Laozi presenting himself as unique in some chapters, which I do not think was the author's intention. Thus, I have translated both words as "we" throughout the text. This still leaves the problem of "why have two words for one meaning," but I have three tentative answers. One is that the two words *used* to mean "I" and "we," respectively, but by Laozi's time that linguistic distinction had receded. A second is that he intended 吾 as "I" and 我 as "we," but that he *also* intended that the "I" should usually (but maybe not always) be taken as a euphemism for "we." The third is euphony: it might be the case that one simply "sounds better," in Chinese, than the other to the author's ear in a given sentence. In any case, to me the clarity of the implied logical inclusiveness of "we" slightly outweighs the problems of grammatical precision and of asking readers to sometimes assume that "I" means "we."

4. The "Progenitor" (帝) could refer to the "High Progenitor" (上帝). If so, it probably refers not to a deity but to the primordial and totemic first human. See Sarah Allan, "On the Identity of Shang Di 上帝 and the Origin of the Concept of a Celestial Mandate (*Tian Ming* 天命)," *Early China* 31 (2007): 1–46.

54 | The Annotated *Laozi* 老子

the "mystery" of the Way specified in chapter 1 and underline the epistemic humility of fallibilism implied in chapters 2 and 3. Meanwhile, "the ancestor of the myriad things" is a phrase that occurs only once in this text[5] but is clearly a poetic allusion to the venerated ancestor of a particular family, clan, or tribe. Ancestor veneration, at least for the ruling clan, was central to early Chinese governance and warfare. This is the first anthropomorphic metaphor for the Way used in the *Laozi*.

The next sentence, "It blunts their sharpness; untangles their knots; softens their glare; merges with their dust," is the first clear articulation in this text of just what it is that the Way does. It relaxes things, in general, and more specifically for us humans, it helps us to "abide in formlessness" (ch. 1). "Merges with their dust" refers to its pervasiveness, to its "vague and elusive" nature, and to what we might metaphorically call its "humility," were the Way to be anthropomorphic, which it is not. (Still, what is now called the "pathetic fallacy" is nevertheless a potent poetic device.) This sentence appears in an extended form in chapter 56, where the subject of the verbs appears, interestingly, to be sagely people rather than the Way. This subtle shift in locution implies our embeddedness in, and dependence on, our environment. (It is also another example of ethical realism.) On the other hand, I could be wrong and we should here read the implied grammatical subject as "(We should) blunt the [i.e., our] sharpness," just as in chapter 56. If this is the case, then this sentence tells us to introspect in order to apprehend the "depth" and "unfathomableness" of the Way.[6]

"Unfathomable, it seems as if it persists, but we know not whose child it may be." Both graphs for "seems to" used in the first two sentences are employed here, creating an impression of almost theatrical doubt, and

---

5. Chapter 70 has "(Our) words have an ancestor" (言有宗), but this a different kind of metaphor, though in both cases the Way is the "ancestor."

6. Aside from the (admittedly weak though not negligible) evidence of the implied subject deriving from the previous sentence, in deciding on which understanding to follow we might ask: Would the author use the same locution in two places with two different implied subjects? I think the answer is yes: Laozi is cleverly using identical tropes to different effect in different places. Two examples: chapters 17 and 23 both use the phrase "If trust in them / it is insufficient, then there will be a lack of trust in him / us" (信不足焉，有不信焉), but in chapter 17 the implied subject is "a leader," while in chapter 23 it is "the Way." And chapters 37 and 48 both use the phrase "uncontrived/ly, yet / and nothing is / will be left undone" (無為而無不為), but in chapter 37 the subject is clearly "the Way," while in chapter 48 the implied subject is us.

they are used to modify the seemingly simple claim that the Way "persists" (存).[7] This is a surprising move for an author whose central cosmological claim, implied in the important opening sentence of chapter 1, is that there *is* such a thing as "the abiding Way." Nevertheless, this existential doubt is important for addressing the reification of the Way from an ordering principle to an "existing," concrete thing. Chapter 25 does refer to the Way as a "thing" (物), but its "thingness" should not be construed as implying that it is made of matter, but rather that concepts can colloquially be called "things," just as we might casually refer to a "thing" called gravity, even while knowing that it is not something that can be touched. The "we know not whose child it may be" leads directly to the next sentence:

"It appears to have preceded the Progenitor." The "Progenitor" (帝) appears nowhere else in this text, and if we infer that the author was in fact referring to the "(High) Progenitor" (i.e., Shang Di 上帝), then it is a reference either to the spirit of the first ancestor of the people (or even "all people") or to its memory. It was associated with the Pole Star, the one unmoving star in the sky around which all other stars appear to revolve. It was more popular in the preceding Shang dynasty than in the contemporaneous Zhou dynasty, but given that it appears only this once, it is unclear if it should be understood as a quaint literary device or if the author literally thought that the first ancestor of his culture (or all humans) was still (in some sense) a conscious entity with power that could be exercised in the human world.[8] Alternatively, the "Progenitor(s)," or "thearch(s)," as this graph is sometimes translated, could refer to the semilegendary, mytho-historical "Five Thearchs" (五帝) that were said to rule before the first Chinese dynasty.[9] Or the word could refer more generally to a class of supernatural entities called "thearchs" (or "progenitors") about which little is known. Perhaps they were long-dead and heroic ancestors, or perhaps they were somehow related to the "spirits" mentioned in chapter 39. In any case, the Way "appears to have preceded" it, or them, which is a declaration that the Way, present from the start,

---

7. Other things that "persist" in this text are "the root of Heaven and Earth" (ch. 6), the "persons" of sages (ch. 7), and "middling scholars," some of whom persist in the Way, some of whom do not (ch. 41).

8. Millennia later, Christians chose this term to translate their word "God."

9. These were Huang Di 黃帝, Zhuan Xu 顓頊, Di Ku 帝嚳, Tang Yao 唐堯, and Yu Shun 虞舜.

56 | The Annotated *Laozi* 老子

certainly precedes the existence of humans.[10] The "empty vessel" metaphor that opens this chapter is reiterated with a specific kind of empty vessel in the next chapter.

---

10. David Pankenier had the fascinating idea that the Way preceding the Progenitor derives from the fact that before the stars in the northern hemisphere appeared to revolve around the Pole Star, they appeared to revolve around an empty space. See Pankenier, *Astrology and Cosmology in Early China* (New York: Cambridge University Press, 2013), 91–92: "It can hardly be coincidental that during the two millennia while this mystical vision was taking shape *there was no star* located precisely at the Pole such as we have today, no obvious physical presence at the pivot of the heavens, so that the marvel of an efficacious 'nothing' at the center of the rotating dome of the sky was nightly on display, inviting wonder."

Chapter 5

Key Ideas

Heaven, Earth, and sages are impartial and inexhaustible; much speaking is not as good as preserving what is within.

天地不仁，以萬物為芻狗；聖人不仁，以百姓為芻狗。
天地之間：其猶橐籥乎？虛而不屈，動而愈出。
多言數窮，不若守中。

Heaven and Earth are not (contrivedly) good, because they take the myriad things to be as straw dogs. Sages are not (contrivedly) good (either), because they take the people[1] to be as straw dogs.

The space between Heaven and Earth: Isn't it like a bellows? Empty, but not expended; moving, but emitting ever more.

Much speech and frequent exhaustion is not as good as preserving what is within.[2]

---

1. There are three words that I translate as "people" or "the people" in this text: the most common is just "people" (人), which I also translate as "humans" or "others"; the next is "the people" (民), indicating the people of a given community or state; and the least common is "the hundred clans" (百姓), where "hundred" simply indicates "many," used only in chapters 5, 17, 49, and 75. A fourth word that could also be translated as "the people" is "the masses" (眾人), which appears in chapters 8, 20, and 64.

2. "Preserving what is within" (守中) occurs only here (though the GD A text also has it in ch. 16). The word "preserve" is also translated as "safeguard" in chapter 9 and "defense" in chapter 67.

58 | The Annotated *Laozi* 老子

Chapter 5 Explanation

The cosmic dyad of Heaven-Earth, as well as those sages who work in harmony with it, are not anthropocentric. Thus, they "are not (contrivedly) good" because they do not have only humanity in mind. (Another example of ethical realism.) Just as the Way precedes the appearance of the human species, so, once humans appeared on the scene, it did not (so to speak) rearrange its "priorities" to make humans the center of its "attention." Furthermore, the articulations of human ethical codes, including what constitutes "goodness," are subject to change, over both space and time, and are always problematically tied to impermanent language. The "straw dogs" were items used in sacrifice: ceremonially important during the sacrifice, but forgotten and trampled on after it. These "straw dogs" are described in greater detail in *Zhuangzi* chapter 14; they are a subset of the "straw numens" (芻靈) mentioned in the *Liji* 禮記 chapter 4.

"The space between Heaven and Earth: Isn't it like a bellows?" A bellows, like the "empty vessel" in chapter 4, is another metaphor for the Way: the useful part is the invisible, formless, open part, just as with the "doors and windows" in chapter 11. It is invisible, yet eminently useful, like gravity. Thus: "Empty, but not expended; moving, but emitting ever more."[3] The first paragraph describes a twofold open-mindedness: being open to different definitions of "goodness" in human society, and being open to "goodness" that is not anthropocentric. The openness implied in those first two sentences is then brought to the fore in the bellows imagery of the next two sentences.

The final sentence, "Much speech and frequent exhaustion is not as good as preserving what is within," shifts the focus from the cosmic to the human. The sage's "wordless teaching" (ch. 2) is alluded to and extended with the "frequent exhaustion" that may result from the tireless and arbitrary defining of what is beautiful or competent (ch. 2), or worthy or valuable (ch. 3). Here it is ostensible goodness—(anthropocentric) morality—that is rejected in favor of "preserving what is within." This exact phrase occurs only here, but "what is within" (中) the Way (should we wish to extrapolate),

---

3. The "empty" (虛) here is the same word as the "open" in "open the mind" in chapter 3 and "openness" in chapter 16. The symmetry between the usefulness of "empty" things like bellows and an "open" mind is obscured in English because we make use of the spatial metaphor of "open" in "open-minded" but would assign a negative connotation to the spatial metaphor of being "empty-minded." (This was noted in the "key concepts.")

Chapter 5 | 59

described in chapter 21, includes creative essence (精) and genuineness (真). And things that we are asked to "preserve" (守) elsewhere in the text include "tranquility" (靜, ch. 16); "the female," "the black," and "the humble" (雌, 黑, 辱, ch. 28); "the Way" and "the ('uncarved block' of) simplicity" in which it abides (樸, ch. 32); "the Way" and its "non-contrivance" (無 為, ch. 37); and the Way as "the mother" and "flexibility" (母, 柔, ch. 52). All of these certainly seem like worthy things to "preserve" in ourselves, but at this point in the narrative I suspect we are to assume that the thing "within" us that we are to preserve is the Way, even though it is not explicitly mentioned in this chapter. If this is the case, then this marks the first time that the reader learns that the cosmic Way is, in fact, within us all. The next chapter goes on to further describe this Way, again without ever explicitly mentioning it.

Chapter 6

Key Ideas

Three metaphors: the deathless valley spirit, the mysterious female, the root of Heaven and Earth.

> 谷神不死：是謂「玄牝」。玄牝之門：是謂「天地之根」。綿綿若存，用之不勤。

The valley spirit does not die: it is called the "mysterious female."[1]
The gate of the mysterious female: it is called the "root of Heaven and Earth." On and on it seems to persist, using them effortlessly.[2]

Chapter 6 Explanation

The "valley" is a third "empty" metaphor for the Way, after the "empty vessel" (ch. 4) and the "bellows" (ch. 5), all of which remind us of the "formlessness"

---

1. The "female" (牝 and 雌) appears again in chapters 6, 10, 28, 55, and 61, where it implies fecundity (ch. 6); adaptability (ch. 10); humble, stable, adaptability (ch. 28); the female part of male-female sex (ch. 55); and effective, tranquil conciliation (ch. 61). Reading the *Laozi* as a whole we might keep all of these in mind in each instance.

2. The subject and object of the last four graphs are not specified. I have taken the Way as the subject (as "it," because it is the subject of the previous two phrases, assuming "the valley spirit" and "the gate of the mysterious female" are both metaphors for the Way) and Heaven and Earth (as "them") as the object (because it is the object of the previous sentence), but others construe this as "(Heaven and Earth) use it (i.e., the Way) effortlessly" or "(We can or should) use it (i.e., the Way) effortlessly." This is the same grammatical problem that we saw in the third sentence in chapter 4.

Chapter 6 | 61

of chapter 1, but in the *Laozi* the "valley" image also connotes several other things: openness (曠, ch. 15), humility (辱, ch. 28), bounteousness (盈, ch. 39), and conciliation (下, ch. 66). It is clearly a potent motif. I would also suggest that it connotes attractiveness, since things, like rainwater, are pulled downward into the valley (by, of course, gravity). The valley as a symbol of charisma is the Yin opposite of the Yang symbol of charismatic virtuosity used by Kongzi (Confucius), the Pole Star, which seems to "attract" the other stars that appear, from our point of view, to "circle" it.[3]

Here the lowly-yet-powerful "valley" is combined with a deathless "spirit," which may be read as a literal "nature spirit," as a literal part of human (and, probably, all animal) physiology responsible for mental acuity, or metaphorically as mental acuity and foresight (in which case it should be translated as "spiritousness"). Early Chinese Scholars texts are replete with all three locutions. The "valley spirit" does not appear again in this text, though both "valley" and "spirit" do.[4]

This image is then immediately connected to the "mysterious female," and "female" here refers to all animals (the graph for "female human," or "woman," is a different graph: 女), which underlines the implication in the previous chapter that the Way is not anthropocentric. If one is inclined to compare Daoist imagery with that of many world religions, the choice of something "mysterious" may not be all that unusual, but the choice of the "female" would certainly stand out.

Upon the two metaphors of "valley *spirit*" and "mysterious *female*" are piled two more: "The *gate* of the mysterious female . . . the '*root* of Heaven and Earth.'" A female "gate" is no doubt what the reader will infer: a reference to yet another "empty" metaphor (of the womb), combined with an allusion to reproductive fecundity. This Yin "female gate" image is then immediately contrasted with a Yang image in the form of the creative, wellspring-like "root" of the cosmos. The "empty" gate and the multifarious "root" make an incongruous pair, but the two very different metaphors work each in their own way to convey a sense of both fertility and connectedness.

---

3. *Lunyu* 2.1: "The scholar said, 'Create government with virtuosity, comparable to the North Star, which abides in its position while all the other stars pay homage to it'" (子曰：「為政以德，譬如北辰：居其所而眾星共之」). The North Star is the Pole Star of the northern hemisphere. If you find this image puzzling, look for a time-lapse photograph of the Pole Star.

4. "Valley" (谷) is also in chapters 15, 28, 32, 39, 41, and 66, while "spirit" (神) is also in chapters 29, 39, and 60, though in chapters 29 and 60 it is translated as "spiritous" and "spirited," respectively.

62 | The Annotated *Laozi* 老子

Ethical realism is implied in several ways in this chapter: like valleys, be open and humble; like females, be creative; like roots, be supportive and not ostentatious.

The final line reiterates the hesitancy in making strong linguistic or epistemological claims about the Way ("it *seems* to persist"), and ends with a poetic ambiguity. Some scholars take the last phrase to mean that "we (can) use it effortlessly," which certainly fits with the "using it" (用之) in chapter 4, but I read the present chapter as an elucidation of the generative power of the Way, and thus read the final phrase as the Way "using" all of Heaven and Earth, including *us*, to, in a sense, manifest itself.[5] This reading leads naturally to the opening sentence of the next chapter, where it is implied that the Way "produces" (生) Heaven and Earth.

---

5. In this reading, the Way "using" us here would presage the "piping of Heaven" (天籟) metaphor in *Zhuangzi* chapter 2, where Heaven "plays" us like a musician playing panpipes. This may or may not be comparable to Jesus saying, "the kingdom of heaven is within you" (Luke 17:21) or Paul saying, "It is no longer I who live, but it is Christ who lives in me" (Galatians 2:20).

Chapter 7

Key Idea

Heaven and Earth do not produce themselves, and sages put themselves last, yet both "live long and prosper."

天長地久。天地所以能長且久者，以其不自生：故能長生。
是以聖人後其身而身先；外其身而身存。非以其無私邪，故能
成其私？

Heaven is long-lasting and Earth is enduring. The reason why Heaven and Earth are able to be long-lasting and enduring is because they do not produce themselves: thus they are able to long-lastingly live.

This is why sages put their persons last, yet their persons are brought to the fore; why they forget[1] their persons, yet their persons persist. Is it not because they are selfless that they are able to complete themselves?[2]

Chapter 7 Explanation

Giving birth to (i.e., "producing") things is a difficult and dangerous undertaking, as the mortality rate of mothers in the premodern world attests. The

---

1. The word "forget" (外)—literally, "outside," and here, to "put outside" of oneself—occurs only this once in the *Laozi*. I use "forget" to avoid the otherwise-awkward locution of "putting oneself outside of oneself" or "putting your person out of your mind." It is also used this way in the *Zhuangzi*.

2. A phrase similar to "able to complete themselves" (能成其私) appears in chapters 34 and 63 as "able to complete their greatness / large (activities)" (能成其大).

64 | The Annotated *Laozi* 老子

Way, though similar to a "mysterious female" with a productive "gate" (ch. 6), is in fact not a mammalian female: this is why Heaven and Earth, as well as the myriad things, including us, can use it endlessly. With the Way doing the heavy lifting of fundamental cosmic production, the things that are produced, beginning with "Heaven" and "Earth," are relatively free from the danger of "childbearing": thus they can be "enduring." Additionally, a long life was a primary concern in early China, given that the Scholars texts are concerned with well-being in this lifetime (rather than, say, with one's immortal soul spending time in either heaven or hell, as seems to have been a primary concern from the eastern Mediterranean to the southern base of the Himalayas). So the goal of being "able to long-lastingly live" was seen as both a natural and an aspirational good.

Sages match Heaven and Earth with their humility by ascribing ultimate cause to the Way rather than to themselves. (This humility—or perhaps it is simply a recognition that we, like Heaven and Earth, do not create ourselves—is another instance of ethical realism, of humans taking ethical cues from the natural world.) But a social maxim can also be inferred from this cosmological claim. Just as sages defer to the Way ontologically, they also defer to the will of the community socially, insofar as humble people are universally admired. Thus, "sages put their persons last, yet their persons are brought to the fore."[3] This may be why "servant-leaders" are well known in the modern business world. (If the term "servant-leader" makes no sense to you, just think of what elected leaders are supposed to do: carry out the will of those who elected them to leadership positions.) Sages, of course, do not literally "forget their persons"; this locution refers to their lack of self-centeredness, which, ipso facto, is why "their persons persist." In Daoism, fallibility, humility, and selflessness are key elements in self-cultivation, in the (ongoing) "completion" of our selves. And now that the topic of "completing" ourselves has been broached, the next chapter specifies a number of ways that might help in this endeavor.

---

3. This may bring to mind, for some, the "So the last will be first, and the first will be last" line in Matthew 20:16.

Chapter 8

Key Ideas

Ten competencies: (1) benefit others; (2) don't fight; (3) don't fear to do what others disdain; attain competence in: (4) location; (5) depth; (6) goodness; (7) trustworthiness; (8) organization; (9) ability; (10) timeliness.

上善若水。水善利萬物而不爭。居眾人之所惡，故幾於道矣。
居善地，心善淵，與善仁，言善信，政善治，事善能，動善時。
　夫唯不爭：故無尤。

The highest competence is like water. Water is competent at benefiting the myriad things while not being contentious with them. It dwells in places that the masses find repellent and thus is similar to the Way.

In a residence, competence lies in location. In the mind, competence lies in depth. In interactions with others, competence lies in goodness. In words, competence lies in trustworthiness. In government, competence lies in organization. In activities, competence lies in ability. In movement, competence lies in timeliness. Simply not being contentious: thus one can be without fault.

Chapter 8 Explanation

It may seem contradictory to claim in chapter 2 that "competence" should not be ossified in a single, contrived definition, and then, six chapters later, to claim, "The highest competence is like water." But the metaphor of water was chosen precisely because it is something that cannot be ossified.

66 | The Annotated *Laozi* 老子

(True, it can be frozen into ice, but "ice" is a different word.) Water is the ultimate metaphor for flexibility.

Furthermore, water does not take pride in its competence, because, like the "servant-leaders" mentioned in the previous explanation, it is too busy "benefiting the myriad things" and "not being contentious with them." The "humility" of water is signaled in the observation, "It dwells in places that the masses find repellent and so is similar to the Way." (Ethical realism.) Such humility was seen in the "lowly" valley metaphor in chapter 6, and in the deference of Heaven and Earth to the Way for their long-lastingness in chapter 7, but not as clearly as in this passage. After having established competence as this chapter's topic, and providing the image of (lowly) water as inimitably competent, the remainder is an inventory showing how competence is important everywhere.

Reading the chapter as an extended metaphor for how we should act (or for how we should pursue self-cultivation), it can be analyzed as a "ten commandments of competence" that address a variety of contexts. Extracted from their contexts, they may be read as: (1) benefit (利) others; (2) do not be contentious (不爭); (3) do not fear to do what others disdain (居眾人之所惡); (4) live in a suitable location (地); (5) cultivate depth (淵) of mind; (6) be good (仁); (7) be trustworthy (信); (8) be organized (治); (9) cultivate your abilities (能); and (10) be timely (時).

The final line reiterates the importance of the second "commandment," not being contentious with your community, for if you pursue the other nine pieces of advice but not this one, then you will be ostracized, and the other nine will be of no help to anyone. One way to "be contentious" with your community would be to insist on *these* "ten commandments" and not some other version. The next chapter addresses this kind of excess, the excess of arrogance.

Chapter 9

Key Ideas

Self-control versus excess: (1) overfilling a cup; (2) oversharpening a blade; (3) overflowing a room; (4) privileged arrogance; (5) grandstanding.

> 持而盈之，不若其已。揣而銳之，不可長保。金玉滿室，莫之
> 能守。
> 富貴而驕，自遺其咎。
> 功遂身退：天之道也。

Grasping and overfilling it is not as good as stopping in time. Hammer and oversharpen it and you cannot protect (the edge) for long. If gold and jade overflow a room, none will be able to safeguard it.

If you are wealthy and honored but arrogant, you will bring on your own ruin.

When the task is accomplished and you then retire: this is the way of Heaven.

Chapter 9 Explanation

This chapter illustrates the importance of humility (ch. 7) and non-contentiousness (ch. 8) with three situational images: an overfilled cup ready to spill,[1] an overbeaten knife-edge ready to chip, and an overflowing

---

1. This image is employed to good effect in the opening passage of the *Shasekishū* 沙石集 (1283) by Mujū Dōkyō 無住道曉 (1227–1312), wherein an academic visits a Zen monk who proceeds to overfill the visitor's teacup. When asked why, the monk replied,

68 | The Annotated *Laozi* 老子

treasury ripe for theft. All of these are metaphors for the main topics of this chapter: arrogance and grandstanding.

"Arrogance" (驕) is only explicitly mentioned twice in the *Laozi* (chs. 9 and 30), but it is implicit throughout. Chapter 1 implies that anyone who thinks they can fully describe the Way is arrogant; chapter 2 implies the same about those who claim a monopoly on defining beauty or competence; chapter 3 is on ostentatiousness, itself a form of arrogance. Here, arrogance in the "wealthy and honored" only sharpens our distaste for it.

The final sentence rhetorically turns the chapter around, from what we should *not* do to what we should, delivering a coup de grâce in a simple yet evocative description: "When the task is accomplished and you then retire: this is the way of Heaven." When you have accomplished something, walk away: no need for self-promotion or attention-grabbing or pontification. After all, other people may have accomplished the same thing in a different manner, more suited to their abilities, but no less effectively. No one likes a show-off. After this cautionary interlude, the next chapter returns to the narrative of self-cultivation, adding six more "commandments" to the ten of the previous chapter.

"Like this cup, you are full of your own opinions and speculations. How can I show you Zen unless you first empty your cup?" Nyogen Senzaki and Paul Reps, *Zen Flesh, Zen Bones* (London: Pelican Books, 1971 [1957]), 17.

Chapter 10

Key Ideas

Six steps: (1) embrace the One; (2) focus; (3) polish your "mysterious mirror"; (4) be without (contrived) knowledge; (5) be "feminine"; (6) be uncontrived; mysterious virtuosity produces / acts / leads inconspicuously.

載：營魄抱一，能無離乎？專氣致柔，能如嬰兒乎？
滌除「玄鑒」，能無疵乎？愛民治邦，能無知乎？
「天門」開闔，能為雌乎？明白四達，能無為乎？
生之畜之：「生而弗有，為而弗恃，長而弗宰」：是謂「玄德」。

Ah: controlling your corporeal soul while embracing the One,[1] can you not depart from it? Focusing your physical energies[2] while achieving flexibility, can you be as (supple as) an infant?[3]

---

1. Early China also had an ethereal *hun*-soul (魂), which does not appear in the *Laozi* (but it is in *Zhuangzi* chs. 2.2, 11.5, 13.2, 15.2, and 22.5). The corporeal *po*-soul (魄) appears only here (and in *Zhuangzi* chs. 13.10, 22.5). "Embracing the One" (抱一) is also in chapter 22. "One" as a metaphor for the Way is in chapters 10, 22, and 39, and might be implied in the "togetherness" (同) of chapter 1. Cf. *Laozi* chapter 39 and *Zhuangzi* chapter 6.3, where the "attain the One" (得一) of *Laozi* becomes "attain it" (得之), that is, "attain the Way" (得道), for *Zhuangzi*.

2. "Physical energies" (氣) refer to the fundamental constituents of matter and energy; here the referent is to one's body and mind. This term also appears in chapter 42 and 55.

3. The metaphor of the "infant" (嬰兒 or 赤子) appears in chapters 10, 20, 28, and 55, though it does not always indicate flexibility as it does here.

70 | The Annotated *Laozi* 老子

> *Cleaning off the "mysterious mirror"*[4] *(of your mind), can you make it spotless? Caring for*[5] *the people while organizing the state, can you do it without (contrived) "knowledge"?*
>
> *While the "Heavenly gate" opens and closes, can you play the role of the female? While perceiving clearly all within the four directions, can you be uncontrived?*
>
> *Produce them and nurture them:*[6] *"produce, but without possessiveness; act, but without expectation; lead, but without dominating":*[7] *this is called "mysterious virtuosity."*[8]

Chapter 10 Explanation

"Ah: controlling your corporeal soul while embracing the One, can you not depart from it?" This opening line introduces two new technical terms: the "corporeal soul" and the "One." Early Chinese Scholars texts refer to two different kinds of souls: an ethereal *hun*-soul (魂), which does not appear in the *Laozi*, and a corporeal *po*-soul (魄), which occurs in this text only here. These two kinds of soul reflect the Yin-Yang, stable-active analysis of things common in early China. At death, the Yin corporeal soul was thought to remain with the interred body, while the Yang ethereal soul could haunt the area around the grave. But while they logically go together, there is

---

4. HSG and FY have "mysterious vision" (玄覽) instead of "mysterious mirror" (玄鑒), which the earlier BD exemplar has; within the context of this sentence, the latter makes more sense to me.

5. To "care for" (愛) uses a graph that in modern Chinese means "love," and while that translation just might be appropriate in the *Laozi*, it seems a bit strong for its ancient meaning. The word appears in chapters 10, 13, 27, 34, 44, and 72, each time as "care for," except for chapter 44, where it is translated as "affections."

6. "Them" (之) could refer to the preceding six competencies, or it could just refer to "things" in general. This locution (i.e., 生之畜之) is also used in chapter 51, where "them" refers to "the myriad things." Grammatically, it should refer to the six preceding competencies.

7. These three phrases in quotes also occur in chapter 51. The topic of leadership is an important one in the *Laozi*, and at least fifteen terms are implicated in it. See "lead, leader (disambiguation)" in the index for a list and for where these terms appear throughout the text.

8. "Mysterious virtuosity" (玄德) also appears in chapters 51 and 65.

Chapter 10 | 71

much precedent for referring to them individually, as in this passage. Here it refers to our corporality, our embodiedness, and this sentence challenges us with the same kind of form-formless advice as that given in chapter 1, but with a slight difference.

In chapter 1, we were implicitly asked if we can both (simultaneously or sequentially) function as a "form," a body with all the desires and distractions this state entails, *and* as a mind able to "abide in formlessness." And that chapter ended by declaring that form and formlessness were a "mysterious" (玄) "togetherness" (同). That togetherness derives from the Way conceived as the "One" (一), due to its presence in both formlessness and form. In this chapter, we are asked if we can both function as a body and embrace the two-sides-of-one-coin oneness of form and formlessness, of regular, outward-oriented consciousness and relaxed, introspective consciousness.[9]

The second line, not to be outdone, introduces three important concepts: physical energies, flexibility, and the infant metaphor. "Focusing your physical energies while achieving flexibility, can you be as (supple as) an infant?" Physical energy, as we saw in the "key concepts," is a dynamic, ever-evolving, self-structuring, fundamental substance. Different things, including different parts of the body, entail different kinds of physical energies: the physical energy-substance of one's bones is decidedly less rarified that that of one's blood or breath. Here the physical energies in question are predominantly psychological because this makes the best sense as the object of the verb "focus" (專). But Yang focus is immediately balanced with Yin flexibility. "Flexibility" (柔), as in the flexibility of living bamboo or an infant able to effortlessly put its toe in its own mouth, is an antidote to ossification. Physical ossification, while a real concern for those concerned with longevity, is here still primarily a metaphor for the ossification of ideals like "beauty," "competence," and the like, discussed earlier. The metaphor of the infant as

---

9. The Way, as the "One," is in some later texts called the "Great One." *Lü shi chunqiu* 呂氏春秋 chapter 5.2: "The Way is ultimate essence, cannot become a form, and cannot be named; forced to articulate it, (I) would call it the Great One" (道也者，至精也，不可為形，不可為名；彊為之謂之太一). This principle may have been anthropomorphized as (or, perhaps, conflated with) a spirit called the "Great One" (太一). We are fortunate to have a pre-168 BCE drawing of this spirit on silk discovered in 1973 at Mawangdui, and a description of its cosmological creativity in a pre-300 BCE text called *The Great One Creates Water* (太一生水) discovered in 1993 at Guodian. But since the term "Great One" does not appear in the *Laozi*, there seems to be little warrant for assuming that spirit is the object of this sentence.

72 | The Annotated *Laozi* 老子

an aspirational figure for maximal flexibility, the Yin to the wizened sage's Yang, persisted as an unlikely aspirational ideal for Daoists, showing up in *Zhuangzi* chapters 19 and 26.

But a much more influential metaphor appears in the following line: "Cleaning off the 'mysterious mirror' (of your mind), can you make it spotless?" Zhuangzi makes use of this image too,[10] which centuries later went on to be immortalized in the famous exchange of Zen poems between contenders for the position of sixth patriarch.[11] This notion of a reflective mind works well for both its "abiding in formlessness" and "abiding in form" modes. For the former, we apprehend things without becoming attached to any particular thing that we sense or imagine or think: it works against confirmation bias (which in this metaphor would be like dust on a mirror). In the latter, it is a metaphor for objectivity, for responding only to what is actually there, rather than to what we think *ought* to be there: it stands for clarity and truthfulness.

The next line builds on the role of government that was briefly mentioned in chapter 8, which said, "In government, competence lies in organization." Both chapters 8 and 10 stipulate "organization" (治) as fundamental to government (and indeed *zhi* 治 also means "to govern"), but here two more actions are stipulated: caring and unbiased knowing. "Caring for the people while organizing the state, can you do it without (contrived) 'knowledge' [of confining mental categories]?" "Caring" as a government duty does not appear again in the *Laozi*, though chapter 27 does say that competent teachers will care for their students. In chapter 3 we saw that sages "cause the people to be without (contrived) knowledge [of confining mental categories]," but here it is the ruler, and by implication the sage-ruler, that is described as being without such constrictive "knowledge." This advice, combined with the rejection of a variety of categorical inflexibility in chapters 2, 3, and 5, and the objectivity implied in the preceding sentence, leads one to infer that the author is recommending to rulers that they reject nepotism in their hiring practices and "open their minds" to anyone who is competent at benefiting the people, no matter how "ugly," "low-born,"

---

10. *Zhuangzi* chapter 7.6: "Accomplished people use their minds like mirrors: going after nothing, welcoming nothing, responding but not storing; this is why they can succeed with things without harm" (至人之用心若鏡：不將不迎，應而不藏；故能勝物而不傷). *Zhuangzi* ch. 22.12 expands on this.

11. See the *Platform Sutra*. Huineng, however, uses the metaphor for his own, Buddhist, ends.

or unconventional they are. Of course, this advice need not be directed only to rulers; even citizens of a democracy may want to be similarly open-minded when choosing their representatives. In any case, the remainder of the chapter is not confined to rulers.

"While the 'Heavenly gate' opens and closes, can you play the role of the female?" reiterates the central role of the "female" first encountered in chapter 6 (and which will appear again in chapters 28 and 61). And while we also saw "the gate of the mysterious female" in that chapter, the "Heavenly gate" here is a slightly different metaphor. The "gate of the mysterious female" is a metaphor for the productive fecundity of Heaven and Earth. It emphasizes the directionality of formlessness to form. The "Heavenly gate" here is a metaphor for the unity of the One, for the cyclical return of formlessness to form and form to formlessness, like an opening and closing door. *Zhuangzi* chapter 23 defines the expression thus: "Forms are produced and those forms die: forms come out and forms go in. This going in and coming out without yet manifesting their shapes, this is called the Heavenly gate. The Heavenly gate is formlessness and form, and the myriad things come forth via formlessness and form" (有乎生，有乎死：有乎出，有乎入 。入出而無見其形，是謂天門。天門者，無有也，萬物出乎無有).[12] The "opening of the Heavenly gate," then, refers to normal, everyday consciousness of form, while the "closing of the Heavenly gate" refers to the introspective state of "abiding in formlessness." "Playing the role of the female," meanwhile, similar to the "infant" metaphor, refers to the flexibility and adaptability of switching between these modes.

The next sentence, "While perceiving clearly all within the four directions, can you be uncontrived?," can be construed as recommending rulers to be knowledgeable about their states, but it is more fundamentally important in underlining that "perceiving clearly" must be done without the contrivance of biased preconceptions.

It is perhaps noteworthy that each of the preceding three pairs of advice begins with a metaphor (embrace the One, clean your mirror, play the role of the female) followed by practical advice (be mentally flexible, be an objective leader, be uncontrived).

---

12. Some English translations of this passage take 無有 as "nonbeing" rather than as "formlessness and form." I follow Chen Guying's understanding. Chen Guying 陳鼓應, *Zhuangzi jinzhu jinyi* 莊子今註今譯, 2 vols. (臺北: 臺灣商務印書館, 1974; rev. ed. 1999), 2:630–32.

74 | The Annotated *Laozi* 老子

In the final sentence, we are not only advised to "produce" and "nurture" all six of the competencies outlined in the preceding sentences, but to do so detachedly. This method is articulated in the poetic " 'produce, but without possessiveness; act, but without expectation; lead, but without dominating,' " the middle phrase of which we saw in chapter 2 (and we will see all three again in ch. 51). While these phrases describe just *how* we should "embrace the One" and pursue the rest of this chapter's advice for self-cultivation, we might also extrapolate to the relationship between humans and the myriad things, or between humans and their possessions (the "nurture them" implies domesticated animals in particular) or between rulers and their (human) "possessions." In both scenarios—with rulers and us regular people—we are advised to simultaneously "produce," "act," and "lead" things but without "possessing," "expecting (contrived outcomes from)," or "dominating" them. That is to say, we should be detached (i.e., "disinterested" in the technical, philosophical sense, but not "uninterested" in colloquial parlance) from both social conventions and material possessions. This echoes the non-contrivance of the previous sentence and also the anti-ostentatiousness of "When the task is accomplished and you then retire" in the previous chapter.

Finally, "this is called 'mysterious virtuosity.' " This is the first appearance of "virtuosity" (德), which appears in fifteen of the eighty-one chapters of this text. Virtuosity in early China originally referred to the charismatic power of a popular leader, but its semantic parameters then broadened to include the intrinsic, effective properties of any given thing. (*Zhuangzi* ch. 19 refers to the virtuosity of a chicken.) Zhuangzi often described human virtuosity in terms of "harmony."[13] This might refer to the harmonization, the balancing, of our individual inclinations with the expectations of our community. When construed as deriving from the Way, it may be called "mysterious." And what is more mysterious, more understated, than the usefulness of nothingness, the topic of the next chapter?

---

13. For example, *Zhuangzi* chapter 16: "Virtuosity is harmony; the Way is principle" (德，和也；道，理也).

Chapter 11

Key Idea

Form is profitable, but openness makes form useful.

三十輻共一轂：當其無有，車之用。
埏埴以為器：當其無有，器之用。
鑿戶牖以為室：當其無有，室之用。
故有之以為利，無之以為用。

When thirty spokes come together in one hub: precisely its openness and form create the usefulness of the carriage.

When you knead clay in order to make a vessel: precisely its openness and form create the usefulness of the vessel.

When you chisel out a door or window in order to make a house: precisely its openness and form create the usefulness of the house.

Thus, it is form that makes a thing profitable, but it is openness that makes it actually useful.

Chapter 11 Explanation

Chapter 11 adds three more metaphors of openness to the empty vessel (ch. 4), the bellows (ch. 5), the valley (ch. 6), and the gate (chs. 6, 10) employed so far. Here it is the usefulness of open spaces that is emphasized (though utility was also implied in the previous metaphors). In all four of the preceding sentences, *wu* 無 is translated as "openness" rather than "formlessness" because the "openness" of wheel hubs, bowls, and doors makes more sense than their "formlessness." But we should remember that the Chinese word

75

76 | The Annotated *Laozi* 老子

is the same and that this is a translation issue. The form-formless dichotomy of chapter 1 is thus echoed again in the final line: "It is form that makes a thing profitable, but it is openness that makes it actually useful." That is, we *pay for* wheels, bowls, and doorframes, but actually *use* the open spaces embedded within them. This openness, or emptiness or formlessness, is certainly a nod toward open-mindedness, to being open to creativity that springs from the "formlessness" of a relaxed mind. Creativity, as every artist knows, is eminently useful. With the metaphorical usefulness of openness established in this chapter, we can now turn to some practical applications of open-mindedness in the next.

Chapter 12

Key Ideas

Open-mindedness: conventional categorizations blind you to other possibilities; follow your gut instead.

「五色」令人目盲;「五音」令人耳聾;「五味」令人口爽。
馳騁田獵,令人心發狂;難得之貨,令人行妨。
是以聖人為「腹」,不為「目」。故去彼取此。

The "five colors" make people's eyes blind. The "five sounds" make people's ears deaf. The "five flavors" make people's mouths dull.

The chase and hunt[1] make people's minds go crazy, and difficult-to-attain goods impede people's actions.

This is why sages are for the "belly" but not for the "eye." Thus, they abandon that and adopt this.[2]

Chapter 12 Explanation

This is a particularly elliptical chapter, with two main interpretations. Here is how I understand it: "[The conventional, contrived categorization of] the 'five colors'—that is, the standard color scheme in early China—make people's eyes blind [to all the other colors, shades, and hues that we can see].

---

1. The "chase" (馳騁) appears again in chapter 43 as the verb "run circles around."

2. The phrase "Thus, they abandon that and adopt this" is also at the end of chapters 38 and 72.

77

78 | The Annotated *Laozi* 老子

[The conventional, contrived categorization of] the 'five sounds'—that is, the standard music scheme in early China—make people's ears deaf [to all the other notes and sounds that we can hear]. [The conventional, contrived categorization of] the 'five flavors'—that is, the standard taste scheme in early China—make people's mouths dull [toward all the other flavor profiles that we can taste]." This is the minority interpretation.

The traditional, majority reading, backed by the elucidation of these same lines in *Hanfeizi* 韓非子 chapter 20 and *Huainanzi* 淮南子 chapters 7.4 and 8.10, is that the "five colors, sounds, and flavors" refer to the many distractions of the external world of forms. This interpretation assumes that this chapter is advising us not to be seduced by that world, but rather to alternate between "abiding in forms" and "abiding in formlessness." If we note that the preceding eleven chapters have (at least) two major themes of introspection-extrospection and non-contrivance, then we might notice that the traditional view of this chapter follows the former theme, while my explanation follows the latter theme of non-contrivance. Perhaps the best way to resolve the issue would be to allow the poetic language to simultaneously carry both implications: we should *both* not neglect interior formlessness for the attractions of exterior form, *and* we should not be constricted to contrived mental categories. That is, be introspective sometimes *and* "think outside the box."

The fourth sentence can also be read in these two ways. The traditional reading would be "The chase and hunt [for attractive external forms] make people's minds go crazy [in pursuit of the external] (just as always working without sleeping can make us go 'crazy'), and difficult-to-attain goods impede people's actions [from pursuing introspection by focusing desire on external forms]." My preferred reading is "The chase and hunt [after contrived fashions dictated by others] make people's minds go crazy [by constricting our creative choices], and difficult-to-attain goods impede people's actions [from valuing goods that we personally find attractive, but which are not valued by the majority or by the arbiters of taste]." The "contrived fashions" after which we might "chase and hunt" include both fashions in physical "beauty" (ch. 2) as well as ethical conceptions of "goodness" (ch. 5). "Difficult-to-attain goods" also has two levels: the sentence implicates both the particular values placed upon specific objects as well as the larger, societal "rat race" that impels us to acquire those objects.

It should come as no surprise that the fifth sentence can similarly be read to support both interpretations (i.e., as a call to introspection and as a call to non-contrivance). In the traditional interpretation, the "belly"

Chapter 12 | 79

is an "empty" and inner vessel contrasted with the outward-looking "eye," and the rejection of the "eye" for the "belly" is actually a rejection of the imbalance that constantly favors the outer over the inner. The minority reading that I follow interprets the "belly" as our intuitive "gut" (as in: "I have a gut feeling about this"), in contrast with the "eye" as the "mind's eye," where we avariciously imagine the things we need to do and acquire in order to rise in the social hierarchy.[3] In this latter reading, this sentence would mean "follow your (uncontrived) gut, your conscience, and not your faddish whims that you imagine will get you 'ahead' in life." A corollary of this second understanding is that following your gut represents (or results in) a simpler life, while chasing after the shiny objects that your eyes always see on the horizon represents (and results in) an extravagant life. We will see these themes in later chapters.

The phrase "Thus, they abandon that and adopt this" that closes this chapter is evidence for the minority understanding that this chapter is a call to reject contrivance in the form of (imperfect) categorization schemes. The majority view of "balance extrospection with introspection" is a both-this-*and*-that bit of advice, whereas the minority view of "ignore contrivance and follow your individual creativity" is an "abandon that and adopt this" bit of advice. In addition, this phrase occurs twice more in the *Laozi*, in chapters 38 and 72, and in both instances it fits somewhat better with the second, minority reading here. Chapter 38 rejects contrivance in favor of non-contrivance (which is how I read this chapter), and chapter 72 rejects ostentatiousness in favor of humility. We should usually abandon contrivance and ostentatiousness in favor of non-contrivance and humility, while the world of forms should only be temporarily "abandoned" in favor of the world of formlessness. Thus, I read this final sentence as "Thus, they [i.e., sages] abandon that [i.e., contrived, conventional categories] and adopt this [i.e., sagely open-mindedness and creativity]." Such open-mindedness is related to the detachment that is the topic of the next chapter.

---

3. Slingerland, *Trying Not to Try*, says the "belly" is "hot, system 1" thinking informed by our emotions—our "gut"—while the "eye" is "cold, system 2" thinking that is primarily logical and relatively untouched by emotion (88).

Chapter 13

Key Ideas

Be detached from favor or disgrace from others; be detached from your person, even as you value and care for it.

寵辱若驚。貴大患若身。

何謂「寵辱若驚」？寵為下：得之若驚，失之若驚，是謂「寵辱若驚」。

何謂「貴大患若身」？吾所以有大患者，為吾有身：及吾無身，吾有何患？

故貴以身為天下者，若可以託天下矣；愛以身為天下者，若可以寄天下矣。

Favor and disgrace (should be seen) as surprising. Values and great vexations (should be seen) as personal.

What does it mean to say, "Favor and disgrace (should be seen) as surprising"? Favor is for subordinates: thus, both getting it (should be seen) as surprising and losing it (should be seen) as surprising. This is why it is said, "Favor and disgrace (should be seen) as surprising."

What does it mean to say, "Values and great vexations (should be seen) as personal"? That by which we have great vexation is due to our having persons: If we were without (contrived) personhood, what vexation would we have?

Thus, those who value their persons the same as everyone else in the world are those that can be entrusted with the world, and

80

those who care for their persons the same as everyone else in the world are those that can be given the world.[1]

Chapter 13 Explanation

The attitude of detachment implied in chapter 10 with the mind-as-mirror metaphor returns here to be applied not to the mind but to the emotions, as well as to our own persons. Humans are a social species that crave "favor" and recoil from "disgrace," but we should nevertheless try to ameliorate this preference through the cultivation of detachment. This detachment encompasses both detachment from the vagaries of how others perceive and treat us, as well as how we define and value ourselves. The first sentence addresses how others see us, and the second how we see ourselves.

The second paragraph explanation for the first sentence is perhaps more elliptical than usual, given that the rhetorical weight of the entire paragraph rests entirely on the first three graphs of its second sentence: "Favor is for subordinates" (寵為下). Both favor and disgrace are, by definition, hierarchical: generally speaking, only superiors can bestow them on inferiors. The *Laozi*, given its penchant for undermining contrived (and sometimes arbitrary) social conventions, is more focused on individual freedom and not on hierarchal structures (even if the latter are, to a very real degree, unavoidable; cf. ch. 20). Hence, it is best to (emotionally, if not practically) ignore such relationships and, when the particulars of these relational dynamics are publicized, or when they shift (as they probably will), it is best to treat them *both* as surprising events. Thus: "Favor is for subordinates: [and, since you should not consider yourself existentially 'subordinate' to anyone, you should treat favor—as well as disgrace—equally] thus, both getting it (should be seen) as surprising and losing it (should be seen) as surprising." Many of us cannot avoid having bosses, but just as we do not need to accept other people's ideas of "beauty," we also do not need to accept their ideas of "competence," even when the latter comes with praise and blame, favor and disgrace.

---

1. The grammar here of 以 X 為 Y (to take or regard X as Y) is, literally, "to take (or regard) yourself as (the same as) everyone else." I continued with the use of "persons" to match the locution of the preceding lines (with "personal," "persons," and "personhood" for 身), even though it makes the English in this last sentence somewhat stilted.

82 | The Annotated *Laozi* 老子

The other bit of advice that opens this chapter is the Yin personal to the first sentence's Yang interpersonal. "Values" are subjective, and "great vexations"—as distinct from minor vexations like an inconvenience or a temporary sickness—are those that we bring upon ourselves.[2] I noted in the "non-contrivance" (無為) section of the "key concepts" that there are several other negative locutions that resonate with non-contrivance, and to be "without (contrived) personhood" (無身) is one of them. Here the "great vexations" are precisely our own contrived ideas about ourselves, and the antidote to such vexations is to not be contrived *toward ourselves*. Without such contrivance, "what vexation would we have"? Clearly, we would still have small vexations like stubbed toes, catching colds, or being "disgraced" by our boss, but we would thereby avoid the "great vexations" of self-delusion.

The final sentence ties one's self-conception or, perhaps, self-regard, to leadership. All of the previous sentences in this chapter promote a kind of individualism, but the last sentence warns against *selfish* individualism. Pursuing self-cultivation and avoiding self-contrivance are great, but the larger context of the community should not be forgotten. We can each define "beauty" and "competence" as we see fit, but so can everyone else, and our personal definitions of such "names," while they may work best for us, are not thereby somehow superior. Those with this kind of self-awareness *and* other-awareness are thereby fit to be "entrusted with" or "given the world," which is to say, are fit for positions of leadership. It would not be unwarranted to presume that such leaders would be chary with dispensing "favor and disgrace." Humble people such as these, however, still need to have a grasp of the cosmic Way in order to be effective leaders, and so we return again to the topic of the Way in the next chapter.

---

2. The grammar of the opening two sentences of this chapter has perplexed many. The "A, B (should be seen) as C" construction is complexified by the "great" (大), as it breaks the symmetry by adding a third word before the verb. Some scholars resolve this anomaly by construing "values" (貴) as a verb. ("Values" can also be translated as the verb or noun "honor"; see the index for both uses in this text.) But I take the symmetry-breaking "great" to be an indication that the author is not referring to ordinary "vexations" (患)—a term that appears nowhere else in the *Laozi*—but rather to a special kind of vexation. A second problem is whether to take "person" (身) as referring to one's physical body or one's whole physical and psychological person. I take it as the latter, and thus might also translate it as "self," as I do in the term "self-cultivation" (修身).

Chapter 14

Key Idea

Although the Way is elusive and vague, grasping it allows us to "steer" ourselves through life.

視之不見，名曰夷；聽之不聞，名曰希；搏之不得，名曰微。此
　三者不可致詰，故混而為一。
其上不皦，其下不昧。繩繩不可名，復歸於無物。是謂「無狀之
　狀，無物之象」。是謂惚恍。迎之不見其首，隨之不見其後。
執古之道，以御今之有，以知古始：是謂「道紀」。

Looking for it without seeing it, it is called unobtrusive; listening for it without hearing it, it is called faint; grasping for it without obtaining it, it is called inconspicuous. These three cannot be extensively interrogated, thus it is unfathomable yet is one.

Above, it is not bright, and below, it is not dark. Endless, it cannot be named; it returns and goes back to nothingness.[1] It is called "a shapeless shape, a semblance[2] in nothingness." It is called elusive and vague. If you meet it you will not see its front, and if you follow it you will not see its back.

---

1. "Nothingness" (無物) occurs only in this chapter and means the same thing as "formlessness" (無).

2. The term "semblance(s)" (象) is also in chapters 21, 35, and 41; it appeared in chapter 4 as "seems."

84 | The Annotated *Laozi* 老子

Grasp the ancient[3] Way in order to steer today's forms, in order
to know the ancient beginnings: this is called "deciphering[4] the Way."

Chapter 14 Explanation

Chapter 14 returns us to the opening line in chapter 1 and gives an answer to the question: Why is it that "the way that can be (fully) conveyed is not the abiding Way"? Already in chapter 1 we knew that it had something to do with the inadequacies of language and with its connection to "formlessness," and here we further learn: because it is difficult to perceive with our senses. Thus, we can describe it as "unobtrusive," "faint," and "inconspicuous." "These three"—that is, the unobtrusiveness, faintness, and inconspicuousness of the Way—"cannot be extensively interrogated" because they mostly elude our senses. Because it so eludes our senses we can conclude that it is "unfathomable, yet" nevertheless, is still "one," a single principle.

The second paragraph distinguishes the Way from Heaven and Earth, insofar as Heaven is "above" and "bright," while Earth is "below" and "dark." Further, Heaven and Earth can be "named," though whether they can be construed as "endless" is unclear. The Way "returns and goes back to nothingness" but it does not stay that way because it is a cyclical principle: formlessness to form to formlessness, without end (well, so far as we know). It may be difficult to perceive this, but not impossible. (Again, a comparison to gravity may be helpful.)

The "shapeless shape" locution occurs only here, but it sets up an important technical term that we will meet again in chapters 21, 35, and 41—the "semblances" of things on the cusp of form and formlessness: the unobtrusive, faint, and inconspicuous indications of things yet to come, the "elusive and vague" signs that are only perceived by percipient sages.[5]

---

3. MWD A, B both have "today's" (今) instead of "the ancient" (古), but BD and all later exemplars have "the ancient."

4. The verb "decipher" (紀) literally means both "thread" and "unravel," but I think in the context of this chapter "deciphering the Way" works better than "unraveling the Way," even though the visual metaphor is lost. (Since in the Chinese "deciphering" follows the "Way," it is more properly a gerund; literally, "the Way's deciphering.")

5. One may be reminded of "the still, small voice" (RSV) or the "sound of sheer silence" (NRSV) in which Elijah recognized his god Yahweh (1 Kings 19:12).

Chapter 14 | 85

It is, however, the last line that most clearly situates this chapter between the previous one on rulers and the subsequent one on officials: "Grasp the ancient Way in order to steer [literally, "steer a chariot"] today's forms." Though we have already seen that the Way is "useful" (chs. 4, 6, 11), and that "abiding in" its formless and formed states allow us to "observe its mysteries . . . [and] manifestations" (ch. 1), this is the first time that the utility of the Way itself is described in practically effective terms. The claim that "grasping" the Way will allow us to "steer" the forms, the things of this world, is an attractive claim. (If the intended audience of the *Laozi* were solely, or even primarily, the rulers of Laozi's day, then the author probably should have started the book with this line.) Given the opening phrases of this chapter, we can be sure that "grasping" is a metaphorical grasping, a grasping with the mind, an understanding. Further, the verb "to steer" implies *not* "to have absolute or dictatorial control over" but rather "to deal with," or even "to cooperate with," just as a charioteer can effectively influence the horses pulling a chariot, even while those horses may have their own agendas outside the ken of the charioteer.

The closing image of "deciphering the Way" fits beautifully with the rest of the chapter because this chapter paints a picture of the Way as "unfathomable" and "vague," yet amenable to being "grasped" and "known." So, as with creatively theorizing the existence of gravity, we must do some detective work before we can apprehend the not-(yet)-fully-comprehensible principles that govern our selves and our world. The tentative nature of this deciphering is amplified in the next chapter.

Chapter 15

Key Ideas

Competent Daoists are: (1) prepared; (2) hesitant; (3) tentative; (4) yielding; (5) solid; (6) open; (7) unfathomable; they use both tranquility and movement to grow and avoid stasis.

> 古之善為道者，微妙玄通，深不可識。夫唯不可識，故強為之
>   容：
> 豫兮若冬涉川，猶兮若畏四鄰，儼兮其若客，渙兮其若釋，敦兮
>   其若樸，曠兮其若谷，混兮其若濁。
> 孰能「濁以靜之徐清」？孰能「安以動之徐生」？
> 保此道者，不欲「盈」。夫唯不盈，故能蔽而新成。

Anciently, those competent at according with the Way[1] were inconspicuously wondrous, mysteriously penetrating, and incomprehensibly deep. Precisely because they cannot be comprehended is why we are forced to make for them a description:

Prepared, as when fording a creek in winter; hesitant, as when reverent[2] of all one's neighbors; tentative, as if they were a guest;

---

1. MWD B and FY have this reading, while GD A, BD, and nearly all other exemplars have "those competent at being officials" (善為士者), a phrase that is found in chapter 68. In chapter 68 this locution makes good sense, while there seems to be nothing in this chapter that is specific to "officials," so I have gone with the minority reading because I think it makes better sense. The phrase "those competent at according with the Way" is also in chapter 65.

2. *Wei* 畏 means both "fearful" (as in chs. 17, 53, 72, 74) and "reverent" (chs. 15, 20); I chose "reverent" here because I don't think "those competent at according with the Way" would be fearful people.

86

Chapter 15 | 87

yielding, like melting (ice); solid, like an uncarved block of wood;[3]
open, like a valley; unfathomable, like muddy water.

*Who is able, "when muddied, to use tranquility to calmly
become clear"?*[4] *Who is able, "when settled, to use movement to
calmly grow"?*

Those who protect this Way do not desire to be "full."[5] *Precisely not being full is why they are able to be hidden, yet renewed
and complete.*[6]

Chapter 15 Explanation

The usual aspirational figure in the *Laozi* is the "sage" (who appears in twen-
ty-five chapters), while "Those competent at according with the Way" is used
only here and in chapter 65. I suspect they are pretty much synonymous.
Such people are "wondrous," "penetrating," and "deep" because they are in the
process of "deciphering the Way" (ch. 14), a process that requires both internal

---

3. The "uncarved block of wood" (樸) is elsewhere a metaphor for potentiality (ch. 28)
and simplicity (chs. 19, 32 37, 57).

4. "Muddied" refers to a doubtful, tentative, fallibilist frame of mind, that only becomes
clear after patient evidence-gathering. Cf. chapters 20, 49.

5. Here being "full" (盈) signifies a state of stasis and complacency; it also has a negative
connotation in chapter 9, but it is a good thing in chapters 39 and 45, and is neutral
in chapters 4 and 22.

6. Exemplars differ on the last several graphs: MWD B, FY (敝而不成), HNZ (弊而不
新成), BD (敝不成), XE (弊復成), HSG, DZ (蔽不新成), FYY (敝不新成). Two other
potentially relevant passages in the *Laozi* are chapters 22 (敝則新: "worn out then
new"), where sources are split on 敝 / 弊, and 45 (大成若缺，其用不弊: "[Although]
great completion [may] seem flawed, using it does not wear it out"), where sources
mostly use 弊, though MWD B and BD use 敝. The graphs for "hidden; ignorant"
(蔽), "worn out" (敝), and "torn down; used up; flawed" (弊) are similar and the second
two are often interchangeable (as in chs. 22 and 45). Since I don't think "Those who
protect this Way" can be "worn out" or "used up," I follow WB's note, HSG, DZ for
"hidden" (蔽); and since "not complete" (不成) or "not renewed and complete" (不新
成) would imply a negative connotation for "complete"—whereas the many instances
of "complete" in LZ (see index) *all* have positive connotations (ch. 7 notes that sages
"complete themselves": 成其私)—I follow the majority of exemplars for "renewed and
complete" (新成), while dropping the "not" (不), though XE's "repeatedly completed"
(復成) remains an intriguing alternative. "Renewed" appears only here, and in chapter
22 as "new."

88 | The Annotated *Laozi* 老子

"focus" (ch. 10) and external detachment (chs. 12–13). That they "cannot be [fully] comprehended" is because they have individual differences: Daoist sages are not identical. At the very least, they will likely have different ideas about beauty, competence, goodness, and the rest. But, though they cannot be "comprehended," they certainly can be apprehended (i.e., we can know *some* things about them, just not everything). Hence the author feels that they can make a description of such people, even if that description is "forced."

The seven-part description that follows highlights the careful nature of what it means to "grasp the ancient Way" such that we may "steer" things. Such people are: (1) prepared (豫); (2) hesitant (猶); (3) tentative (儼); (4) yielding (渙); (5) solid (敦); (6) open (曠); and (7) unfathomable (混). That is, they have foresight and are cautious, polite, flexible, trustworthy, open-minded, and doubtful (i.e., humble).

The second paragraph pivots on the multivalence of the image of water: sometimes "muddied" and sometimes "clear" or "settled." "Muddied" is a metaphor for the aspirational state of fallibilism, of knowing that you don't know everything, and that new evidence might always crop up to undermine your knowledge. Being "settled," on the other hand, recalls a previous metaphor: if we are (or at least strive to be) objective, like a spotless mirror, then a certain amount of confidence in our (fallible) knowledge is justified. And the means for getting from muddied uncertainty to clear (albeit tentative) certainty is "tranquility" (靜). This term, appearing first here but also in chapters 16, 26, 37, 45, 57, and 61, will become a central Daoist theme, also one picked up much later in Zen. Unless I am reading too much into this term, it seems to be construed here as an early antidote to what we (much later) will come to call "confirmation bias." We should move from uncertainty to certainty slowly, cautiously, and objectively, and not by cherry-picking evidence to fit our preconceived notions. A tranquil attitude is thus the basis for the steady "movement" necessary for us to "calmly grow." (Our emulation of changing water clarity is another example of ethical realism.)

But no matter how confident we might grow in our knowledge, even knowledge that is steadily and calmly gained, we should never feel as if there is nothing left to learn on any given subject. That is, we should never be, or feel, "full."[7] This would indicate stasis, the opposite of "steady movement," and overconfidence, the antithesis of fallibilism.

---

7. James Legge translated this single graph as "full of themselves," a delightful colloquialism that was apparently around even back in the nineteenth century. See James Legge, *The Texts of Taoism*, 2 vols. (New York: Dover, 1962 [1891]), 1:58.

Chapter 15 | 89

The last line unfortunately has two textual problems, due to the several variations among exemplars for the last part of the sentence (see note 6). As I read it, it is a reiteration of the movement from doubt to clarity, wherein the humble fallibilist, being "not full" (不盈), is nevertheless still able to move, in their humble "hiddenness," to "renewal" (新) and "completion" (成), that is, confidence. This reading might remind us of another Yin-to-Yang phrase from chapter 7: "Is it not because they [i.e., sages] are selfless that they are able to complete themselves?" (非以其無私邪，故能成其私？). To be "selfless" seems akin to being "not full," with both of these states resulting in our "completion," which, despite the potential implication of finality, certainly refers to a dynamic state of mind that is sometimes "muddied" and sometimes "clear." What is "completed" is the attitude of fallibilism, the 'full circle' of Yin-Yang, formless-form, muddied-clear, settled-growth that is always in motion, always being renewed, always completing—becoming— itself. The goals of being tranquil and being "not full" in this chapter are resumed in the opening sentence of the next chapter.

Chapter 16

Key Ideas

Openness and tranquility enable us to return to abide in destiny, and the resulting percipience leads to tolerance, impartiality, wholeness, the Heavenly, the Way, and durability.

致虛極，守靜篤。萬物並作，吾以觀其復。

夫物芸芸，各復歸其根，曰靜。靜曰「復命」。復命，常也；知
常，明也；不知常，妄作凶。

知常容，容乃公，公乃全，全乃天，天乃道，道乃久，沒身不
殆。

Achieve utmost openness; preserve deep tranquility. The myriad things arise together, and we use these to observe their return.

Things thrive in abundance, but each again returns to its root, which is called tranquility. Tranquility is called "returning to destiny."[1] To return to destiny is to abide. To know how to abide is percipience.[2] To not know how to abide is to foolishly incite inauspiciousness.

Knowing how to abide brings tolerance; tolerance brings impartiality; impartiality brings wholeness; wholeness brings the Heavenly;

---

1. I distinguish "destiny" from "fate" by defining fate as those things that we cannot avoid or change (e.g., who our parents are, our genetic makeup, where we were born) and destiny as the potential that we discover in ourselves. We can fail our destiny but cannot fail our fate. *Ming* 命 has both meanings.

2. This "to know how to abide is percipience" (知常，明也) is, in later exemplars, "to know how to abide is called percipience" (知常曰明), which appears in chapter 55.

Chapter 16 | 91

*the Heavenly brings the Way; and the Way brings durability, such
that for the rest of your life you will be free from danger.*[3]

Chapter 16 Explanation

"Openness," or open-mindedness, is a central theme in the *Laozi*, already
discernable in the warnings about contrived social conventions in chapters
2, 3, and 5, and in the "open" metaphors for the Way in chapters 4, 6,
and 11. The term *xu* 虛 literally means "empty" (as in the empty bellows
in chapter 5 and the empty granary in chapter 53), and sometimes "empty"
works metaphorically (as in the "empty words" in chapter 22). But other
times the metaphor doesn't work in English. In chapter 3, where sages were
said to "open [i.e., empty] the minds" (虛其心) of the people, and in this
chapter, "empty" is the same kind of spatial metaphor as the "open" in
"open-minded" (insofar as an "open-minded" person's mind is not literally
open, like an open window). Here, this literal "emptiness" as metaphorical
"openness" is the same as, or at least resonant with, the "abiding in formlessness" of chapter 1, and it functions just as the tranquility did in the
previous chapter: as the Yin basis for Yang activity. If one is open-minded
and tranquil, then one can see the ebb and flow of forms, of things, as
they come and go.

"The myriad things arise together, and we use these [i.e., openness
and tranquility] to observe their return." If you are closed-minded or caught
up in the hustle and bustle of life, you will be unable to see how things
return, how form reverts to formlessness.

"Things thrive in abundance, but each again returns to its root,"
the root of formlessness, from which all things stem. This root "is called
tranquility" because the introspective state of "abiding in formlessness" is
a tranquil one. "Tranquility is called 'returning to destiny'" because when
we return, in tranquility, to the root of formlessness, of potentiality, then

---

3. GD A, but no other exemplar, has as its entire chapter 16: "Perfect openness is
'abiding.' Preserving what is within is 'depth.' The myriad things arise together, and
dwell by means of necessarily returning. The way of Heaven is circular, each (thing)
returning to its root" (至虛，恆也；守中，篤也。萬物旁作，居以須復也。天道員員，各
復其根). The meaning is roughly the same, but this version repeats the "preserving what
is within" from chapter 5.

92 | The Annotated *Laozi* 老子

we can discover our own potential, our own destiny.[4] This introspective state, which actually includes both the knowledge of our individual potential and our inevitable mortality, "is to abide" (常), synonymous or nearly synonymous with the "abiding" (恆) used for both the Yin and Yang states in chapter 1. The "abiding in formlessness" in chapter 1 led to being able to "observe . . . wonders" (觀 . . . 妙), and here it leads to "percipience" (明), so the perceiving *of* wonders—both universal and individual—is not an unwarranted conclusion to draw. "To not know how to abide is to foolishly incite inauspiciousness," because then we will interact with the world (i.e., the myriad things of the first two sentences) in a wrong-footed manner, *and* we will struggle to discover the individual potential that we all have (i.e., the destiny to which we might return). In both cases, inauspiciousness is sure to manifest.[5]

Beginning with the "root" of open-mindedly and tranquilly "abiding" in formlessness is the start of accepting and abiding in the Yin-Yang, form-formless nature of the Way. This beginning sets off a chain reaction, predicated on "percipience," which then (ideally) results in "tolerance" (容), then "impartiality" (公), then "wholeness" (全), then "the Heavenly" (天), then "the Way" (道), and finally, "durability" (久).

That is: *perception* of the ebb and flow; *tolerance* for other ways of being beautiful, competent, and the rest; *impartiality* in dealing with those other ways; *wholeness*, insofar as the objectivity of impartiality leads to personal growth (as we saw in chapter 15); *the Heavenly*, insofar as we will then be free of (contrived) social conventions and thus be able to realize our individual, natural destinies;[6] and *the Way*, of harmonizing our individual destinies with the community (contrived social conventions and all) and the environment. All this should result in not just a peaceful and fulfilling life, but a long one as well. The "danger" we should be free of, "for the rest of your life," is the danger of "foolishly incit[ing] inauspiciousness" by (in reverse order) *not* abiding, *not* being percipient, *not* returning to destiny,

---

4. Alternatively, or rather, additionally, if you want to read *ming* 命 here as "(unchangeable) fate" rather than "(changeable) destiny," then this would refer to the fact that all things are fated to death or disintegration rather than, as I read it, to the situation of individuals discovering their raison d'être. I suspect both readings are correct.

5. "Inauspiciousness" (凶) appears again in chapters 30 (as "bad") and 31.

6. "Heavenly" is often a euphemism for "natural" in the Scholars texts.

Chapter 16 | 93

not being tranquil or open. People who practice this Way thus begin in openness and tranquility, within themselves, and end in durability, within their community, and progress from the one to the other (and back again) smoothly and unobtrusively. It is this smoothness and unobtrusiveness that are the topics of the next chapter.

Chapter 17

Key Idea

The best leaders are unobtrusive and trusting.

太上，下知有之；其次，親而譽之；其次，畏之；其次，侮之。
信不足焉，有不信焉。猶乎其貴言。成功遂事，而百姓曰我自
　然。

*For the top leaders,[1] their subordinates know only that they are there;
for the next (type of leader, their subordinates) are close to them and
praise them; for the next (type of leader, their subordinates) fear them;
and for the next (type of leaders, their subordinates) insult them.*

*(If a leader's) trust in them is insufficient, then there will
be a lack of trust in him.[2] Hence, he values his words. (Thus, he)
completes tasks and accomplishes activities, yet the people say that
they did it themselves.[3]*

---

1. The word *shang* 上 has two general meanings in this text: literally, "above" (as in ch. 14) or "highest" (as in ch. 8) or "best" (as in ch. 31), but also "to lead" (as in chs. 66 and 75).

2. This phrase appears again in chapter 23, but there the subject is the Way, while here it is leaders.

3. Gendered pronouns did not suddenly appear in the narrative; rather, the contrast is between "leaders" and "the people" but I wanted to avoid referring to both of them as "they," so for "leaders" I switched to the singular and used "he / him."

Chapter 17 Explanation

Returning to the topic of leadership (hinted at in chapters 3, 5, 7, and 8; addressed more clearly in chapters 10, 13, and 15), the best "leaders" are described as those who are not obtrusive or intrusive. So much so that the better the leader the less their subordinates, and we the people, even know about them. (The word "subordinates" could refer primarily to a leader's officials, the subject of chapter 15, or it could refer to the people in general.) The first paragraph sketches four types of leaders: those whom we can safely forget about, knowing "only that they are there"; those we watch and, on occasion, "praise"; those we watch and "fear"; and those that are contemptible, worthy only of "insult."

"Trust" underlies many important aspects of political and economic culture. This chapter is a brief vignette of a government system that is so in tune with the wishes of the people that it seems invisible. If the expectations of the people are met, and the government neither goes further than expected nor falls short of what is expected, the result is that the government is neither praised nor blamed but rather more or less forgotten. This political paradigm is another instance of Daoist "emptiness," added to the ontological and psychological paradigms already adduced, but in this paradigm, a Yin state of formless "invisibility" is always preferred; only when a Yang state of warfare is necessary[4] will the government intrude upon the daily life of the people.

Thus, "(If a leader's) trust in them [i.e., their subordinates and the people, to make competent decisions about things] is insufficient, then there will be a lack of trust in him." This, again, might be taken to imply a good and competent human nature (as we saw in chapter 3), but in the context of this chapter, it more probably points to the trust that happy officials and a happy populace who agree with the plans of their leaders, have in that leader. "Hence,[5] he values his words," because he will not want to break the bond of trust with others (recall chapter 8: "In words, competence lies

---

4. As implied in chapters 30, 31, 68, and 69.

5. By Wang Bi's time, the "Hence" (猶乎) was instead read as "Leisurely" (悠兮), which also makes sense, because good leaders will delegate authority to subordinates and will feel safe among their own people.

96 | The Annotated *Laozi* 老子

in trustworthiness"), and because he will not need to say much, given his trust in his subordinates and his people.

The last sentence more clearly brings in all "the people" that leaders lead, and not just a leader's immediate subordinates. When good leaders lead, even in a leisurely and quiet manner, they still have "tasks" and still do things, of course. But when such a leader "completes" those tasks and "accomplishes" the "activities" that needed doing, the people nevertheless do not think to give them credit, due to their being servant-leaders (ch. 7), to their being unobtrusive (ch. 9), and to the mutual trust between those who lead and those being led. Now that a competent leader has been given a first sketch (with more to come later), the next chapter turns to the opposite: the state of affairs when incompetent leaders try to dictate ethics to a people that the author assumes are naturally good.

Chapter 18

Key Ideas

For person, family, and government: innate virtuosity is better than (contrived) goodness, filiality, and correctness.

大道癈，焉有仁義。六親不和，焉有孝慈。邦家昏亂，焉有正臣。

When[1] the great Way is abandoned, then there is (contrived) goodness and propriety. When the six familial relationships[2] are not in harmony, then there is (contrived) filiality and (parental) compassion. When the state and its families are benighted or disordered, then there are (contrivedly) correct ministers.[3]

---

1. GD C; MWD A, B; BD all begin chapter 18 with a "Therefore" (故), implying that chapters 17–18 were read together; I omit this because the connection is tenuous. Perhaps this chapter was, in an unknown earlier exemplar, preceded by a chapter that connected to this one better.

2. The six are those between parents and children, elder and younger siblings, and husband and wife.

3. The Chinese text derives from GD C; nearly all later exemplars, beginning with MWD A, add another sentence after "propriety" and before "When the six familial": "When (contrived) wisdom and intelligence come forth there is great contrivance" (智慧出，有大偽). GD C; MWD A, B; BD all add the three instances of "then" (焉) that XE and HSG omit. I also follow GD C with "correct" (正), rather than the "steadfast" (貞) that MWD A, B and BD have, or the "loyal" (忠) that *Huainanzi* chapter 12, XE, HSG, and others have.

98 | The Annotated *Laozi* 老子

Chapter 18 Explanation

Chapter 18 expands upon the topic of the relativity of ethics broached in chapter 5, where the hierarchy of a particular community's ideas of "goodness" was challenged with the evenhandedness of objectivity. Here the Yin-Yang, form-formless analytical lens is once again employed, and the three arenas of ethics, the family, and the state are considered. In each case the ideal is one of unarticulated, non-contrived, open-minded, tolerant objectivity.

In the area of individual ethics, when we fall short of this ideal, when we articulate and force upon others community-specific, binding ideals of "goodness and propriety," oblivious to the fact that they will surely change over time (and will surely differ from other contemporaneous communities), then we bring intolerance and disharmony.

Second, when dealing with family members, the "filiality" that children show to parents and the "(parental) compassion" that parents show to children are, ideally, informed by unspoken love and not formal ethics. *Zhuangzi* chapter 23 notes: "If you step on another person's foot in the marketplace, then you apologize for your carelessness; but if you do this to your elder brother, then (you apologize) with a wordless glance of empathy; and if you do this to one of your parents, then you do not need to do anything" (蹍 市人之足，則辭以放驚；兄則以嫗；大親則已矣). The "great Way" is one of mutual trust, of good faith, as we saw in the preceding chapter. Laozi, once again, is aiming for a society in which good faith is the norm.

Finally, government service, ideally, should function in a similar manner. Only when things are not going well will people have to talk about "correct ministers," otherwise their loyalty can be assumed, just as the parents assume contrition on the part of their children in the preceding *Zhuangzi* quote. The best-case scenario is that ministers will simply "complete [their] tasks, but without dwelling (on them)" (ch. 2), in which case, their "doing their job" will be a matter of unselfconsciously meeting expectations and not a matter of ostentation, of contrivance. The denigration of the contrived values in this chapter continues in the next, but the next adds some positive advice as well.

Chapter 19

Key Ideas

For person, family, and government: aim for benefit, filiality, and guilelessness, though these are insufficient.

> 絕知棄辯，民利百倍。絕偽棄詐，民復孝慈。絕巧棄利，盜賊
> 無有。
> 此三言，以為文不足；故令之有所屬：見素抱樸，少私寡欲。

Relinquish (contrived) knowledge and disregard (contrived) eloquence, and the people will benefit a hundredfold. Relinquish contrivance and disregard artifice, and the people will return to filiality and (parental) compassion. Relinquish guile and disregard the profit motive, and of thieves and robbers there will be none.[1]

---

1. The Chinese text derives from GD A; all later exemplars, beginning with MWD A, have a slightly different first three sentences: "Relinquish (contrived) sageliness and disregard (contrived) wisdom, and the people will benefit a hundredfold. Relinquish (contrived) goodness and disregard (contrived) propriety, and the people will return to filiality and (parental) compassion. Relinquish guile and disregard the profit motive, and of thieves and robbers there will be none" (絕聖棄智，民利百倍。絕仁棄義，民復孝慈。絕巧棄利，盜賊無有). This paragraph provides good examples of how context is crucial to translation. Here (good) "benefit" and (bad) "profit motive" both translate the single word *li* 利. The same is true of (bad) "guile" (巧), which is also bad in chapter 57 (there translated as "cunning"), but good in chapter 45 (where it is translated as "skill"). Similarly, "filiality and (parental) compassion" were denigrated in the preceding chapter (though presumably only the contrived kinds), but here describe an aspirational state. "Knowledge" (知) and "eloquence" (辯) are also portrayed as both good and bad in the *Laozi*. These are all good examples of the author's language skepticism, of "a name that

99

100 | The Annotated *Laozi* 老子

These three sayings function as ornaments and are insuffi-cient; thus, have them keep to that which they should attend to:[2] manifest purity, embrace simplicity, reduce selfishness, and decrease (contrived) desires.

Chapter 19 Explanation

Chapter 18 opened with the rhetoric of "If (bad thing) A happens, then (unexpected not-ideal thing) B will result," whereas chapter 19 opens with the rhetoric of "If you get rid of (bad thing) A, then (unexpected not-ideal-but-relatively-acceptable thing) B will result." In this rhetorical sense, they may be said to fit together. But let us first look at chapter 19 by itself. The three pairs of targets change from the ostensibly good (knowledge and eloquence), to the always bad (contrivance and artifice), to the sometimes good and sometimes bad (guile / skill; profit / benefit).

We met "(contrived) knowledge" (知) in chapters 2, 3, and 10, but "knowledge" was also used in a positive sense in chapters 4, 14, and 16. We have not yet met "(contrived) eloquence" (辯), but it appears with a positive connotation in chapter 45 and a neutral or perhaps negative con-notation in chapter 81 (there translated as "persuasive"). Here the two are clearly playing the role of villains, since if we are rid of them both then "the people will benefit a hundredfold."

The two subjects in the second sentence, however, are never good. "Con-trivance" (偽) is the bête noire of the entire *Laozi*, appearing in this graphic form only here, while the nearly-synonymous "artifice" (詐) appears nowhere else in this text. As for the "return to filiality and (parental) compassion," it is interesting that in chapter 18, these things were the less-than-ideal result

---

can be (fully) descriptive is not an abiding name" (ch. 1). I should also note that in ancient Chinese texts, "knowledge" (知) and "wisdom" (智) were interchangeable graphs. In this passage, MWD A, B have "knowledge" but BD and HSG have "wisdom." For modern scholars, this issue is nearly irresolvable, but it is my opinion that the *Laozi* is against contrived knowledge, beginning with the "knowledge" of what constitutes "beauty" and "competence" in chapter 2 and continuing on throughout the text. Thus, in my reading of this text, "wisdom" only occurs in chapter 33.

2. The word "attend to" (屬) occurs only here; one of its fundamental meanings is "to enjoin," which would also work here, but as it is also cognate with "to fix one's gaze on" (矚), I chose "attend to."

Chapter 19 | 101

of "When the six familial relationships are not in harmony," whereas here they are the relatively good result of getting rid of bad "contrivance" and "artifice." Clearly, if the author is to avoid self-contradiction, the pair in chapter 18 must be construed with an implied "(contrived)," while here they should be construed as uncontrived. Far from courting self-contradiction, I think the author is making two points, one about language skepticism and another about some goals being less than ideal, but still better than nothing.

Continuing with this theme of language skepticism, the two targets in the third sentence sometimes carry a positive connotation and sometimes carry a negative connotation. Here they are both bad, but "guile" (巧) appears as "skill" in chapter 45 and is again bad "cunning" in chapter 57. Meanwhile, "the profit motive" (利) means "benefit" in chapter 8 and in the first sentence here, "profitable" in a good sense in chapter 11, "beneficial" in chapter 73, and describes the "benefit" that characterizes the "way of Heaven" in chapter 81. Rather than translate these as "(contrived) skill" and "(contrived) benefit," I went with "guile" and "the profit motive." But their rhetorical flexibility still stands in pretty stark contrast with "knowledge" and "eloquence," both of which need an implied "(contrived)" to make sense.[3]

As noted earlier, we might also examine the three opening sentences of chapter 19 in light of those from chapter 18. Both chapters deal with ethics, family, and the state, though chapter 19 concludes with an important addendum.

First, "Relinquish (contrived) knowledge and . . . eloquence, and the people will benefit a hundredfold." We saw in chapter 18 that "when the great Way is abandoned, then there is (contrived) goodness and propriety." Since knowledge and eloquence are used (or can be used) to articulate and define goodness and propriety, as "knowledge" tried to do with beauty and competence in chapter 2, these fit together naturally. Though neither "knowledge" nor "eloquence" appears in chapter 5, the common "knowledge" of what constitutes "goodness" was certainly challenged there, and such contrived "knowledge" is also implied with both goodness and propriety in chapter 18 (and will be again in chapter 38).

Second, "Relinquish contrivance and disregard artifice, and the people will return to filiality and (parental) compassion." In chapter 18 we saw

---

3. For "(contrived) eloquence" I might have used "sophistry" (or even "disputatiousness," which is another meaning of *bian* 辯), but I don't know of a word for "knowledge" that has a negative connotation. If "assumptions" works, then perhaps the opening sentence here should be "Relinquish assumptions and disregard sophistry."

102 | The Annotated *Laozi* 老子

that "when the six familial relationships are not in harmony, then there is (contrived) filiality and (parental) compassion." Pairing these two implies that "(contrived) filiality and (parental) compassion"—with the "(contrived)" applying to both—are types of "contrivance" and "artifice," which they by definition are. So these two also seem to make a fitting pair.

Third, "Relinquish guile and disregard the profit motive, and of thieves and robbers there will be none." We saw in chapter 18 that "when the state and (its) families are benighted or disordered, then there are (contrivedly) correct ministers." Since government ministers are responsible for curtailing "thieves and robbers,"[4] and since "guile" might be construed as "benighted" skill, and "the profit motive" might be construed as "disordered" benefit, these two also make a rather natural pair. Thus, while chapters 18 and 19 function well enough on their own, they may also be read together with some benefit.

The three goals of chapter 19—benefiting people, returning to filiality and (parental) compassion, and having no thieves or robbers—are better than their alternatives but are still not ideal: they set a low bar, as far as aspirational goals go. Thus they are "ornaments and are insufficient." They are near-term goals, steps on the road to the things we should ultimately "attend to."

The four-part advice for our ultimate goal is delivered at the end: "manifest purity, embrace simplicity, reduce selfishness, and decrease (contrived) desires." We have already met the "decrease desires" idea in chapter 3, and "selflessness" in chapter 7, but "simplicity" and "purity" are new.[5] "Simplicity" we will meet again in chapters 32, 37, and 57. "Purity" appears only here, though near-synonyms appear elsewhere: literal "whiteness" (白) is translated as "purity" in chapter 41, and the "clear / clarity" (清) in chapters 15, 39, and 45 is close in meaning. The attack on contrived virtues in the previous chapter and this one comes to a conclusion in the next chapter, after addressing just one more target arena: education.

---

4. In chapter 57, "thieves and robbers" (盜賊) are the result of too many "laws and statutes" (法令).

5. The word for "simplicity" (樸), literally, "an uncarved block of wood," was used as a metaphor for "solidity" in chapter 15, so the Chinese graph isn't entirely new to us here, though this meaning is. The word for "purity" (素) is literally an undyed knot of cloth.

Chapter 20

Key Ideas

For learning: be flexible but mindful of your community; be placid amid the teeming masses; value the "Mother."

絕學無憂：唯之與阿：相去幾何？美之與惡，相去何若？人之所
　　畏，不可不畏。荒兮其未央哉。
衆人熙熙，若享太牢，若春登臺。我泊焉未兆，若嬰兒之未孩；
　　儽儽兮若無所歸。
衆人皆有餘，而我獨若遺。我愚人之心也：沌沌兮。
俗人昭昭，我獨若昏。
俗人察察，我獨悶悶。忽兮若海，飂兮若無所止。
衆人皆有以，而我獨頑似鄙。我獨異於人，而貴食「母」。

*Relinquish (contrived) learning and be without anxiety: (polite)
agreement and a (desultory) "yeah": What difference is there between
them? Or, beauty and ugliness:[1] How are they different? Yet that
which people revere must be revered. The periphery: it is not yet
the center.[2]*

---

1. HSG has "competence and inadequacy" (善之與惡); the reading I use derives from GD B; MWD A, B; BD. In addition to this being the earlier reading, I find the juxtaposition of "beauty-ugliness" (美惡) a more plausible comparison in early China than "competency-inadequacy" (善惡), though both make sense.

2. The first sentence implies situation ethics (i.e., modify rules to fit the situation); the second implies ethical pluralism (i.e., accepting a variety of norms within a group); the third implies majoritarianism (i.e., following the dominant norms of the group); the fourth implies ethical evolution. The fourth sentence could also be translated "The uncivilized

104 | The Annotated *Laozi* 老子

The masses are busily happy, as if they were enjoying a grand festival, as if ascending a terrace in springtime. We are placid among them, without any outward sign, like an infant that has not yet smiled; sedate, as if there were no place to return home to.

The masses all have more than enough, but we alone[3] seem to be without. We (seem to) have the minds of stupid people: turbid.

Ordinary people (seem) bright; we alone seem dim.

Ordinary people (seem) clear; we alone (seem) hazy.[4] Dispassionate, like the ocean, yet blown about, as if without a place to stop.

The masses all have expediency, but we alone are rustic and seem coarse.[5] We alone are different from the others and value feeding from the "Mother."

Chapter 20 Explanation

As with chapters 5, 12, 18, and 19, where I do not take the author to be denigrating goodness, the five colors, five sounds, five flavors, propriety, filiality, parental compassion, correctness, knowledge, or eloquence, per se, but rather as denigrating a certain *kind* of these virtues and categorizations: namely, *contrived* goodness, and so forth, so with this chapter. As noted in the translator's note, but perhaps worth repeating, this analysis derives from the wider context of the entire *Laozi*, where other passages hold these same virtues to be aspirationally good. For example, if the author thought "goodness" was in fact not good, then they could not say, "In interactions with others, competence lies in goodness" (ch. 8) without contradicting "sages are not good" (ch. 5). This analysis finds a clear basis in chapter

---

is not yet ended" (荒兮其未央哉), which, though a completely different reading, would have the same implication: unjust social expectations (i.e., the "periphery" or "the [so-called] uncivilized") sometimes only change slowly, with patience.

3. It is possible that the five uses of "alone" (獨) in this chapter should be read as "detachedly." The same may be said of the "alone" in chapter 25.

4. Chapter 58 uses the same words "clear" (察察) and "hazy" (閔閔), but there they are translated as "definitive" and "tentative."

5. The word "expediency" (以) is usually used as a transitive verb, "to use" X, or as a conjunction, "by means of" X or "in order to" X; here it is contrasted with "rustic" and "coarse" and implies a contrived single-mindedness, as opposed to a bucolic versatility.

38, which begins "People of lofty virtuosity are not (contrivedly) virtuous, and this is why they can have (real) virtuosity" (上德不德，是以有德). This claim, without the parentheticals, can be read either uncharitably as a category error (insofar as "lofty virtuosity" is logically and necessarily a subset of "virtuosity") or charitably as having the parenthetical annotations I have added. This analysis takes "non-contrivance" (無為) to be a central component of the text, implied even when unstated.

Chapter 20 adds "learning" (學) to the list articulated in chapter 19 and further supports the analysis in the preceding paragraph, for if we should "relinquish" (絕; literally, "sever from") *all* learning, then why would we continue to read this book? Rather, taking our cue from several previous chapters, particularly chapters 2 and 12, we should sever ourselves from the contrived and conventional learning of the socially accepted hierarchies of beauty and competence, and of the socially constructed categories of (only) five colors, sounds, and flavors, and so on. As chapter 64 will say, we should "learn to not learn (contrivedly)" (學不學) what we have been taught as children so that we may reimagine our articulated (or imagined) relationship with reality. This is how we may avoid "anxiety," the anxiety of negotiating what we are told with what we feel is right,[6] even if it has been "passed over by the masses" (ch. 64).

Chapter 20 is the first to (implicitly) broach the topics of situation ethics and majoritarianism,[7] as distinct from the ethical pluralism and eth-

---

6. I am not a psychologist, but this negotiation seems to be at least implied by Freud's three-part psychology, with the ego negotiating the conflict between the superego and the id.

7. As I construe them, "situation ethics" is a combination of the "follow your conscience" and "ethical pluralism" paradigms described in the "non-anthropocentrism and ethics" section of the "key concepts." It relies on the individual (conscience) to navigate a variety of ethical norms. The ethical flexibility inherent in "situation ethics" involves two kinds of binary choices. The first is that between your individual conscience and the prevailing ethical norm for the situation in which you find yourself. The second is that either the norm should always be followed, regardless of potentially extenuating circumstances, or the rules may sometimes be bent. Let us return to the example of situation ethics found at *Mengzi* 4A17, discussed in the section on "unlearning" in the "key concepts," which says we should "act according to circumstances" (權), even if it contravenes established protocol (禮). The example given was having the ethical norm of "men should not touch women they do not know," but this can be contravened, for the author, in some circumstances: for example, if the woman is drowning. Conversely, an example of inflexible ethics may be found in the 2002 Mecca girls' school

106 | The Annotated *Laozi* 老子

ical realism of previous chapters. Ethical pluralism was implied in chapters 2 and 3, which ask us to acknowledge a range, rather than a hierarchy, of competencies and worthiness. Normative ethical realist advice is found in many successive chapters: chapter 5 implies that goodness is impartial (like Heaven and Earth); chapter 6 implies that we should be creative (like "females" and "roots"); chapter 7 encourages humility (like Heaven and Earth); chapter 8 promotes flexibility (modeled on water); and chapter 10 asks us to be mentally flexible (as infants are physically flexible). Chapter 15 includes a list of seven qualities that may be construed as ethical, four of which are derived from natural phenomena; and chapter 16 adds tolerance, derived from observing the life cycles of living things. Chapters 18–19 drive home the point that whatever ethical norms are under discussion, they are better if genuine and uncontrived, as other animals (presumably) are. Most of the ethical realist advice given in these chapters is explicitly connected to natural phenomena (even if, as Hume would insist, they are *selectively* chosen [see the "key concepts," note 18]).

The first sentence of this chapter, then, can be read as implying situation ethics (viz., "read the room"); the second sentence implies ethical pluralism (viz., "to each their own"); the third, ethical majoritarianism (viz., "majority rules"); and the fourth, ethical evolution, thus:

"(Polite) agreement and a (desultory) 'yeah': What difference is there between them [across a variety of situations]?" I do not think that the author is saying that there is no difference between saying, "Yes, ma'am" and "Sure thing, girl," but rather that different people will use different expressions in different situations. In the end, they do mean the same thing, but "that which people revere must be revered," and "the people" in most communities and cultures (that I know of) would insist that "there is a time and a place" for each of these expressions. This example, then, is one of situation ethics, wherein the "rule" is to say "Yes, ma'am" in formal situations and "Sure thing, girl" in informal situations. Both of these responses are acceptable in ethical pluralism, but we must follow our own conscience in deciding just which situation we currently find ourselves in.

---

fire, in which Saudi firemen followed the rule of "men should not touch women they do not know," thereby allowing fifteen schoolgirls to die in a fire rather than touch them. In *Zhuangzi* chapter 2, the recognition that one can be ethically flexible across situations or communities is called "equalizing" (齊) their various norms. Situation ethics should not be conflated with "cultural relativism" ("When in Rome, do as the Romans do") or "ethical relativism" ("all ethical systems are equally good").

Chapter 20 | 107

Similarly, the second sentence—"Or, beauty and ugliness: How are they different [across a variety of individual preferences]?"—is not implying that beauty and ugliness are interchangeable, but that they are different for different people. This is a comment on aesthetic pluralism, but we may extrapolate from this to ethical pluralism.

The third sentence brings us to majoritarianism: "Yet that which people revere must be revered." This is not always easy for an individualist to admit, but the fact is that we humans mostly exist within communities that do not always share our personal values, and we must make adjustments to ourselves for the sake of social harmony (or, at least, in order to not be ostracized). We must, to a very real degree, respect others, even when we disagree with them. That does not mean that we should be spineless "sheeple" and just follow the crowd, but we do have to be able to articulate the reasons for our preferences, pick our battles, and sometimes, yes, just go with the flow. The third sentence, in context, says that we can have our own, individual ideas about ethics, but this does not give us license to always contravene or ignore the will of the majority. Though Laozi focuses more on individualism, there is nevertheless a Yin-Yang balance between the individual and the community that undergirds the Daoist project.

The fourth sentence, "The periphery: it is not yet the center," expresses the hope that our own, individual ideas about ethics may one day *become* the norm. This describes an ethical "razor's edge" that may also be seen in the idea of "contentment," first obliquely broached in chapter 12 (with the "belly" over the "eye"), but later explicitly endorsed in chapters 33, 44, and 46. Just as modern people strive for a "work-life" balance, so does this author imply a Yin-Yang-like "contentment versus work-to-improve-the-world" balance that has its roots in the psychological "form-formless" and "active-introspective" cycles introduced in chapter 1. We should surely strive for contentment, but not for a do-nothing, turn-a-blind-eye attitude toward the suffering of others. Ethically, though this may be more difficult for some to countenance, the author suggests that we should have an ethical "backbone," so to speak, but that we should simultaneously be flexible when dealing with others. Hence the previous "non-contentiousness" advice of chapters 3 and 8 (and chs. 22, 66, 68, 73, and 81 later). It is a complicated dance, a difficult needle to thread.

The remainder of this chapter is something of a "call and response" between "we" Daoists, and "the masses," wherein Daoist fallibilism is contrasted with the ethical certainty of the larger community. This back-and-forth has five stanzas, comparing "their" busyness, acquisitiveness, cleverness,

108 | The Annotated *Laozi* 老子

confidence, and opportunism with "our" (Daoist) sedateness, simplicity, skepticism, fallibilism, and easygoingness.

The metaphor of "feeding from the 'Mother'" is continued in the next chapter with its description of "creation."

Chapter 21

Key Idea

Cosmogony no. 1: the Way, semblances, things, essences, and genuineness: use the Way to examine the inceptions of things.

> 孔德之容，唯道是從；道之為物，唯恍唯惚。惚兮恍兮，其中有象；恍兮惚兮，其中有物。窈兮冥兮，其中有精；冥兮窈兮，其中有真。
>
> 自古及今，其名不去，以閱眾甫。吾何以知眾甫之然哉？以此。

The expression of pervasive virtuosity follows only the Way, but the Way as the maker of things is vague and elusive.[1] Elusive and vague, yet within it are semblances; vague and elusive, yet within it are things. Obscure and hidden, yet within it are essences; hidden and obscure, yet within it is genuineness.[2]

---

1. "The Way as the *maker of* things is vague and elusive" (道之為物，唯恍唯惚) can also be read "The Way *as a* thing is vague and elusive." How you construe "make / as" (為) depends on whether you think this chapter is a description of the Way's creation of things or a description of the Way itself. I think it is the former.

2. I have made two changes to the third sentence. First, all exemplars have "its essences are very genuine" (其精甚真) instead of "hidden and obscure," but (a): this breaks the clear AB, AC symmetry in sentences two and three; and (b), describing "essences" as "genuine" (or "non-genuine") makes no sense to me. Second, all exemplars have "within it is trustworthiness" (其中有信), instead of "within it is genuineness," but "trustworthiness" (信) graphically implies speech (言), and the Way does not speak, so I replaced it with the "genuine" from the excised "its essences are very genuine." I think an ancient scribe made a mistake that resulted in a garbled passage that I have attempted to restore. Also, "genuineness" should be plural, to match the prior three, but "genuinenesses" is a little too awkward.

110 | The Annotated *Laozi* 老子

> *From antiquity until today, its name has not been discarded, as it is used to examine the inceptions of the multitudes.[3] How do we know the inceptions of the multitudes are thus? (Precisely) by means of this (Way)![4]*

Chapter 21 Explanation

The "Mother" in the previous chapter is here described as "the maker of things." Each and every thing has its own "virtuosity" and its own way of "expressing" that virtuosity, hence "The expression of pervasive virtuosity follows only the Way" could just as well be in the plural: "The expressions of virtuosities in all cases follow the Way." In chapter 14 we saw the Way is "elusive and vague" (惚恍) and while that description is here employed once again, the implication goes all the way back to chapter 1, to "the way that can be (fully) conveyed is not the abiding Way."

Laozi's Yin "creation story" is in five steps.[5] First is the Way. Second, there are "semblances," a term that in chapter 14 was used to describe the Way itself: "a semblance in nothingness" (無物之象). "Semblances" is an "elusive and vague" term that is nevertheless quite fascinating. It appears in the text five times, in five chapters. In chapter 4 it is used in a grammatically distinct way, as the verb "seems to." The other four uses are all as the noun "semblance(s)." Chapter 14 describes the Way as "a semblance in nothingness," while here in chapter 21 it is said of this selfsame Way that "within it are semblances" (其中有象), semblances of the myriad things within the "great semblance" of the Way: "mystery and more mystery" (ch. 1). And, in fact, with the fourth use of the term, in chapter 35, the Way is described

---

3. To "examine the inceptions of the multitudes" (閱眾甫) is an interesting phrase, but it occurs only in this chapter. MWD A, B have "follow along with the father of everything" (順眾父), and BD has "explain the father of everything" (說眾父) here (父 and 甫 were sometimes interchangeable in antiquity). My translation, which infers that the earlier "father" (父) was a proxy for "inception / father" (甫) is from HSG and is supported by WB's note, which says, "The 'inceptions of the multitudes' are the beginnings of things" (眾甫，物之始也).

4. The last two sentences (i.e., 吾何以知 . . . 以此), with slight modifications, are also in chapters 54 and 57.

5. Their Yang cosmology is in chapter 51, which has four steps that shape us: the Way, virtuosity, (other) things, and circumstances.

Chapter 21 | 111

precisely as the "great semblance" (大象). The fifth and last appearance of the word underlines Laozi's genius as a wordsmith: in chapter 41 we will see that "great semblances may (seem to) have no definite shape" (大象無形), where, in context, it is (relatively) clear that "semblances" is used as a generic term, but the inclusion of "great" cannot but insinuate that this is a double entendre meant to recall the previous, chapter 35, use. Brilliant. But to return to the present chapter: just as all children carry the genetic imprint of their mothers, so each of the myriad things carries a "semblance" that, while unique, is nevertheless traceable to its source.

Step three articulates the mother's children: the "things" (物) that constitute the myriad things. This step is rather straightforward. Steps four and five, however, go past mere "thingness" to express two stages of the uniqueness of everything. Step four is a thing's "essence" (精). For living things, this describes both the ability to physically reproduce and the ability to be cognitively inventive: creativity times two. Finally, step five depicts a thing's "genuineness" (真). All extant things necessarily complete the first four steps, but the fifth step is reserved as an aspirational step attained only by some things. This step characterizes "fulfilling one's destiny"; in Zen terms it is realizing your "suchness" (*tathātā*; 真如); in Christian terms it is following "God's plan" for you;[6] but in secular terms it is simply realizing your potential.

"From antiquity until today, its name has not been discarded, as it is used to examine the inceptions of the multitudes." The idea of the Way, the "elusive" ordering principle of the cosmos, is an old idea. The Way "has not been discarded" because it figures foundationally in the creation story articulated in the previous paragraph, which the author is implying was a creation story that has been around since "antiquity." One potential wrinkle in this claim is that the Way has a "name," even though later chapters imply that the Way is "nameless" (chs. 32, 37, 41), but this is merely a rhetorical quibble.[7] The "inceptions of the multitudes" (衆甫) is an interesting phrase,

---

6. Jeremiah 29:11: "For surely I know the plans I have for you, says the Lord, plans for your welfare and not for harm, to give you a future with hope." In context, this verse applies particularly to the Jews exiled to Babylon, but some Christians extrapolate the sentiment to all humans.

7. In fact, chapters 32, 37, and 41 do not say the Way *is* nameless but rather "*abides in* nameless simplicity" (恆無名樸) and "*is hidden in* namelessness" (隱無名). If you read this as a distinction without a difference, then I would return to the "this is merely a rhetorical quibble" explanation. Additionally, there are two other ways to read the

112 | The Annotated *Laozi* 老子

but it occurs only in this chapter.[8] The import of this sentence is that the Way is a fundamental ontological and cosmological concept, one that cannot be easily "discarded."

Let us review your own creation story, as one of "the multitudes" described here. First, the Way is the impetus for everything, including you. Second, your Way-made "semblance," when you were but a zygote or, perhaps, when you were but "a twinkle in your mother's eye." Third, you as a Way-guided "thing," which is to say, you as a human. Fourth, you as having Way-influenced physical and cognitive "essence(s)": you as an animal capable of reproducing, as a human capable of reproducing your specific genes, and you as a human capable of critical thinking and of creating explanatory knowledge. Fifth, you as having Way-inspired "genuineness," as having aspirations to realize your unique potential. In this scenario, the Way is the initial impetus that "expresses" itself in four successive steps, and this unfolding "expression" is the manifestation of your "virtuosity," both actually *and* aspirationally rooted in the Way, but still your own. The Way is thus like a rock thrown in a pond, with the ripples its virtuosity, and the discrete ripples having the names "(liminal) semblance," "(formal) thingness," "(reproductive) essence," and "(teleological) genuineness."

The uncertain fallibilism of chapter 20 is thus in this chapter ostensibly and momentarily balanced by the seemingly simple "rule" of tying "the expression of pervasive virtuosity" to following "only the Way." The simplicity of this declaration certainly may impart a degree of psychological respite from the unrelenting ambiguity of ethical pluralism, but the confidence that comes with simplicity is genuinely warranted: even fallibilists can

---

word "name" here. First, we can read it as "renown" or "fame," but it sounds a little less natural to "discard" "renown," though it is not impossible. Second, we can read the sentence as "*these names* have not been discarded, (as we) use (them) to examine the inceptions of the multitudes." In this reading, "these names" would refer either to the names of the "things" that the Way has created, or to the names "semblances," "things," "essences," and "genuineness."

8. "Inceptions" (甫) occurs only here, but "multitudes" (衆) appears in chapters 1 and 31 as "many," and the same graph constitutes part of "the masses" (衆人) in chapters 8, 20, and 64. It might be tempting for us to construe "inception" as "inceptor," as a "begetter," as the Yang "Father" to the Yin "Mother" of the previous chapter. I don't read it this way because to say the Way, the Mother, "is used to examine the Father of the multitudes" would be metaphorical mayhem, and, in my opinion, a mistake.

Chapter 21 | 113

be confident in what they (currently) know.[9] Why did form spring from formlessness? Why did life evolve from non-living elements? If the answer to these questions is "There is no 'why,' these things simply happened as a matter of course," then we can continue to use the Way as an expression of that "course."

The idea of the Way, the "elusive" ordering principle of the cosmos, is an old idea. One of the reasons why such an idea has persisted for so long is that we can use it to explain origin stories, that is, "the inceptions of the multitudes." "How?" we might ask. The phrase given in response to this question, "by means of this," occurs three times in this text; here, and in chapters 54 and 57. Each time, it seems to be a tongue-in-cheek, almost flippant, response implying that the answer should be obvious by now. In this case, given that the Way is the ordering principle of the cosmos (and all things in it), how could it *not* be used to explain the beginnings of the cosmos (and all things in it)? If the author had a smiley face icon to append at the end of a sentence, I suspect they would have used one here. After the consideration of the Way's creativity in this chapter, the next chapter turns to the creative human "agents" of the Way: sages.

---

9. That is, one can be a good fallibilist and still speak with a degree of confidence about the theory of gravity or the theory of evolution. That "theory" in the previous sentence means different things to different people (i.e., a "guess" versus a "testable explanation") is a good example of why Daoists are language skeptics.

Chapter 22

Key Ideas

Sages embrace the One behind change; they are unobtrusive and thereby become illustrious and extolled.

> 曲則全，枉則直；窪則盈，敝則新；少則得，多則惑。是以聖人
> 抱一為天下式。
> 不自見，故明；不自是，故彰；不自伐，故有功；不自矜，故
> 長。夫唯不爭，故天下莫能與之爭。
> 古之所謂「曲則全」者，豈虛言哉？誠全而歸之。

Bent then whole, crooked then straight; empty then full, worn-out then new; without then with, abundant then uncertain.[1] This is why sages embrace the One to become models[2] for the world.

(Sages) do not advertise themselves, which is why they become illustrious, and do not advocate themselves, which is why they are extolled; do not brag, which is why they succeed, and do not boast,

---

1. It is odd that the first five phrases all change from bad to good, and this sixth phrase doesn't seem to fit in: Should it be reversed to "uncertain then abundant"? Either way, all six point to the principle of change. On the other hand, read with the preceding chapter, perhaps this reversal is meant to indicate that not everyone will reach their "genuineness."

2. The idea of the "model" (式) also appears in chapters 28 and 65. MWD A, B and BD have "shepherd" (牧) instead of "model" here. (They have "model" in chapters 28 and 65.) "Shepherd" appears nowhere else in the text.

Chapter 22 | 115

which is why they endure.[3] *Simply not being contentious is why no one in the world is able to contend with them.*

That which was said by the ancients—"bent then whole"—was this empty talk? To be truly whole, return to it.

Chapter 22 Explanation

The first sentence is clearly about binary change, which recalls and elaborates on the formless-form dynamic of chapters 1 and 2. "This [principle of Yin-Yang change] is why sages embrace the One," because the theory that they derive from their observations of change is, of course, the ordering principle that they call the Way, also known as "the One," so called because it encompasses all these changes in a relatively balanced way. It is due to both of these factors of encompassing and balancing that sages thereby "become models for the world."

The four clauses of the third sentence, which we meet again (in a somewhat different form) in chapter 24, all pretty much say the same thing, but do serve to situate the opening sentence within the social sphere, though it does repeat, in different words, what was said in chapter 7: "This is why sages put their persons last yet their persons are brought to the fore," and so on. The fourth sentence adds "not being contentious" to the humility and unostentatiousness of the third sentence, thereby recalling a major theme of chapter 8.

The last two sentences reiterate the opening sentence of this chapter, which may imply that the opening sentence was a known quote that the author was borrowing. The "empty talk" (虛言) may well just be an inconsequential rhetorical device. Or perhaps the intended question was: "Was this open(-minded) talk?" As noted in the "key concepts," *xu* 虛 means both "open(-minded)" (as in chs. 3 and 16) and "empty" (as in chs. 5 and 53). Simply realizing that things change—for example, from being "bent" to being "whole"—is itself a form of open-mindedness. In any case, I went with the more literal reading here. These sentences also repeat the idea of

---

3. These four activities are also in chapter 24: "Those who advertise themselves are not illustrious; those who advocate themselves are not extolled. Those who brag about themselves do not succeed; those who boast of themselves do not endure" (自見者不明，自是者不彰。自伐者無功，自矜不長).

116 | The Annotated *Laozi* 老子

"return" (歸) that we saw in chapters 14 ("returns . . . to nothingness") and 16 ("returns to its root"), with the object of the verb here being the Oneness behind the ceaseless change.

The narrative thread of this chapter, then, is: embracing the Yin-Yang principle of change as a unity should lead to a broader perspective that will induce one to become more humble and unostentatious, and less contentious, which in turn leads to social success. Understanding this one principle may also help us to realize the final stage of "genuineness" in the five-part creation story in the previous chapter. The philosophical "oneness" of the Way in this chapter returns to a poetically anthropomorphized Way (last seen in ch. 20) in the next.

Chapter 23

Key Ideas

Heaven and Earth change naturally; to accord with the Way, and not lose it, means trusting it.

> 希言自然。故飄風不終朝，驟雨不終日。孰為此者？天地。天地
> 尚不能久，而況於人乎？
> 故從事於道者同於道，德者同於德，失者同於失。故同於德者：
> 道亦得之；同於失者：道亦失之。
> 信不足焉，有不信焉。

To rarely speak is natural.[1] Thus, a blustery wind does not last all morning, nor does a sudden rain last all day. Who is it that does these? Heaven and Earth. If even Heaven and Earth cannot be so persistent, then why should humans?

Thus, those who pursue activities with the Way, accord with the Way, just as the virtuous accord with virtuosity, and the lost accord with loss.[2] Furthermore, those who accord with virtuosity:

---

1. The two graphs translated here as "natural" (自然) appear together in the *Laozi* five times. In chapter 17 it was translated as "themselves," in chapter 25 as "itself," in chapter 51 as "naturally," and in chapter 64 as "naturalness." It may help to connect these translations to each other by considering the two graphs as meaning "self-so."

2. Since "virtuosity" (德) is a homophone with "gain" (得), the virtuosity-loss (德失) is a play on gain-loss (得失).

117

118 | The Annotated *Laozi* 老子

the Way also gains them; and those who accord with loss: the Way also loses them.[3]

If trust in it is insufficient, then it will not have trust in us.[4]

Chapter 23 Explanation

Chapter 2 said that sages "implement wordless teaching" (行不言之教), which, while somewhat ironic in a book—of *words*, meant to *teach*—implies that sages prefer to teach by example rather than by decree. Here that advice is recontextualized as being inspired by the ways of nature (another example of ethical realism), asking: "If even Heaven and Earth cannot be so persistent, then why should humans?" This kind of thinking may account for why the *Laozi* is such a short book.

The wordplay of virtuosity / (gain) and loss (see this chapter's note 2) does not distract from the underlying message that the truly virtuous, those who have "gained" the Way, accord with what motivates them (i.e., the Way), just as those who have "lost" the Way are motivated by things that will ultimately result in personal and social loss.

The final sentence appeared in chapter 17, where it referred to the dynamic between ruler and ruled, but this chapter is not about ruling, and the "it" refers to the Way. This final line—"If [our] trust in it [i.e., the Way] is insufficient, then it will not have trust in us"—should be read as advice that we *should* trust in the Way, despite it being "vague and elusive" (ch. 21) and verbally reticent. That the Way will "not have trust in us," should we fail to heed this advice is, once again, a bit of poetic anthropomorphization. It is like saying, "If you don't believe in gravity, then gravity will exact its revenge upon you." There will be more poetic anthropomorphizing in future

---

3. MWD A and B have a single graph variant: "Those who accord with virtuosity: the Way also *is virtuous to* them; those who accord with loss: the Way also loses them" (同於德者，道亦德之；同於失者，道亦失之). HSG, meanwhile, has an interesting variant that anthropomorphizes the three subjects: "Those who accord with the Way: the Way also *delights in* gaining them, (just as) those who accord in virtue: virtuosity also *delights in* gaining them, and those who accord with loss: loss also *delights in* gaining them" (同於道者，道亦樂得之；同於德者，德亦樂得之；同於失者，失亦樂得之).

4. This last line is also in chapter 17, where it refers to the trust between rulers and the people. Here the same locution is used to refer to the trust that humans should have in the Way.

chapters, as with Heaven ostensibly "saving" (救) people in chapter 67, finding presumptuousness "repellent" (惡) in chapter 73, and "abiding with" (恆與) competent people in chapter 79 (assuming one reads this "abiding" as a conscious decision rather than a description of an unavoidable state of affairs). Such anthropomorphizing is attractive to those who prefer a more "personal" relationship with the cosmos.

We saw in this chapter that humans who accord with the Way do not talk too much, but in the next chapter we see that there are certain kinds of talking that they *especially* eschew.

Chapter 24

Key Ideas

Do not be contrived or ostentatious; those with the Way detest this.

> 企者不立，跨者不行。
> 自見者不明，自是者不彰。自伐者無功，自矜者不長。
> 其在道也，曰：「餘食贅行」。物或惡之，故有道者不居。

> *Those who stand on tiptoe cannot stand (firmly); those who straddle a gap cannot walk (normally).*
>
> *Those who advertise themselves are not illustrious; those who advocate themselves are not extolled. Those who brag about themselves do not succeed; those who boast of themselves do not endure.[1]*
>
> *Those who are with the Way call these "leftover food and useless practices." (All) things seem to detest them; thus, those with the Way are not occupied with them.*

Chapter 24 Explanation

Chapter 24 offers evidence for the previous chapter's claim that the Way is trustworthy by way of a physics lesson. To "stand on tiptoe" or to "straddle a gap" is to be off-balance, given human physiology. The two observations in the first sentence are used as metaphors for four claims that nearly say the same thing, which is, as a popular expression has it: "pride goeth before a

---

1. The four activities in the two sentences of the second paragraph are also in chapter 22.

120

Chapter 24 | 121

fall."[2] The second and third sentences consist of ethical extrapolations from the physical situations in the first sentence (and are thus a kind of ethical realism); we met them in chapter 22.

In the penultimate sentence, the unstated but implied object "these"[3] refers back to the four verbs, "advertise," "advocate," "brag," and "boast." But whereas in chapter 22 the motivation to avoid these activities is a desire for success, here the motivation is to avoid opprobrium, which is, of course, not unrelated. Nobody likes a braggart. This chapter on humility is balanced in the next chapter, which reminds us of the greatness of the Way.

---

2. This is a popular elision of Proverbs 16:18: "Pride goes before destruction, and a haughty spirit before a fall."

3. It is implied because there is no 之 ("these") following the 曰 ("call"); I added the "these."

Chapter 25

Key Idea

The Way precedes Heaven and Earth, does not change, is cyclical, and complies only with itself.

有物混成，先天地生。寂兮寥兮：獨立而不改，周行而不殆，可
　　以為「天下母」。
吾不知其名，字之曰「道」，吾強為之名曰「大」。大曰逝，逝
　　曰遠，遠曰反。
故道大，天大，地大，王亦大。域中有四大，而王居其一焉。
人法地，地法天，天法道，道法自然。

There is a thing, nebulously complete, prior to the production of Heaven and Earth. Quiet and empty: it stands alone and does not change;[1]

---

1. This word for "change" (改) occurs only here. Ames and Hall argue that "does not change" should be read transitively, as "is not open to alteration by appeal to something other than itself" (210). They are concerned that "does not change" may be read to mean the Way is some transcendent godlike entity, and I agree this is not what is being said here. Ziporyn supports the Ames and Hall reading by noting, "In fact, this moral-normative sense is perhaps the dominant use of the term *gai* [i.e., "change"] in pre-*Daodejing* Confucian and Mohist texts, which *never* use it to mean natural or value-neutral change" (117). I find this almost convincing and would change my translation to "is not changed" if I thought it fit the context of this chapter better. But there is no entity in this chapter (or anywhere else) that might be construed as being up to the task of "changing" the Way; still, perhaps the *Laozi* is simply stating the obvious here. Ames and Hall further note that "does not change" ostensibly contradicts the following "it moves all around," insofar as movement entails change. But I read "does not change" to simply mean it is dependable, like gravity, which is the "same" everywhere,

it moves all around and does not endanger anything; it can be taken as "the mother of the world."[2]

We do not know its name, so we style-name it the "Way." Pressed further to make for it a name, we would call it "Great." Great implies moving on; moving on implies going far; and going far implies (eventual) return.[3]

Thus, the Way is great, Heaven is great, Earth is great, and the king[4] is also great. Within the universe[5] there are these four greats, and the king occupies a unifying place among them.[6]

People comply with the Earth, Earth complies with Heaven, Heaven complies with the Way, and the Way complies with itself.

Chapter 25 Explanation

The "thing"-ness of the Way does not imply materiality; it simply establishes the Way as a topic of conversation. It is "nebulous" (混; translated as

---

though in a sense it may be "less" on the moon than on earth. See Roger Ames and David Hall, *Dao De Jing: "Making This Life Significant"; A Philosophical Translation* (New York: Ballantine Books, 2003), and Brook Ziporyn, "Vast Continuity versus the One: Thoughts on *Daodejing 42, Taiyishengshui,* and the Legacy of Roger T. Ames," in *Appreciating the Chinese Difference,* ed. Jim Behuniak (Albany: State University of New York Press, 2018), 111–32.

2. While GD A, WB's note, and HSG support this reading, MWD A, B and BD have "the mother of Heaven and Earth" (天地母), which I think goes better with the first and final lines of this chapter, but I'm not ready to overturn the majority of tradition in this instance.

3. This might be a reference to the seasons: "great" summer, "moving on" autumn, "far (away)" winter, and the "return" (of life) in spring.

4. Chen Guying, following the FY and FYY exemplars, thinks that, given the last line in this chapter, "king" here should be "people." I agree with this suggestion, but I will take "king" here as a representative of "people" in the cosmic scheme of things. See Chen Guying 陳鼓應, *Laozi jinzhu jinyi* 老子今註今譯 (臺北: 臺灣商務印書館, 1970; 3rd ed., 2000), 147–48, note 10.

5. The word *yu* 域 (territory; region), which occurs only here, is a generic term, but since in this sentence it must logically include Heaven and Earth, I used "the universe."

6. People, and perhaps sage-kings in particular, can "unify" the cosmos by being able to "steer" the things of this world (ch. 14) and by being able to "be a model" for the world (chs. 22, 28). Or, "the king occupies *a unifying place* among them" (王居其一焉) could, more prosaically, be read instead as "the king occupies *one* of them."

124 | The Annotated *Laozi* 老子

"unfathomable" in chs. 14 and 15) in the same way that it is "vague and elusive" (chs. 14, 21), but this does not mean that it is incomplete. We already know from chapter 7 that it was around "prior to the production of Heaven and Earth." All material things change, as implied in chapters 22 and 23, but the Way that orders them, like the principle of gravity, "does not change."

Because it is so nebulous, it cannot be fully described, as the opening line of the text avers, but we might nevertheless agree to call it the "Way" and agree that it is indeed "Great." That something "great" necessarily implies "moving on" may imply envisioning the Way as a river, always moving but never changing.[7] Or perhaps the entire three-part line should bring to mind the always "moving" seasons (see this chapter's note 3).

The *Xunzi* and *Liji* will later famously say that we humans can and should "form a triad with Heaven and Earth."[8] The *Laozi* predates these texts, but the "quadrangle" of the four "greats" of the Way, Heaven, Earth, and humans may imply a similar dynamic. In any case, the phrase at the end of this seventh sentence could be read in either a quite banal or quite surprising way. Given that the author just stipulated what the four "greats" were, it is slightly repetitive to then say, "Within the universe there are these four greats, and the king [or 'people'] occupies *one* of them." On the other hand, the same phrase could be read, "Within the universe there are these four greats, and the king [or 'people'] occupies *a unifying place* among them." This reading would place quite a bit of responsibility on us humans, responsibility that is not repeated elsewhere in this text as clearly as this. Yet chapter 1 implies that we are in a rather unique position, able to observe both the "mysteries" and "manifestations" of the Way. Chapter 5 says that the sages among us can be as objective as Heaven and Earth, which may also be construed as an ability that separates humans from other

---

7. Sarah Allan, *The Way of Water and Sprouts of Virtue* (Albany: State University of New York Press, 1997), 77: "The *dao* like water—and time—is amorphous, something that continually passes by, which may contain things but can never be grasped. That 'going far away' is called 'going back' or 'returning' (*fan*) may refer to an idea that streams replenish themselves from the waters of the underworld, the Yellow Springs."

8. *Xunzi* 荀子 chapter 17: "Heaven has its seasons, Earth has its resources, and humans have their orderliness, and these are said to be able to form a triad" (天有其時，地有其財，人有其治，夫是之謂能參). *Liji* 禮記 chapter 31 (中庸): "In this world, only those with full honesty. . . . can participate in the development and nurturing of Heaven and Earth; and thus can form a triad with Heaven and Earth" (唯天下至誠. . . . 可以贊天地之化育，則可以與天地參矣).

·Chapter 25 | 125

animals. Chapter 14 says we humans are in a position to be able to "steer" the things of this world, which I suppose no other animal can do. Chapter 22 (and ch. 28) says that sages can "become models for the world," which might be construed as a "unifying" activity. These passages, to my mind, do constitute sufficient evidence for reading this line in the more interesting way (i.e., reading *yi* 一 as "unifying" rather than as "one"), which makes this relatively obscure line one of fundamental cosmic importance.

The final sentence, "People comply with the Earth, Earth complies with Heaven, Heaven complies with the Way, and the Way complies with itself," is the one that typically garners the most attention in this chapter (and indeed, is one of the most famous passages in the entire book). We humans, despite being the "unifying" factor among the "four greats," depend upon the Earth for sustenance. Earth, in turn, depends upon Heaven for the rain necessary for Earth to produce things. Heaven's dependable seasonality depends upon the ordering principle of the Way. And the Way itself is but a tentative descriptor of an obvious order that exists spontaneously. This is as profound an antitheological statement as has ever been made.

The final "the Way complies with itself" can be construed as an interesting text-critical issue. Rhetorically, "X complies with Y" implies that X is not Y, which is certainly the case with the first three phrases in the sentence. But for the fourth, even while there is no change in *rhetoric*, there is a *semantic* change. That is, rhetorically, we might expect the final term to be something that is not the Way, but which the Way complies with, and we might translate that "thing" as "the self-so," thus: "Heaven complies with the Way, and the Way complies with the self-so." Rhetorically, this translation works, but I didn't use it because a reader might infer that the "self-so" is another entity or principle, one that the Way complies with. This is certainly not the intended meaning. If you read "the Way complies with the self-so" as a category shift, something like "gravity complies with physics," that might be fine, but I opted for (semantic) clarity over (rhetorical) elegance. Note 1 in chapter 23 lists the other four uses of the word *ziran* 自然 in the *Laozi*, and none of them use it as a stand-alone term denoting an ontological entity, principle, or category. It is, rather, a linguistic term that means "of itself," so when paired with a pronoun, like "it" or "my" or "them," it means itself, myself, themselves, and so on (as in chs. 17 and 25). And when it appears by itself, then "self-so" or "of itself" is translated more smoothly as "natural" or "naturally" or "naturalness" (as in chs. 23, 51, and 64). Thus, one *might* translate the sentence here as "the Way complies with nature," but that, too, might suggest that "nature" was some separate

126 | The Annotated *Laozi* 老子

entity or principle that the Way complies with. And that is not the case: the ordering principle of the cosmos complies with nothing other than the ordering principle of the cosmos "itself."

After the conspicuously prominent role given to kings in this chapter (even though I suspect "kings" should really be "people," as then it would match the closing sentence), the next reminds said kings of how to be sage-like rulers.

Chapter 26

Key Idea

Be rooted in the heavy and tranquil (Way) to dwell detachedly, not frivolously or agitatedly.

> 重為輕根，靜為躁君。是以君子終日行，不離其「輜重」。雖有
> 榮觀，燕處超然。
> 奈何萬乘之主，而以身輕於天下？輕則失本，躁則失君。

The heavy is the root of the light; the tranquil is the ruler of the agitated. This is why noble people[1] travel all day without leaving their heavy "supply wagon."[2] Even when there are glorious sights to behold,[3] they calmly dwell detachedly.

How then can leaders of ten-thousand-chariot states deal with their persons lightly within the world? If (too) light, then they will lose the root; if (too) agitated, then they will lose the position of being ruler.

---

1. This chapter is one of only two (the other is ch. 31) to use the term "noble people" (君子), usually characterized as a Ruist (Confucian) term, though "ruler" (君) appears in chapters 26 and 70. HSG and other exemplars use "sages" (聖人) here instead.

2. Adjectives typically precede the nouns they modify, and here the "heavy 'supply wagon'" (輜重) is in fact a two-noun phrase that would be more literally translated as "supply wagon that is also a heavy wagon." For *zhong* 重, which typically means "heavy," as "heavy wagon," cf. *Zuozhuan* 左傳 "Duke Xuan" (宣公), year 12: "Chu's heavy wagons arrived at Bi" (楚重至於邲).

3. There are variations of "Even when there are glorious sights to behold" (雖有榮觀) across exemplars. For example, MWD A has: "Only (when they) have encircling palaces" (唯有環官) do they calmly dwell detachedly. But most exemplars support the text I translated.

128 | The Annotated *Laozi* 老子

Chapter 26 Explanation

Chapter 2 described the complementarity of "form and formlessness," "difficult and easy," and other dichotomies. There the focus was on their relativity; preference for one over the other was not the issue. A preference for the Yin side of things was implicitly discernable in chapter 6 (with "the mysterious female"), but there was no explicit comparison to a male. Chapter 10's "can you play the role of the female" is similarly suggestive. Chapter 24's preference for standing firmly over standing on tiptoe does clearly prefer one over the other, and it isn't difficult to see standing firmly as calm Yin and standing on tiptoe as energetic Yang. This chapter continues in that vein, postulating, "The heavy is the root of the light; the tranquil is the ruler of the agitated," with "root" and "ruler" in clearly superior positions. The word "root" implies a tree, with "light" branches and leaves blowing in the wind, possibly in an "agitated" manner.

The metaphor of the "supply wagon" for the Way is a whimsical addition to the previous metaphors of "empty vessel," "bellows," "valley spirit," "mysterious female," and so on. It also might be construed as a metaphor for "heavy," given the literal weightiness of wagons laden with supplies.

The idea of "detachment" was implied in chapter 13's "Favor and disgrace (should be seen) as surprising." Here "detachment" (超)—literally, "to go above" or "to transcend"—is introduced explicitly in noble people who "calmly dwell detachedly." The term does not occur again in this text, but the idea pervades it.

Advice to government "leaders"—"a ten-thousand-chariot state" being shorthand for "a large state"—appeared previously in chapters 13 (where they should "value" [貴] and "care for" [愛] their "persons" [身] as much as everyone else's) and 17 (where they should be practically invisible). Here the advice to be "heavy" and "tranquil" is signaled in the rhetorical question: "How then can leaders of ten-thousand-chariot states deal with their persons lightly within the world?" Which is to say: "How could it be possible that a successful leader could ignore the 'root' and 'supply wagon' of the Way, and flit about frivolously? (It isn't.)" Why? Because "lightness" (輕), here a metaphor for carelessness or frivolousness,[4] results in losing "the root," while being "agitated" (躁), the opposite of being tranquil, results in losing the job of being a leader. Laozi returns to the "heavy root" theme in chapters 39 and 59.

This chapter describes how good leaders deal with themselves, while the topic of the next is how they deal with everyone else.

---

4. "Light, lightness, underestimate" (輕) occurs eight times in four chapters and never has a positive connotation in the *Laozi*.

Chapter 27

Key Ideas

Sages subtly help people via "continuous percipience," via respect for both the competent and the incompetent.

善行者無轍迹。善言者無瑕謫。善數者不用籌策。善閉者無關楗
而不可開。善結者無繩約而不可解。
是以聖人恆善救人，而無棄人；恆善救物，而無棄物。是謂
「襲明」。
故善人，不善人之師；不善人，善人之資。不貴其師，不愛其
資，雖「知」必大迷：是謂「要妙」。

Competent travelers leave no tracks. Competent speakers utter no mistakes. Competent accountants count without using tallies. Competent gate-closers lock up without a crossbar, yet their gates cannot be opened. Competent fasteners bind without ropes, yet their knots cannot be untied.

This is how sages are always competent at helping people, without disregarding anyone; how they are always competent at helping things, without disregarding anything. This is called "continuous percipience."[1]

Thus, competent people are the teachers of incompetent people, and incompetent people are the "material" for competent people. Those who do not value their teachers and those who do not care

---

1. Cf. the "continuous abiding" (襲常) in chapter 52; these are the only two uses of "continuous" in the *Laozi*.

130 | The Annotated *Laozi* 老子

for their "material," though "knowledgeable," will certainly[2] *be greatly deluded: this is called "crucially wondrous."*

Chapter 27 Explanation

The common denominator of the opening five competencies lies in the *unseen* aspects of their respective skills, their ability to do what is required without leaving a trace.[3] Sages, competent by definition, similarly help people and things without their knowing it or, at least, do so unostentatiously. Thus, "*how* sages are always competent at helping people" and "things" is: subtly and discreetly. Their unostentatious and non-contentious methods do not exhaust either the people being helped or the sages doing the helping: sages do not forsake people (or things) because their style(s) of helping is flexible and, so to speak, relatively "free and easy." This is mutually beneficial because, in a manner of speaking, as we will see in chapter 81, "the more they give to others, the greater their abundance." Given how frustrating other people can sometimes be, the commitment to not write them off is characterized as "continuous," which modifies "percipience," the perception that everyone has the potential for the improvement that may be necessary for both realizing their own "genuineness" and for social harmony.[4]

This discernment leads to the rather startlingly liberal conclusion: "Thus, competent people are the teachers of incompetent people, and incompetent people are the 'material' for competent people."[5] Incompetent people are neither derided nor rejected. Those who disagree with this assessment, who do not have the requisite "continuous percipience," are described as "deluded," but the more interesting observation is that, given

---

2. The "certainly" (必) is only in BD; MWD A, B have something like a comma here (i.e., 乎), but most exemplars have nothing.

3. Competent travelers can walk where they leave no tracks, competent speakers can practice their speeches, competent accountants can count in their heads, but I do not know what competent gate-closers and fasteners do to achieve their goals. Maybe they use latches and pins rather than crossbars and ropes?

4. "Everyone" may be slightly hyperbolic; some psychopaths may be beyond help. *Lunyu* 19.3 discusses both sides of this issue but comes to no obvious conclusion.

5. By "liberal," I mean the idea of protecting (and even celebrating) the individual, despite the proclivities of the majority (whose proclivities, nevertheless, must still be "revered," as we saw in chapter 20).

the oft-contentious state of human society, we should nevertheless not give up hope on our fellow humans. Overcoming the potential implausibility of this advice is described as "wondrous," and its importance is aptly termed "crucial." That is, it is "crucial" because a significant number of people are incompetent; it is "wondrous" because an otherwise "knowledgeable" teacher may well conclude that unmotivated students are not capable of improving and so trying to teach them would be a waste of time. The author is perhaps being counterintuitive to claim that (nearly) *everyone* can improve. As we saw earlier, though this text does not use the term "(human) nature," the implication is nevertheless that humans (generally) have good human natures. The invisibility of the competencies described in the opening sentences of this chapter carries over into the (slight) Yin preference of the next chapter.

Chapter 28

Key Ideas

Sometimes be Yang aggressive, but Yin receptive is flexible, limitless, and full of potential.

> 知其雄，守其雌：為天下「谿」。為天下谿，恆德不離，復歸
> 於嬰兒。
> 知其白，守其黑：為天下「式」。為天下式，恆德不忒，復歸
> 於無極。
> 知其榮，守其辱：為天下「谷」。為天下谷，恆德乃足，復歸
> 於樸。
> 樸散則為器，聖人用之，則為官長。故「大制不割」。

Know the male, but preserve the female: be a "mountain stream" for the world. For in being a mountain stream for the world, you will not depart from abiding virtuosity and will return to being as (flexible as) an infant.

Know the white, but preserve the black: be a "model" for the world. For in being a model for the world, you will not err in your abiding virtuosity and will return to the limitless.[1]

Know the glorious, but preserve the humble: be a "valley" for the world. For in being a valley for the world, your abiding

---

1. The "limitless" (無極) will become a main feature of Neo-Confucianism in the Song dynasty, a millennium and a half later, but this term only appears this once in the *Laozi*. The word "limit" (極) however appears in chapter 16 as "utmost," in chapter 58 as "turning points," in chapter 59 as "limits," and in chapter 68 as "utmost."

virtuosity will be sufficient and you will return to the "uncarved block" (of potentiality).

When the "uncarved block" is dispersed, then "vessels"[2] are made from it, and when sages use them, then they become ministers and leaders. Thus, "great crafting does not hack."

Chapter 28 Explanation

As with the psychological interior-exterior balance in chapter 1, this chapter opens with three Yin-Yang dualities that we are advised to balance, albeit with a slight preference for the latter, the Yin. (That is, "to preserve" is slightly more important than "to know.") Thus, balance the "male" with the "female," but treat the female as "the root"; balance the "white" [i.e., clarity and exteriority] with the "black" [i.e., open-mindedness and interiority], but treat the black as foundational; balance "glory" with "humility," but remain grounded in humility. These three pairs describe (cognitive) flexibility, (fallibilist) epistemology, and (destined) potentiality; they relate to attitude, methodology, and practice, respectively.

The "male" and "female" here are juxtaposed with two images. The first is a "mountain stream," which is, by definition, in relation to its surroundings, "lowly," and thus a metaphor for humility. It is probably also winding, and thus a metaphor for adaptability. The second is "an infant," a metaphor for flexibility. Thus, the "male" here symbolizes the soaring mountains among which relatively lowly streams windingly flow, and the relatively inflexible adults who care for infants, while the "female" connotes the humility, adaptability, and flexibility of the two images.[3]

The "(fallibilist) epistemology" of the white-black antipodes results in a "limitless" potential for open-ended knowledge-gathering: the "limit" here is the same as the "utmost" in the advice to "achieve utmost openness" (致虛極) that opens chapter 16. In chapter 22, being a "model" involved embracing the One, which, in that chapter and this, implied a balancing of opposites.

---

2. "Vessels" (器) are (sometimes) a metaphor for people, and particularly for people's "capacity" for community or government service. See chapter 67 for a similar usage, or *Lunyu* 2.12, 3.22, 5.4, and 13.25.

3. The "female" (雌 and 牝) appears in this text in chapters 6, 10, 28, 55, and 61; the "male" (雄 and 牡) appears in chapters 28, 55, and 61.

134 | The Annotated *Laozi* 老子

The previous chapter spoke to the sage's unostentatious influence on people in general; this chapter speaks to sages who specifically facilitate some people becoming "ministers and leaders." That is, one kind of potentiality of the "uncarved block" is realized when capable people, guided by sages (in this case, overlapping with the "teachers" of the previous chapter), become government ministers and leaders. But sages are able to "craft" such people only to realize their students' own individual potentiality: they do not randomly "hack" at people, mistakenly thinking that all humans have the capabilities to be ministers and leaders. To "hack" at the potentiality of people who are not so inclined to be leaders would be an example of contrivance, a topic we have already met with, and yet one that is important enough to be repeated in the next chapter.

Chapter 29

Key Ideas

Sage leaders are uncontrived, yet careful; are responsive to change; and discard excess, extravagance, and pomposity.

> 將欲取天下而為之者：吾見其不得已。天下「神器」，不可為
> 也。為者敗之，執者失之。
> 故物「或行或隨，或呴或吹，或強或贏，或培或墮」。是以聖人
> 去甚，去奢，去泰。

Those who want to gain (leadership of) the world and be contrived with it: we see their lack of success.[1] The world is (like) a "spiritous vessel"[2] and cannot be contrived. Those who are contrived will fail in it; those who are attached will lose it.[3]

---

1. The "lack of success" translates *budeyi* 不得已, literally, "simply will not get (what they are after)." But 不得已 is also a stock phrase that means "inevitable." The phrase 不得已 occurs three times in the *Laozi*: here, and in the next two chapters, where they mean "inevitable" (though in chapter 31 it is translated as "unavoidable"). So this sentence *could* read: "Those who want to gain (leadership of) the world and act (contrivedly) upon it: we see that this is (sometimes) inevitable." The next two sentences would then go on to advise against this.

2. A "spiritous vessel" is a delicately created object that was interred in tombs in place of practical vessels; for example, a fragile clay water pot rather than a sturdy bronze one. This is similar to the reference to frying a small fish in chapter 60, a different metaphor for a political context: "Organizing a great state is like cooking a small fish." Both "spiritous vessels" and "small fish" need to be handled with care.

3. This same sentence is in chapter 64, but there the "it" is not implied as it is here (as "the world").

135

136 | The Annotated *Laozi* 老子

Thus, things "sometimes go and sometimes follow, sometimes blow hot and sometimes blow cold,[4] sometimes are strong and sometimes are weak, sometimes build up and sometimes tear down." This is why sages discard excess, discard extravagance, and discard pomposity.

Chapter 29 Explanation

In chapter 3 we were told that non-contrivance brings "organization" (治), and here it similarly says that contrivance is not, ultimately, going to be successful. Certainly, *short-term* success may be expected for following cultural contrivances, to the extent that we are assessed and rewarded by those invested in such norms, so the "lack of success" here must refer to long-term success. The "spiritous vessel" metaphor for our (ecological and social) environment(s) implies that we should act in these contexts with a "light touch."

The third sentence connects uncontrived success and prudent action with the "detachment" touched upon in chapter 26. This point is illustrated with the Yin-Yang, "this too shall change" and "for everything there is a season"[5] motifs of the following sentence, where things "sometimes go and sometimes follow." Non-contrivance and detachment are both responsive to the situation at hand, whether going or following, whether the situation calls for us to "build up" things or to "tear down" things. Timeliness always plays a role in such decisions.

The final sentence articulates three things to discard—"excess . . . extravagance . . . [and] pomposity"—which could, in a pinch, be related to three of the things chapter 19 asked us to rid ourselves of: (contrived, ostentatious) knowledge can be pompous; artifice can be excessive; and an (excessive) profit motive can lead to extravagance. They also overlap with the "three treasures" of chapter 67: compassion (not excessive displays of pity), frugality (not extravagance), and not presuming to lead the way (not pompous). This sentence begins with "This is why" because responsiveness to

---

4. This phrase should be taken literally, as sometimes breathing out warm air from the lungs and sometimes breathing out cold air through pursed lips, and not as in the English expression that denotes being sometimes angry and sometimes calm.

5. Ecclesiastes 3:1.

Chapter 29 | 137

the differences and changes described in the preceding sentence requires the simplicity described in this sentence. (This theme of "frugality" for leaders returns in chapters 59 and 67.) The ordinary extravagance denounced in this chapter is specifically situated in the context of war in the next.

Chapter 30

Key Ideas

The Way in war: achieve the goal and then stop; discard boasting, bragging, and arrogance.

> 以道佐人主者，不以兵強天下，其事好還。「師之所居，荊棘生焉。」「大軍之後，必有凶年。」故善者果而已：不敢以取強。
> 果而勿矜，果而勿伐，果而勿驕：果而不得已，果而勿強。物壯則老：是謂不道，不道早已。

Those who serve leaders by using the Way will not force the world with weapons,[1] for such activities are likely to cause retaliation. "The places where armies dwell are where thistles and brambles grow." "After a great military campaign, there is certain to be a bad harvest."[2] Thus, competent people achieve the goal and then stop: they do not presume thereby to take things by force.

Results without boasting, results without bragging, and results without arrogance are results that (seem) inevitable and are results that are unforced. Things that are overbearing get old (prematurely): this is called not (being in accord with) the Way, and things not (in accord with) the Way will come to an early end.[3]

---

1. The word for "weapons" (兵) can also mean "soldiers," "armies," "troops," and so forth.

2. I've put these two sentences in quotation marks because they sound to me like "sayings" that the author is quoting. But I could be wrong and both sentences are the author's own words. Also, the second saying does not appear in the GD A or MWD A or B exemplars.

3. The last sentence is also the last sentence of chapter 55 (with one minor change).

Chapter 30 Explanation

This is the first of seven chapters that address the issue of "weapons / soldiers / the army" (兵).[4] The defensive position of the author is given straightaway: Daoists "will not force the world with weapons." Three reasons are given for this position: first, it is "likely to cause retaliation," it will cause "a bad harvest," and taking "things by force" is not a "competent" way of obtaining things.[5] Diplomacy should always be tried first.[6]

That "competent people achieve the goal and then stop" is reminiscent of the "When the task is accomplished and you then retire: this is the way of Heaven" in chapter 9. Both passages combine humility with competency.

The injunction against "boasting" and "bragging" we saw in chapters 22 and 24, while "arrogance" was advised against in chapter 9. If one has to engage in battle, then a "get in and get out" strategy will doubtless cause less consternation in, and pushback from, the conquered than a protracted and "overbearing" occupation. The chapter wraps up neatly with a return to the "early end" that was implied by the "retaliation" in the opening sentence.

This chapter on humility in war is expanded upon in the next chapter with the memorable advice to treat military victory like a funeral.

---

4. The seven are: chapters 30, 31, 50, 57, 69, 76, and 80.

5. I don't know if the "bad harvest" is literal superstition, is pointing to the potential for soldiers to steal crops, or is just a poetic metaphor.

6. Several centuries later, the father-son team of royal librarians, Liu Xiang 劉向 (79–8 BCE) and Liu Xin 劉歆 (45 BCE–23 CE) created a ten-part classification system for intellectual history. Ruism (Confucianism) and Daoism are the two most famous, but another lesser-known category was of "Diplomatists" (縱橫家). However, what little remains of those books is now only in fragmentary form.

Chapter 31

Key Ideas

Noble people do not glorify war; military victory should use mourning protocol.

夫兵者，不祥之器，物或惡之；故有道者不居。君子居則貴左，
　用兵則貴右。
兵者，不祥之器，非君子之器，不得已而用之：恬憺為上。
故不美也，若美之，是樂殺人也。夫樂殺人者，不可以得志於
　天下矣。
故吉事尚左，凶事尚右。是以偏將軍居左，上將軍居右，言以
　喪禮居之。
殺人衆多，則以悲哀泣之：戰勝以喪禮居之。

Weapons are inauspicious instruments, and all things probably detest them; thus, those with the Way are not occupied with them. Noble people at home value the (Yang) left, but when using weapons then they value the (Yin) right.[1]

　Weapons are inauspicious instruments, and are not the instruments of noble people, but when unavoidable they use them: (still,) peace and quiet are best.[2]

---

1. The "left" refers to Yang-active matters, like making a living, and the "right" to Yin-stable matters, including death and death-related things.

2. Some scholars see the last phrase, "peace and quiet are best," not as a counterpoint to the use of weapons but rather as describing the best way of using them: use weapons when you have to, but do so "peacefully and quietly."

140

Chapter 31 | 141

Thus, (weapons) are not glorious,[3] and if one glorifies them, this would be to delight in killing humans. Those who delight in killing humans will not realize their ambitions in the world.

Thus, for auspicious activities one values the (Yang) left, while for inauspicious activities one values the (Yin) right.[4] This is why lieutenant generals are situated on the left, while commanding generals are situated on the right, which is to say they are situated with mourning protocol.[5]

When great numbers of people have been killed, then one should weep for them with sorrow and sympathy: military victory should be treated with mourning protocol.

Chapter 31 Explanation

Chapter 30 gave three reasons why military weapons might be considered "inauspicious instruments," and here a fourth reason is adduced: "all things probably detest them." (I cannot tell if the "probably" was prudence or playfulness.)

The Yin-Yang analysis of "right" and "left" makes clear that "noble people at home" are busy getting things done, busy living life, "but when using weapons then they" adopt a more cautious attitude, receptive to ideas that will allow them to avoid contention and war. Nevertheless, the text is not advocating pacifism, given that "when unavoidable they [i.e., noble people] use them."

Perhaps the most memorable line about warfare in the *Laozi* is the counterintuitive and trenchant saying: "Thus, (weapons) are not glorious, and if one glorifies them, this would be to delight in killing humans." The

---

3. The word "glorious" (美) also implies literal "beauty," so Laozi may also be stating a preference for plain weapons over fancy, decorated, "beautified" weapons. Weapons, then, should be like garden tools.

4. There are two terms in this chapter that I translate as "inauspicious" (不祥 and 凶). The first (i.e., 不祥) occurs only here (twice) and in chapter 78, though the ostensibly "auspicious" (祥) part of "inauspicious" is also in chapter 55, translated as "ominous." (It is one of those words that, like "cleave" in English, means both one thing and its opposite.) The second (i.e., 凶) is also in chapter 16 as "inauspiciousness" and in chapter 30 as the "bad" in "bad harvest." The word translated here as "auspicious" (吉) occurs only here.

5. "Protocol" (禮) occurs only in this chapter and in chapter 38.

142 | The Annotated *Laozi* 老子

following sentence, "Those who delight in killing humans will not realize their ambitions in the world," calls to mind the aphorism: "Conquering the world on horseback is easy, it is dismounting and governing that is hard."

The Yin-Yang, right-left analytic is used again in the reference to the "lieutenant generals" (who are doing the actual fighting and Yang-active killing) and the "commanding generals" (who are overseeing the fighting and doing the Yin-stable planning). It is the "commanding generals" who will be the ones to exercise Yin-stable caution in both "reading" a dangerous military situation that will likely lead to death, and who will, or should, feel "sorrow and sympathy" in overseeing the bloody response to that situation. Literal "mourning protocol" is of course also an Yin-stable enterprise, as caution in dealing with dead bodies is both a genetic inclination (to avoid contamination) and an ethical choice (to show respect).

This chapter introduced the counterintuitive language of "mourning victory," so the next chapter's return to the chapter 1 motif of language skepticism seems fitting.

Chapter 32

Key Ideas

Daoist leaders use nameless simplicity to be modest and equitable; exclusivity in naming is presumptuous.

道恆無名樸。雖小，天下莫能臣。侯王若能守之，萬物將自賓。
天地相合，以降甘露，民莫之令而自均。
始制有名，名亦既有，夫亦將知止，知止所以不殆。譬道之在天
下，猶川谷之與江海。

The Way abides in (the) nameless ("uncarved block" of) simplicity.[1]
Though modest,[2] no one in the world is able to make of it a servant.
If governors and kings could preserve it, the myriad things would
subject themselves to them. By the mutual union of Heaven and
Earth, sweet dew falls and, without any human laws, is naturally
equitable.

In the beginning, when things were made, there were names
(given to them), but once there were names, there also should have

---

1. This sentence reads, "The Way abides in nameless simplicity" or "The Way abides in the nameless uncarved block," so the parentheticals are added to remind the reader of the underlying image of an "uncarved block" of wood. This "uncarved block" connotes "solidity" in chapter 15 and "potentiality" in chapter 28, but more often is a metaphor for simplicity.

2. The primary meaning of "modest" (小) is "small," though chapters 18 and 25 call the Way "great" (大), as do chapters 34, 53, and 67; thus, the great Way abides in modesty (or, more literally, abides in "the small"), for example, modest or small things like dew. The Way is also called "modest" in chapter 34.

144 | The Annotated *Laozi* 老子

been a knowing of when to stop, for knowing when to stop is a
means of avoiding danger.[3] *Metaphorically, the Way is in the world*
as creeks in valleys flow into rivers and oceans.

Chapter 32 Explanation

The "('uncarved block' of) simplicity" (樸) was a metaphor for "solid" in chapter 15 and for "potential" in chapter 28, but given the context of modesty here, the metaphor is of "simplicity" (which is also the case in chapters 19, 37, and 57). Here it is described as "nameless" and "modest" (小), meaning "(ostensibly) negligible," yet it is nevertheless quite powerful when people make use of it. In particular, "if governors and kings could preserve it, the myriad things would subject themselves to them." This is so because, as we saw in the previous three chapters, no one likes arrogant, aggressive, bloodthirsty leaders.

The fourth sentence relates to the third sentence because "governors and kings" are to "the myriad things" as "Heaven" is to "Earth," and as the latter pair have a relationship that is a "mutual union," so should leaders with those whom they lead. (Ethical realism, again.) Thus, just as "sweet dew" falls naturally from Heaven to Earth (or so it was thought), so should good leaders treat people in an "equitable" manner, "without any human laws" that forcibly stipulate they be that way.[4]

The second two sentences of the first paragraph display a Yin-Yang tension between "subject themselves" (自賓) and "naturally equitable" (自均), insofar as the first necessitates a hierarchy, while the second celebrates equality. But just as Yang Heaven and Yin Earth are hierarchical, with Heaven above and Earth below, and are also a complementary pair that "mutually" come together to create "sweet dew," so leaders and followers can, ideally, make for a good team.

The two key terms that connect the first and second paragraphs are "modest" and "equitable," which, in the first paragraph, apply to the Way, Heaven and Earth, and good leaders. The second paragraph asks us to exercise a bit of modesty in our desire to (fully and completely) describe the

---

3. Locution similar to the last phrase of this sentence is also in chapter 44 (i.e., 知止不殆).

4. I suspect that this, too, is a reference to "Goodhart's law," mentioned in chapter 3, note 5, insofar as rulers should ideally want to be naturally equitable and not forced to be that way through laws (that often seem to have loopholes).

world. But the sentence, by itself, may at first be a little perplexing: "In the beginning, when things were made, there were names (given to them), but once there were names, there also should have been a knowing of when to stop, for knowing when to stop is a means of avoiding danger." Why? What does Laozi have against naming things? Sure, the *Way* might be intrinsically "nameless," but what about everything else? I can think of five answers.

The first (Yang) answer is that Laozi has nothing at all against naming most things, but only with naming—defining—certain contrived things as definitive. Recall the denigration of presuming to be able to define "beauty" and "competence" in chapter 2, "goodness" in chapter 5, the so-called "five" colors, sounds, and flavors in chapter 12, and the various virtuosities in chapters 18 and 19. An example in this chapter is in saying the "great" Way is, counterintuitively, also "modest" (see note 2), just as great Heaven is present and active in modest dew. In this reading, it is not "names" per se that are bad, only the presumption of trying to define subjective and individual assessments as if all people had the same sensibilities.

The second (Yin) answer returns us to the advice to "abide in form-lessness" from chapter 1. When one is introspecting, the verbal "train of thought" is quieted, "names" recede, and "peace and quiet are best" (ch. 31). In this reading, too, it is not "names" per se that are bad, only the name-filled "stream of consciousness" that seems to never quit unless we consciously stop it. In such an introspective state, from which we can "observe . . . wonders" (ch. 1), names—that is, conscious analysis—take a back seat to the *experience* of wonder.[5] The "danger" in the first reading is in a lack of fallibilism, a lack of humility, and of alienating those who do not share your definitions, while the "danger" in this second reading is a lack of interiority, a lack of the "in-sight" gained from introspection.

Third, holding to "simplicity" in speech might seek to avoid the danger of jargon. Consider the proliferation of jargon that accrues in various (academic) fields: that jargon may be helpful to those in the know, but to the vast majority of people it is less than useless.[6] Fourth, there is also the

---

5. *Zhuangzi* chapter 2 has an anecdote about five stages of knowing, with the first and highest being a state of mind wherein one "apprehends the not yet beginning to be (discrete, named) things" (以為未始有物).

6. Though I cannot be certain that these are the people the author had in mind, early China did have rhetorists (名家) who apparently delighted in making claims like "A white horse is not a horse" (白馬非馬). There was no doubt jargon that could "explain" such claims, but I think Laozi was just having none of it. See the closing pages of the *Zhuangzi* for a list of such claims.

146 | The Annotated *Laozi* 老子

chance that some people might assume that once things are named, then we will thereby fully comprehend them. Consider the writing of laws. If laws were clearly written and self-explanatory, then we would not need courts to interpret them. But they often are not, which invites the danger of misapprehension or of misuse,[7] and thus we do need judges to interpret what lawmakers write.

And fifth, if we take the "uncarved block" at the beginning of this chapter to refer to both "simplicity" *and* "potentiality," then consideration of that nameless potentiality is yet another Daoist goal, one that supports the "unlearning" discussed in the "key concepts" and that we saw in chapter 20 (and will see again in chapters 48 and 64). Considering your own potentiality should help you avoid the danger of living your life in a way that is not genuine. For example, if you see yourself as, say, a "scientist," that should not thereby preclude you from appreciating poetry. Thus, this chapter echoes the language skepticism of chapter 1: language can obscure as much as it illuminates. The "danger" of trying to name everything in the hope of having perfectly clear human communication is both quixotic (insofar as language is always evolving) and detrimental to the imaginative perception of the unity and simplicity of nature, which robs it of its mystery and potentiality.

The humility implied by the geographically lower position of "rivers and oceans" in the final sentence has three referents. First, it is related to the "knowing when to stop" humility of the previous sentence. Second, it connects back to the "simplicity" and "modesty" of the first two sentences. And third, it functions as a nod to another meaning of the Chinese word for "names" (名), which means both linguistic "naming" as well as social "fame." There is a danger in naming too much, and another danger in becoming too famous. Thus, this chapter begins with "nameless simplicity," the correct use of which may result in fame for good leaders, even though we should keep in mind that Heaven and Earth are not interested in praise or fame, and it continues with the overzealous activity of naming and the proliferation of jargon, ending as it began, with the simple, useful, equitable, and humble Way. The final image of humility in this chapter is continued in the next, with yet another Yin-Yang framing.

---

7. Chapter 57 says, "The more laws and statutes are proclaimed, the more thieves and robbers there will be."

Chapter 33

Key Ideas

Know yourself, control yourself, be content, persevere, keep your place, live long.

知人者智也，自知者明也。
勝人者有力也，自勝者強也。
知足者富也，強行者有志也。
不失其所者久也，死而不亡者壽也。

Those who know others are wise; those who know themselves are percipient.

Those who conquer others have power; those who conquer themselves are strong.

Those who know contentment are rich; those who persevere have determination.

Those who do not lose their place will endure; those who die without (such) loss are long-lived.

Chapter 33 Explanation

This chapter is rather self-explanatory, but there are two things that might be noted. The first concerns the "conquer others" line, which *could* be read as contradicting the non-contention advice of chapters 8 and 22 (as well as 30 and 31), but I think this should be understood as advice to "overcome (the challenges raised by) others" and not as advice to compel others to do your will.

148 | The Annotated *Laozi* 老子

Second, if we read this chapter with a Yin-Yang analysis, similar to that in chapter 28, we may construe the first half of each sentence as outer Yang, describing the social sphere, and the second half as inner Yin, describing the individual sphere. This is clear in the first two sentences, but less so in the following two. Though one might "know contentment" apart from society, we might nevertheless imagine being "rich" comparatively, in relation to those caught in the so-called "rat race," condemned to never feel content.[1]

The final sentence, too, can be so construed. I take "Those who do not lose their place" to refer to those who steadfastly follow their own individual paths within society at large, with its pressure to conform acting as an inducement for us to "lose our place." The Yin side of this equation focuses on the inner loss of our destiny, of the path we (ideally) know we should be on, and if we are on that inner path to our own "genuineness," we will find ourselves in the proper outer place, and this will be conducive to living a long life.[2] This chapter exclusively on humans is immediately balanced by the next chapter exclusively on the Way.

---

1. Three of the four pairs of adjectives that conclude each of these sentences are nearly synonymous—wise / percipient, power[ful] / strong, and endur[ing] / long-lived—but the pair in the third sentence are decidedly not. I don't know if this indicates a mistake, but it certainly draws one's attention.

2. Both MWD texts have "forget" (忘) instead of "loss" (亡), and while it makes perfect sense in a generalized early Chinese context to want to be remembered after death, I don't think this fits particularly well with Laozi's overall philosophy. On the one hand, the MWD reading *could* be construed as "those who die without being forgotten will be long-lived [insofar as they will be remembered for being such exemplary Daoists]," and this may indeed be an early reading. But on the other hand, within the context of the *Laozi* itself, such postmortem "fame" seems out of place. Thus, I take this "loss" (亡) to be congruent with the preceding "lose" (失), both reiterating the common *Laozi* theme of pursuing one's individual path in life, tempered, of course, with the exigencies of living in a community of others.

Chapter 34

Key Ideas

The Way gives things life, but is desireless and thus modest; it does not make itself lord and thus is great.

> 大道氾兮，其可左右。萬物恃之以生而弗辭，成功而弗名有。愛
> 養萬物而不為主。
> 恆無欲，可名於小。萬物歸焉而不為主，可名為大。
> 是以聖人以其終不自為大，故能成其大。

The great Way flows everywhere; it can go to the left and right. The myriad things rely on it for life, and it does not deny them; it completes its tasks, but it does not claim ownership.[1] It cares for and nourishes[2] the myriad things but does not make itself lord.

It abidingly is without desire, and thus can be called modest. The myriad things return to it, yet it does not make itself lord; thus, it can be called great.

This is why sages with it never consider themselves great; thus, they are able to complete their greatness.[3]

---

1. Rhetorically similar phrases are in chapters 2 and 77. Chapter 2: "The myriad things arise, but (sages) do not deny them. (Sages) 'act, but without expectation; and complete tasks, but without dwelling (on them)'" (萬物作而弗辭。「為而弗恃，成功而弗居」). Chapter 77: "Sages 'act, but without expectation; complete tasks, but without dwelling (on them)'" (聖人「為而弗恃，成功而弗居」).

2. This phrase is from HSG and XZ; BD has "cares for and benefits" (愛利); FY and FYY have "clothes and covers" (衣被); DZ has "clothes and nourishes" (衣養).

3. A nearly identical sentence appears in chapter 63 (i.e., 是以聖人終不為大，故能成其大), but with a somewhat different translation.

149

150 | The Annotated *Laozi* 老子

Chapter 34 Explanation

Cosmologically, we learned in chapter 21 that the Way "is used to examine the inceptions of the multitudes," and in chapter 25 we saw that there was a something that was "prior to the production of Heaven and Earth," and from these we might have guessed that the Way "flows everywhere."

Biologically, we saw in chapter 25 that it "can be taken as 'the mother of the world,'" and in chapter 30 that "things not (in accord with) the Way will come to an early end," so it is no surprise that here we learn "the myriad things rely on it for life." It is, in a germinal sense, "responsible" for everything, yet "it does not claim ownership." This is a matter both of humility and of the reality, seen in chapter 25, that it "complies with itself."

That the Way is "without desire" is not surprising either, given that it is not sentient. However, given the ethical realism of the text, we humans are advised to emulate the Way in its desirelessness. (This advice is given in chapters 3, 37, 57, and 64; chapter 19 says, less hyperbolically, that we should "decrease desires" [寡欲].) This paragraph describes the Way as both "modest" (小) and "great" (大), which are natural antonyms in Chinese. Both of these adjectives also describe the Way in other chapters. Chapter 32 said the Way is "modest" like Heaven and Earth conspiring in dew, and like the gravity that subtly pulls water downhill toward oceans. Here it is modest because it "abidingly is without desire." We might construe both the "namelessness" (無名) in chapter 32 and the "desirelessness" (無欲) here as two instantiations of ontological tenuousness or ethical humility, as a kind of modesty. Chapter 25 said the Way is "great" but gave no reason why, though the next sentence says, "Great implies moving on . . . going far; and . . . (eventual) return." Here in chapter 34 it is great because "it does not make itself lord" of the "myriad things" that inevitably "return to it." We might connect the Way's motility in chapter 25 with its humility here by noting that it is difficult to be overbearing when always on the move.

After five sentences about the Way and its relationship with the myriad things, sagely people are introduced as those who emulate the Way. Here the specific thing to be emulated is modesty. Thus, "sages with it"—that is, with the Way—"never consider themselves great," and it is by this humility that they thereby "complete their greatness." This is an insight that many of us pick up on in high school: it's one thing to excel at something (beauty, sports, grades), but it's quite another when one becomes obviously aware of that excellence and then to *consider yourself* to be extraordinary. This chapter describes both the greatness and the modesty of the Way; the next continues these themes with its great attractiveness and modest "flavorlessness."

Chapter 35

Key Ideas

The Way is a "great semblance" that results in security and peace, but it is modest and sounds flavorless.

執「大象」，天下往。往而不害，安平太。
樂與餌，過客止，道之出言，淡乎其無味。
視之不足見，聽之不足聞，用之不可既。

> *Hold to the "great semblance," and the world will come to you. It will come without harm, and its security and peace will be great.*
>
> *Music and food induce passing travelers to stop, but when the Way is spoken of, it sounds thin and flavorless.*
>
> *Look for it, but it won't be seen; listen for it, but it won't be heard; use it, but it can't be exhausted.[1]*

Chapter 35 Explanation

The "great semblance" is a metaphor for the Way that we saw in chapter 14 (as "the semblance in nothingness");[2] it connotes the "vague and elusive"

---

1. Cf. chapter 14: "Looking for it without seeing it, it is called unobtrusive; listening for it without hearing it, it is called faint; grasping for it without obtaining it, it is called inconspicuous" (視之不見，名曰夷；聽之不聞，名曰希；搏之不得，名曰微).

2. In chapter 21, the Way contained "semblances" within it . . . mystery within mystery. *Xiang* 象 (semblance; image; form; likeness; seems, seemingly) appears five times in the *Laozi*, in chapters 4, 14, 21, 35, and 41. It may originally have referred to the "images" in the sky: asterisms like the "Big Dipper" or the Dragon in the first hexagram of the *Yijing* 易經. I use "semblance" here to denote the "hazy outline" of the Way in the cosmos.

151

152 | The Annotated *Laozi* 老子

(ch. 21) nature of the Way, which in this chapter is articulated in the final sentence's "Look for it, but it can't be seen; listen for it, but it can't be heard." But it also connotes incipient activity and productivity. Thus, one who holds to this vague Way will find that it results in attractiveness and, furthermore, "security and peace" in great measure, an abiding usefulness that "can't be exhausted." As "the Way" brings to my mind the analogy of "gravity," so the "great semblance" brings to my mind the image of a tiny shoot, a sprout that is just beginning to break the soil, but one that cannot yet be seen and thus cannot be identified or named. But a careful observer will nevertheless see the broken soil and surmise a sprout, even if they cannot yet predict what it will become.

This Yin-Yang pairing of hazy amorphousness and dependable efficacy is here applied to the images of "music and food" (in, perhaps, a tavern at which "passing travelers" stop): some food and music are florid and widely appealing, while other kinds are subtle and palatable only to certain attenuated sensibilities.[3] Following the Way, as we saw in chapter 14, is like following a thread, even like following the "thread" of a (scholarly) argument: it requires focus and patience but is ultimately rewarding.

That the Way, when "spoken of," may sound "thin and flavorless," perhaps rings more true today than it did two and a half millennia ago. Its themes of individualism, realizing your "genuine" self, "beauty is in the eye of the beholder," "don't be a show-off," be a "servant-leader," be open-minded, embrace change and difference, be inclusive, and don't be a warmonger, are all now widely seen as "common sense." Given the passage at hand, perhaps it was so construed in early China as well. Nevertheless, while the words of this text may not constitute earth-shattering news, we should not thereby dismiss it. It may well appeal to us as something like "thin" broth when we're feeling under the weather, or "flavorless" water when we're thirsty.

The modest, "thin and flavorless" "great semblance" in this chapter manifests itself in an ever-changing variety of circumstances in the next.

---

3. This is not to imply that subtle melodies and flavors cannot be great or tasty: chapters 41 and 80 implicitly say they may.

Chapter 36

Key Ideas

Observe variables with subtle percipience, then be flexible, but not *too* flexible.

將欲翕之，必固張之；將欲弱之，必固強之；將欲廢之，必固舉
之；將欲取之，必固與之：是謂「微明」。
柔弱勝剛強。魚不可脫於淵，邦之利器，不可以示人。

To shrink something, it must already be expanded;[1] to make some-thing supple, it must already be stiff; to reject something, it must already be popular; to have something taken away, it must already have been given: (seeing) this is called "subtle percipience."

(Thereby,) the flexible and supple overcome the inflexible and stiff. (But, just as) fish should not abandon deep water, (so) the sharp instruments[2] of the state should not be paraded before the people.

Chapter 36 Explanation

Perception of the Yin-Yang vicissitudes of material size and resilience, and of interpersonal acclaim and exchange is here called "subtle percipience,"

---

1. A more literal translation would be: "If (one) would shrink something, (someone) must have already expanded it." Some scholars, following Han Feizi 韓非子, read the *yu* 欲 (would, want, desire) with more intentionality: "If (you) want to shrink something, (you / someone) must in fact have (already) expanded it." But I think this is about the changing circumstances in which we should be flexible and not (questionable) advice about how to shrink things. The same locution, with the same rhetorical objective, is used in the following three phrases. Rhetorically, I think the opening sentence here is the same as that which opens chapter 22: "Bent then whole" (曲則全), among others.

2. The phrase "sharp instruments" (利器), meaning weapons, occurs only here and in chapter 57.

153

154 | The Annotated *Laozi* 老子

one of two specialized kinds of percipience found in this text.[3] We can perceive such changes in natural matters where change is inevitable and in those human affairs where change must be consciously brought about. We can use this percipience in at least four ways.

First, simply perceiving that a current situation may be temporary could be a useful observation. If we extrapolate from things that "shrink" and "expand," like our lungs when we breathe, or the waxing and waning moon, then getting from one state to another may just be a matter of waiting. Second, if you know that something "supple" may eventually become "stiff," like overworked muscles or joints, then we can keep an eye out for the signs or "semblances" (ch. 21) of when enough is enough, of when the tide is about to turn.

Third, when situations A and B are logically connected, then when we see A we can infer B. For example, knowing that fashions come and go, when we happen upon a fashion "reject," something out of (current) fashion, we can infer that what is now expressly unfashionable once was "popular." Fourth, in realizing the variability of (a particular set of) current circumstances, we can appreciate the adage that "this too shall pass." This is especially clear in the fourth example, "to have something taken away, it must already have been given."

The second paragraph adds two things to our perception of our subtly ever-changing world. That "the flexible and supple overcome the inflexible and stiff" is an observation that mental flexibility is requisite for being aware of existing circumstances and for prudently dealing with them. We saw this already in several preceding chapters.

The last sentence acts as a brake on the advice to be flexible, just as chapter 20 used "that which people revere must be revered" as a brake on unchecked individualism. The advice in this chapter is to be flexible amid changing variables, but not so flexible that you get yourself killed. "Fish should not abandon deep water" if they don't want to attract the attention of fishermen, just as weapons "should not be paraded before the people" if leaders do not want to incite the people to violence.[4] Juxtaposing fish and weapons makes for a memorable comparison as both should be kept hidden. Further, we might extrapolate from fish and weapons to leaders

---

3. The other is the "continuous percipience" (襲明) in chapter 27, describing the sage's inclusivity.

4. This final sentence is reminiscent of Theodore Roosevelt's "speak softly and carry a big stick."

Chapter 36 | 155

themselves, who may find that being unobtrusive is a more effective way of ruling than ostentatiousness,[5] which is advice that we met as early as chapter 7. Extrapolating from leaders to the rest of us, we might infer that leaders (and empires) come and go, making flexibility a functionally desirable skill, so don't bring out the "big guns" unless you really intend to use them. But it is usually better to remain above the fray or, to change metaphors, to remain in the deep waters in which fish are safe from the nets and lures of impatience and obstinance.

Whereas this chapter focuses on flexibility and unobtrusiveness, so the next reminds us, once again, that these virtues are best grounded in the fundamental virtue of non-contrivance.

---

5. Zhuangzi does this when he equates "sharp instruments" with "sages" in *Zhuangzi* chapter 10. After quoting this passage, he adds: "These sages are the 'sharp instruments' of the world and are not that which (should be) perceived by the world" (彼聖人者，天下之利器也，非所以明天下也).

Chapter 37

Key Ideas

The Way abides uncontrivedly, yet nothing is left undone; tranquility can develop and settle people.

道恆無為而無不為。侯王若能守之，萬物將自化。
化而欲作，吾將鎮之以無名之樸。
無名之樸，夫亦將不欲。不欲以靜，天下將自定。

The Way abides uncontrivedly, yet nothing is left undone. If governors and kings could preserve it, the myriad things would develop themselves.

If, while developing, (contrived) desires arise, we will settle them with (the) nameless ("uncarved block" of) simplicity.

(After being settled with) nameless simplicity, then they will not (contrivedly) desire. (If they thus) do not (contrivedly) desire, by means of tranquility, then the world will settle[1] itself.

Chapter 37 Explanation

The opening line is perhaps the unofficial motto of Daoism (and appears again in chapter 48, where we, not the Way, are the subject). The coun-

---

1. GD C; HSG; DZ have "settle" (定); MWD A, B; BD; FY; FYY have "correct" (正). Chapter 57 has a similar saying, whereby good leadership results in the people "developing" (化), "correcting" (正), "prospering" (富), and "simplifying" (樸) themselves.

Chapter 37 | 157

terintuitive efficacy of following the Way is summarized in its conclusion: "yet nothing is left undone." Cosmologically, that means "everything that is supposed to happen, does happen." (The laws of physics are pretty dependable that way.) For humans who emulate the Way, though, "nothing [*important*] is left undone," since contrived actions are generally useless, at least for self-cultivation (though they may be useful, sometimes, for social harmony).

The "governors and kings" here are political figures, and their ability to "preserve" the Way is crucial for social harmony (and an implicit political hierarchy), but social harmony in this text does not imply a static citizenry. Rather, it is predicated on a dynamic populace, one in which it is expected that people "would develop themselves." The term "develop" (化), which appears only here and in chapter 57, implies both natural evolution in general *and* a natural evolution toward individual competence and ethical goodness.

The kind of natural development that Laozi has in mind does not include us desiring to be what we genuinely are not; that is, it does not include desires for anything contrived. But given that we are social creatures who want approval, such desires may nevertheless "arise."[2] When that happens, one guiding activity that the author approves of is that someone will "settle them with (the) nameless ('uncarved block' of) simplicity," an important term discussed in chapter 32. The "namelessness" of this "simplicity" is also a poetic descriptor of the Way, implied in the opening sentence of chapter 1 but appearing more explicitly in chapter 41 with "the Way is hidden in namelessness" (道隱無名).

The result of being "settled" with "nameless simplicity" is that we then "will not (contrivedly) desire." That this psychological state of "tranquility" is one of inner "development" (and not external coercion) is further implied by the final outcome: "the world will settle *itself*." This chapter, though it includes references to leaders (both "governors and kings" and whoever will be kind enough to help us "settle" our contrived desires), definitely puts the onus of personal development, of self-cultivation, on our own shoulders. The next chapter anticipates our reliance on established community ethics but then undermines that reliance in no uncertain terms.

---

2. The word "arise" (作) appears in chapters 2, 16, 37, and 63, but this is the only instance where it is used with "desire."

Chapter 38

Key Ideas

The Way trumps virtuosity, goodness, propriety, and protocol; and it cannot be predicted.

上德不德，是以有德；下德不失德，是以無德。

上德無為而無以為；上仁為之而無以為；上義為之而有以為；上禮為之而莫之應，則攘臂而扔之。

故失道而後德，失德而後仁，失仁而後義，失義而後禮。夫禮者，忠信之薄也，而亂之首也。

「前識者」，道之華也，而愚之首也。是以大丈夫居其厚不居其薄，居其實不居其華。故去彼取此。

People of lofty virtuosity are not (contrivedly) virtuous, and this is why they may have (real) virtuosity; (while) people of lowly virtuosity do not lose (hold of contrived) virtuosity, and this is why they are without (real) virtuosity.

People of lofty virtuosity may be uncontrived, but they may lack the means of practicing it; people of lofty goodness may contrive it, but they (too) may lack the means of practicing it; (meanwhile,) people of lofty propriety may contrive it, but they have the means of practicing it; and people of lofty protocol may contrive it, but if no one responds to them, then they roll up their sleeves and coerce them.[1]

---

1. Many later exemplars have "people of lowly virtuosity may be contrived, but they have the means of practicing it" (下德為之而有以為) between the first and second phrases of the second paragraph, right after the "lofty virtuosity" phrase. Two of our earliest sources for this chapter, *Hanfeizi* chapter 20 and MWD A and B, do not have

158

Chapter 38 | 159

Thus, when the Way is lost then there is virtuosity; when virtuosity is lost then there is goodness; when goodness is lost then there is propriety; and when propriety is lost then there is protocol. Protocol is the wearing thin of sincerity and trustworthiness, the beginning of disorder.

"Foreknowledge" is superfluous to the Way and is the beginning of stupidity. This is why great people[2] dwell in the thick and not in the thin, dwell in the real and not in the superfluous.[3] Thus, they abandon that and adopt this.

Chapter 38 Explanation

The deleterious effects of "contrivance" were implied as early as chapter 2; these effects were extended to knowledge and desire in chapter 3, and to goodness in chapter 5. "Contrivance" is the unstated-but-implied bugaboo throughout this text, sometimes implicit in the verb "to act, to do, to practice, to contrive" (為). The "contrive" meaning can be highlighted by the slightly altered graph that means "contrive, falsify" (偽), which appears only in chapter 19. Implicitly applied to goodness in chapter 5, and then to propriety, filiality, parental compassion, and correctness in chapter 18, then to knowledge and eloquence in chapter 19, and to learning in chapter 20, here "contrivance" is (implicitly) applied to "virtuosity" in general, implicating all the specific virtues dealt with so far. The first sentence here, then, with its Yin-Yang polarity of (real or genuine) virtuosity versus (contrived) virtuosity is unsurprising, though the use of "lofty" versus "lowly" is

---

this phrase, nor do they have the "lowly virtuosity" phrase in the first paragraph. So why did I choose to keep the first one but not the second? I kept the first because the "lofty" (上) implies a "lowly" (下), otherwise the "lofty" would be kind of pointless as a descriptor in this chapter. I omit the second because then "lowly virtuosity" and "lofty propriety" would have identical descriptions, which seems unlikely to me. So I think somebody along the way mistakenly added the second phrase because the first sentence had it; but it doesn't really make sense.

2. The term "great people" (大丈夫) occurs only here.

3. "Real" (實) and "superfluous" (華) have fundamental meanings of "fruit" (which is important to sustaining life) and "flower" (which is not). "Real" occurs only here and in chapter 3 (as the verb "fill"), but it means about the same thing as "genuine" (真), which is used to similarly describe virtuosity in chapter 54.

160 | The Annotated *Laozi* 老子

a new feature that appears nowhere else.[4] So the first paragraph implies that non-contrivance is a sine qua non of genuine virtuosity, while the second paragraph says that non-contrivance is only one half of the picture, the Yin open-mindedness to the Yang of that mysterious font of creativity . . .

The four parts of the second paragraph unfold around the missing piece that isn't provided until the third paragraph (but is not too hard to guess). "People of lofty virtuosity may be uncontrived," which is why they are able to be genuine, but non-contrivance by itself is evidently not enough: "they may lack the means of practicing it." The "means of practicing it," of practicing genuine virtuosity is, of course, the Way: we must "use" (ch. 4) or "grasp" (ch. 14) or "accord with" (chs. 15, 23) the Way. As chapter 21 said: "The *expression* of pervasive virtuosity follows only the Way" (italics added).

One step down from virtuosity comes "goodness," which also may or may not be contrived: chapter 5 eschewed the contrived sort, while chapter 8 praised the uncontrived kind as the definition of competence in "interactions with others." The difference lies precisely in "the means of practicing it," that is, the Way.

One step down from goodness is "propriety." It differs from "goodness" in two ways: one, there are no passages in the *Laozi* where "propriety" is cast in a positive light (though given the brevity of the *Laozi*, this may not be conclusive); and two, people who practice it "*have* the means of practicing it." The text does not say what those means are, but I think the means of "propriety" is precisely the very next step down: "protocol," because protocol can be codified and written down and appealed to as an external guide (just as the Way is an internal guide, but one that cannot be codified or exhaustively written down, since it may vary from person to person). In this sense, "propriety" is an inner feeling or attitude, while "protocol" is a list of rules. "Propriety" is wanting to be courteous; "protocol" includes, for example, the rule that it is proper to wear a suit to an interview. At this point there has been a category shift: for virtuosity and goodness, the "means of practicing" them can only be the internal guidance of the Way, while for propriety, the "means of practicing" it are the external rules of protocol.

The final step, down and away from the Way, is thus "protocol," and those who blindly follow protocol—contrived social conventions—do not have anything other than protocol itself, anything other than "tradition," to appeal to. Thus, it is portrayed here as appealing to brute force: "if no

---

4. Though "lofty" is used in the "highest competence" (上善) of chapter 8 and the "lofty virtuosity" (上德) of chapter 41.

Chapter 38 | 161

one responds to them, then they roll up their sleeves and coerce them." I feel fairly certain that we are to find this funny, but that doesn't preclude it from being true. Protocol can certainly be useful for social interactions, but it doesn't offer very much in the way of self-cultivation or individual creativity.

The third paragraph lays all the cards on the table. First and best is "the Way," which ought to inform everything. Without it, "then there is virtuosity," in second place. When that "is lost then there is goodness," in third place. And when that "is lost then there is propriety," in fourth place. Fifth and last is "protocol," but the final line adds more information: "Protocol is the wearing thin of sincerity and trustworthiness, the beginning of disorder." This suggests that "sincerity and trustworthiness" precede protocol, which, in this schema, would make them part of propriety. This makes sense because propriety ought to be something like an inner "moral compass" that operates genuinely, and this is the case with sincerity and trustworthiness too. As soon as any of these three are held hostage to protocol—that is, someone else's inflexible idea of what it means to be ethical, to be sincere and trustworthy—then they are no longer your own. They are contrived.

"Foreknowledge" appears only this once in the text, and here it refers to those who presume to know how the Way will operate within individuals, to those who think they know how your or my individual "genuineness" will manifest itself. A second target would be those who claim to know how others should act virtuously, without any (fore)knowledge of potentially mitigating circumstances. (In this sense, "foreknowledge" of what ought to constitute virtuosity may imply a kind of ethical majoritarianism, which is one way to construe Ruist [Confucian] ethics.) Some scholars take this term as referring to *Yijing* 易經 (or other kinds of) divination, or to certain extant ideas about foreknowledge,[5] but that would make it something of a non sequitur in this chapter. In any case, it is described dismissively, if not derisively, as "superfluous" (華: literally, as the practically useless "flower"

---

5. For example, *Liji* chapter 31 (中庸), section 24: "The way of perfect honesty may allow for foreknowledge. When a state is about to flourish, there certainly are good omens and signs, and when a state is about to perish, there certainly are bad omens and signs. (They can be) seen in milfoil and turtle divination, and felt in the four limbs. When misfortune and fortune are about to arrive, any competence will certainly be foreknown and any incompetence will certainly be foreknown. Thus, perfect honesty is like being spiritous" (至誠之道，可以前知。國家將興，必有禎祥；國家將亡，必有妖孽。見乎蓍龜，動乎四體。禍福將至，善，必先知之；不善，必先知之。故至誠如神).

162 | The Annotated *Laozi* 老子

in juxtaposition with the useful "fruit") and as "the beginning of stupidity."[6] The Yin-Yang analysis returns in this paragraph, with "thick-thin," "real-superfluous," and "this-that," the second iteration in this text of the formula "Thus, they abandon that [i.e., being contrived and superfluous] and adopt this [i.e., being uncontrived and real]." So though the Way may *sound* "thin" (ch. 35), it is actually "thick": once again, "The way that can be (fully) conveyed is not the abiding Way." After a relatively long chapter on what the Way is *not* (i.e., contrivedly virtuous), the next chapter returns to a discussion of what it *is*.

---

6. "Stupid / ignorant" (愚) occurs three times in this text, in chapters 20, 38, and 65. In chapter 20, the author says, "We (seem to) have the mind of stupid people," giving the term a potentially positive, albeit ironic, connotation. In chapter 65, sages keep the people "ignorant (of contrived categories)," which I read as having a neutral connotation. Here it seems the connotation should be negative.

Chapter 39

Key Idea

Obtaining the One results in being: clear, calm, numinous, bounteous, correct.

昔之得一者：天得一以清，地得一以寧，神得一以靈，谷得一以
　　盈，侯王得一以為天下正。其致之。
天無以清，將恐裂；地無以寧，將恐癈；神無以靈，將恐歇；谷
　　無以盈，將恐竭；侯王無以正，將恐蹶。
故貴以賤為本，高以下為基。是以侯王自謂「孤、寡、不穀」。
此非以賤為邪？非乎？
故至譽無譽。不欲琭琭若玉，珞珞若石。

*Those who previously attained the One: Heaven attained the One
and became clear; Earth attained the One and became calm; spirits
attained the One and became numinous;[1] valleys attained the One
and became bounteous;[2] and governors and kings obtained the One
and made the world correct. It achieved these.*

*If Heaven were without what made it clear, then it would
probably tear apart; if Earth were without what made it calm,*

---

1. This is the only chapter that mentions literal "spirits" (神) and the only one that uses "numinous" (靈). However, "valley spirit" (谷神) was used as a metaphor for the Way in chapter 6, "spiritous vessel" (神器) was used as a metaphor for the world in chapter 29, and "spirited" (神) characterizes ghosts in chapter 60.

2. While not in MWD A or B, BD, or YZ, HSG and others here have the phrase "the myriad things attained the One and became fecund" (萬物得一以生), and in the next paragraph correspondingly have "if the myriad things were without what made them fecund, (then they) would probably become extinct" (萬物無以生，將恐滅).

164 | The Annotated *Laozi* 老子

then it would probably be abandoned; if spirits were without what made them numinous, then they would probably come to an end; if valleys were without what made them bounteous, then they would probably become exhausted; and if governors and kings were without what made them correct,[3] then they would probably be overthrown.

Thus, the honored is rooted in the common, and the elevated is founded on the lowly, which is why governors and kings refer to themselves as "orphaned," "widowed," and "unfortunate."[4] Is this not taking the common as the root? Is it not?

Thus, the best praise is without (contrived) praise.[5] Do not desire what jingles like jade but rather what rumbles like rock.

Chapter 39 Explanation

In the context of chapters 10 and 22, "the One," as a metaphor for the Way, implied a bringing together of Yin-Yang aspects into a unified whole. Here "the One" is this same singularity, but framed in terms of productivity: the "thing" (like gravity) that makes things what they are. Indeed, here it says unambiguously that "it achieved these." Given that "non-contrivance"

---

3. Most exemplars have "honored and elevated" (貴高) instead of "correct" (正) here, but I find the logic of following the symmetry of using the same word (i.e., 正) in the first and third sentences (as is the case with the four other examples) to be persuasive.

4. These epithets were used by rulers to express the idea that "it's lonely at the top," but here the suggestion is that good rulers, while "honored" and "elevated," remember that they owe their status to both the Way and to the "common" and "lowly" people they lead, hence their self-deprecation. In fact, all five of the things in the first paragraph are "honored" and "elevated" and all are "rooted in" and "founded on" the Way, which is also "lowly," insofar as it is unobtrusive and "vague."

5. The phrase "Thus, the best praise is without (contrived) praise" (故至譽無譽), derives from an unattributed quote in *Zhuangzi* chapter 18 (which has 至譽無譽 without the 故), and from the XE, FY, and FYY exemplars (though these latter three have the causative 致 instead of 至: "Thus, give praise without [contrived] praise"). MWD A, B, *Huainanzi* chapter 12, YZ, and HSG all have some version of a very different sentence, which I might synthesize as "Thus, (we) create numerous carriages from non-carriages," meaning carriages, which are "honored" and "elevated" vehicles, are constructed from "common" and "lowly" parts: wheels, axles, linchpins, floorboards, and the rest. This metaphor would imply that "honored" and "elevated" governors and kings rely on (potentially and/or comparatively) "common" and "lowly" ministers and bureaucrats, but it is a somewhat odd metaphor, and I think the *Zhuangzi*, XE, FY, and FYY readings make more sense.

Chapter 39 | 165

is the modus operandi of the Way, it seems reasonable to construe this "achieved" (致) as something like "facilitates," a more Yin-like verb.[6] In this way, both chapters 25 and 39 give the Way some agency—there as "mother," here in the third paragraph as "root"—yet still allow for things to become so of themselves.

Could "Heaven" have become "clear" *without* the One? No: mothers and roots are necessary for (most) fauna and flora. If these metaphors are not suggestive enough, the entire second paragraph makes clear that the One is needed for success. The qualifier "probably" (恐) is a strong qualifier; not 100 percent certainty, but close. (Fallibilism eschews absolute certainty.) Thus, "attaining the One" is requisite for becoming "clear . . . calm . . . numinous . . . bounteous . . . [and] correct." All five of these adjectives, of course, might be aspirational for humans too. (More ethical realism.) Anthropologically, we may construe "attaining the One" as "arriving at the (mental or physical) space wherein one can grow without undue outside influence," or, more poetically, as "fulfilling one's destiny."

The fundamental Yang-active importance of the Way having been established, the third paragraph brings the Yin-receptive humility back. The Way is surely essential for all of the outcomes described in this chapter, but it nevertheless is unobtrusive, and the implication is that it is also "common" and "lowly" as implied by the "root" metaphor. The Way does not seek glory, and neither should rulers, despite their importance.

"Thus, the best praise is without (contrived) praise." This is seeing Heaven and Earth in lowly "dew" (ch. 32), and forgetting about "top leaders" (ch. 17). It is avoiding hyperbole and obsequiousness, and preferring the "thin and flavorless" (ch. 35) to the "chase and the hunt" (ch. 12). It is describing the "great Way" as "modest" (both from ch. 34). It is also in the final line, "Do not desire what jingles like jade but what rumbles like rock." This is a wonderfully poetic coda to the chapter, adding a musical (or, perhaps, geological) parallel to other Yin-Yang metaphors like valley-mountain, root-branch, and mother-father (the father to appear in chapter 42). This chapter describes a cosmology rooted in the One, a cosmology that connects the "elevated" with the "lowly," while the next has one where form is rooted in formlessness, one that is connected via "cyclicality."

---

6. In fact, *Zhuangzi* chapter 18.2 says, "Heaven is uncontrived via clarity, Earth is uncontrived via tranquility" (天無為以之清，地無為以之寧).

Chapter 40

Key Idea

The Way is cyclical and uses flexibility in producing forms from formlessness.

反者道之動也；弱者道之用也。
天下之物生於有，有生於無。

Cyclicality is the movement of the Way; flexibility is the utility of the Way.

The things of the world[1] are produced in forms; form is produced from formlessness.

· Chapter 40 Explanation

This, the shortest chapter in the *Laozi*, is a brief summary of the cosmology of the text. It brings the narrative back to the "root," after having extended itself to the "elevated" things of this world in chapter 39 and, further afield, to the human attempts to codify ethics in "protocol" in chapter 38. Chapter 25 noted that the Way, in itself, "does not change" (不改), even though it "moves all around" (周行). Here we see again that it does move; its "movement" can be seen in the cycles of the stars in Heaven as well as the cyclical seasons on Earth. The word "cyclical" (反) is appropriate here because the movement from formlessness to form is not linear, but circular.

---

1. Some later exemplars have "the world's myriad things" (天下萬物) instead of "the things of the world" (天下之物), but GD A, MWD B, and YZ agree on the latter.

Chapter 40 | 167

However, the same graph is elsewhere translated as "return," as in chapter 25, where "going far implies (eventual) return" (遠曰反), and in chapter 65, where it says, "Mysterious virtuosity is deep, and wide, and along with (all other) things returns" (玄德深矣，遠矣，與物反矣). This kind of "return" was implied in the previous two chapters: in chapter 38, we are implicitly asked to "return" to the Way in order to vivify hidebound ethics; and in chapter 39, our leaders are implicitly asked to "return" to the One in order to "correct" hidebound political orders. Other examples of advice for us to "return" to our root or our interiority are throughout the text. A translation of "return" works well for short-term analyses, even while "cyclicality" works better on a meta-level.

The efficacy of "flexibility" we have already encountered in chapters 3, 10, 28, and 36. The "form-formless" ontology appeared in chapter 1, and though chapter 2 said they "produce each other" (相生), the precedence of formlessness was implied in chapters 14 (where the One "returns . . . to nothingness," implying that nothingness precedes thingness, or formlessness precedes form) and 28 (where we are asked to "return to the limitless").[2]

The two sentences of this chapter are not unrelated. Though there is no overt grammatical connection, I think they are connected logically and we can read this chapter as saying, "The Way uses cyclicality and flexibility in its manifesting (or "mothering") of forms from formlessness, as well as in its return of forms to formlessness."

From these simple cosmological beginnings, now midway through the *Laozi*, the next chapter turns to how different humans perceive the Way.

---

2. Conversely, some scholars note that GD A, but no other exemplar, omits the second "form" (有), and render the final line: "The world's myriad things are produced from form and are produced from formlessness" (天下萬物生於有，生於無). This GD reading *might* be more congruent with chapter 2, where form and formlessness are said to "produce each other," but is less congruent with chapters 1, 14, and 28, insofar as the first says formlessness is "the beginning of Heaven and Earth" while form is "the mother of the myriad things," the second says the Way "returns to nothingness" (復歸於無物), and the third says we should "return to the limitless" (復歸於無極), each of which implies that formlessness precedes form. However, even the chapter 2 claim of mutual production may only mean that the one logically implies the other, not that they somehow literally and simultaneously "produce" each other. Ultimately, even the GD reading here does not preclude the precedence of formlessness implied by chapters 1, 14, and 28, insofar as we might read it: "The world's myriad things are produced from form, (which was) produced from formlessness."

Chapter 41

Key Ideas

People practice the Way differently; it encompasses contradictions, thus it is nameless but competent.

> 上士聞道，勤能行之；中士聞道，若存若亡；下士聞道，大笑
>   之。不笑，不足以為道。
> 是以建言有之：「明道如昧，進道如退，夷道如纇」。
> 上德如谷，大白如辱，廣德如不足，建德如偷，質真如渝。
> 大方無隅，大器晚成，大音希聲，大象無形。
> 道隱無名，夫唯道，善貸且成。

When the best officials hear of the Way, they are able to assiduously practice it;[1] when middling officials hear of the Way, some persist in it and some lose it; and when the worst officials hear of the Way, they laugh at it. If they did not laugh, it would not be adequate to be the Way.[2]

---

1. GD B and MWD B both have "*able to* assiduously practice it" (堇能行之), while YZ, HSG, and other later exemplars have "assiduous *in* practicing it" (勤而行之). I follow the earlier exemplars. A second issue is that GD B, MWD B, and BD have *jin* 堇 ("scarcely," now usually written as 僅), while YZ and HSG have *qin* 勤 (assiduously), so the question is: Should the former be read as a graphic variant of the latter? I think "they are able to assiduously practice it" makes more sense than "they are scarcely able to practice it." Also, paleographically speaking, I follow Li Ling, *Ren wang dichu zou; Laozi: Tianxia diyi* 人往低处走; 老子: 天下第一 (北京: 三联书局, 2008), 138, in reading 堇 as a variant for 勤.

2. That is, "the way that can be (fully) conveyed is not the abiding Way," and mysterious things that cannot be fully articulated are sometimes laughed at. I suspect Isaac Newton was laughed at when he first articulated his theory of gravity.

Chapter 41 | 169

This is why an established saying has it: "the bright Way may (sometimes) seem dark, the advancing Way may (sometimes) seem to be retreating, the smooth Way may (sometimes) seem knotty."

(Similarly,) lofty virtuosity may (sometimes) seem like a (lowly) valley, great purity may (sometimes) seem disgraceful, extensive virtuosity may (sometimes) seem inadequate,[3] established virtuosity may (sometimes) seem lazy, and substantial genuineness may (sometimes) seem changeable.

(Similarly,) great squares may (seem to) have no corners, great vessels may take a long while to complete, great music may use faint sounds, and great semblances may (seem to) have no definite shape.[4]

(Thus,) the Way is hidden in namelessness, but only the Way is competent at providing and completing.

Chapter 41 Explanation

The opening three-part analysis of "officials [who] hear of the Way" promptly segues into an extended explanation of just why "the worst officials . . . laugh at it." The following three-paragraph explanation takes the general form of "things are not always as they seem," with a roster of twelve counterintuitive claims: three on the Way, three on virtuosity, and one each on purity, genuineness, squares, vessels, music, and semblances. Given that the preceding chapter says that "cyclicality is the movement of the Way," it appears that these twelve claims might simply be examples of that principle of change.[5]

Still, one wonders if these twelve examples might be analyzed with more specificity. (1) The "bright" and "dark" might refer to the rising and setting of the sun, with (2) the "advancing" and "retreating" to the waxing and waning moon, and (3) the "smooth" and "knotty" to the human way of becoming, in general, or self-cultivation in particular. If this is correct, these first three could imply the "triad" of Heaven-Earth-Humans articulated in other early Chinese texts.[6]

---

3. *Zhuangzi* chapter 27.7 quotes these two phrases (i.e., 大白若辱，盛德若不足), except he uses "abundant" (盛) rather than "extensive" (廣), which in *Laozi* chapter 67 I translate as "generous."

4. This rhetoric of "great X may (counterintuitively) be Y" appears again in chapter 45.

5. Another simple analysis of these twelve claims is to assume that X may sometimes appear as Y, but *only* to "the worst scholars."

6. See chapter 25, note 8.

170 | The Annotated *Laozi* 老子

(4) That "lofty virtuosity may (sometimes) seem like a (lowly) valley" is a trope that we have seen implicitly in chapters 6, 15, 28, and 39, and will see again in chapter 66. (5) "Disgraceful" (辱) was paired with "favor" (寵) in chapter 13, and with "glory" (榮) in chapter 28; in the former we were advised to be detached from both states, and in the latter we were advised to "know the glorious but preserve the humble," which may be another way of saying that we should not be overly attached to either one. Here, building upon the prior two examples, the author might be implying that doing what is right (i.e., "having great purity"), rather than, say, being loyal to a corrupt superior, will appear to some as "disgraceful."[7]

(6) That "extensive virtuosity may (sometimes) seem inadequate" could be an early articulation of what we now call "tough love." (7) That "established virtuosity may (sometimes) seem lazy" may be the obverse of the previous phrase: sometimes, in dealing with others, the best thing may be "a kick in the pants," which an observer might consider "inadequate," but other times the best thing might be a hug, which a different observer might consider to be a "lazy" way of solving the problem.

(8) Here the topic changes a third time, and after the Way, virtuosity, and purity, the author now articulates a "substantial genuineness" that "may sometimes seem changeable." "Genuineness" (真) appears in this text in only two other chapters. In chapter 21, where it was the culmination of a five-step creation paradigm, and in chapter 54, which says, "Cultivate it [i.e., the Way] in (your) person and your virtuosity will be genuine." So it seems clear that "substantial genuineness" might be "changeable" because self-cultivation—the pursuit of one's destiny—is a matter of "becoming" and not a matter of arriving at some point of stasis. A second, exterior, Yang way of interpreting this phrase is if "inadequate" virtuosity and "lazy" virtuosity describe two different but complementary types of acting, of trying to help others, then perhaps this "changeability" is the ability to know when to do each. (In the previous hypothetical, this would be like knowing that it is acceptable to sometimes use "tough love" and sometimes to use a hug.) In any case, the topic of Yin-Yang changeability has been a near constant throughout this text, and changing from introspection to action (and back again) is one of its most fundamental messages.

---

7. Alternatively, "disgraceful" (辱) might be a loan graph for "black" (黷), in which case the meaning would be "even things that, from a distance, appear white will, upon closer inspection, contain some black." But this reading would make this phrase incongruous with the "virtuosity" claims that precede and follow it.

Chapter 41 | 171

(9) In an example of being "unable to see the forest for the trees," sufficiently large "squares" (of, say, land) may have "corners" too distant to see. (10) Chapter 29 says the world is a "spiritous vessel," and the world is, given its ever-changing nature, certainly not yet "complete." (11) The variation between loud and faint notes in "music" is now a well-studied phenomenon called "dynamics." (12) As with (9), a "semblance" can be so large that an observer standing too close to it will not be able to see its overall shape, or so vague that you cannot make out just what it is (yet). It is fitting to end this list with "great semblances," because though the context of the preceding three "great" things here implies that "semblances" should be understood in the plural, it will not be lost on us that the singular "great semblance" was used in chapter 35 as a metaphor for the Way.

"(Thus,) the Way is hidden in namelessness."[8] Since none of the preceding twelve pairs of adjectives can adequately describe the Way (as we already knew from chapter 1), it must remain "hidden in namelessness." (Remember, the "Way" is just a "style name," a pseudonym, as we saw in chapter 25.) This "namelessness" implies the Way's practical flexibility, and it is precisely due to such flexibility that "the Way is competent at providing and completing." A less flexible principle would not be able to inform the ever-changing world in which we live.

After noting that the Way encompasses contradictions—both ostensible and real—in this chapter, the next continues this theme by returning to the basics of Yin and Yang.

---

8. Counterintuitively, the "name / renown" (名) of the Way was said to have "never been discarded" (不去) in chapter 21. This may not be a contradiction here with "the Way is hidden in namelessness" if we conflate these two claims as "the renown (名) of the nameless (無名) has never been discarded." On the other hand, chapter 34 describes the Way as simultaneously "modest" (小) and "great" (大), which may be one reason that the author here says it is "nameless," insofar as "the way that can be (fully) conveyed" that is also "the abiding Way" might sound contradictory.

Chapter 42

Key Ideas

The Way produces the myriad things, which use Yin-Yang to be harmonious; leaders should be similarly flexible.

道生一，一生二，二生三，三生萬物。萬物負陰而抱陽，沖氣
　以為和。
人之所惡，唯「孤、寡、不穀」，而王公以自名。故物或損之而
　益，或益之而損。
人之所教，我亦教之：強梁者不得其死。吾將以為教父。

The Way produces one, one produces two, two produces three, and three produces the myriad things. The myriad things carry Yin on their backs and embrace Yang in front and blend these physical energies in order to be harmonious.

That which people detest is being "orphaned, widowed, and unfortunate,"[1] yet kings and dignitaries use these words to describe themselves.[2] Thus, things can sometimes be added to by being reduced, and sometimes they can be reduced by being added to.[3]

---

1. We just saw these three in chapter 39.

2. Though it doesn't affect the meaning (or translation), "uses these words to describe themselves" (以自名) derives from MWD A (and parts of MWD B and YZ), while some later exemplars have "uses these words to describe themselves" (以為稱).

3. That is, sometimes leaders will accrue more prestige by delegating authority, and may reduce their prestige by micromanaging.

172

That which people teach, we also teach it: those who are stiff and overbearing cannot avoid their (untimely) demise. We take this as the father of all teachings.[4]

Chapter 42 Explanation

The *Laozi*'s cosmogony in chapter 21 is briefly recapped here to highlight the harmonious use of Yin and Yang. No one knows for sure what the "one," "two," and "three" refer to, but I think they implicitly borrow the four steps from chapter 21, thus "the Way produces" semblances first, which then produce essences second, then genuineness third, and each of these three steps are followed in each of "the myriad things."[5] In this scheme, we humans are uniquely able to not reach our genuineness, which is why Laozi wrote this book.

There are, however, other theories about this "one, two, three." One is that they could simply be an articulation of the "unfolding" of the cosmos and not refer to any specific things at all.[6] Another is that the "one, two, three" refer to physical energies (氣), Yin-Yang, and harmonized physical energies (和氣). That is: one, a semblance of a form emerges from formlessness; two, the physical energy that constitutes that semblance is influenced by the Yin and Yang states that characterize all physical energies; three, once the semblance has morphed, chrysalis-like, into its final "harmonious" form, it has become a stable entity. (For a time, that is, as all form eventually reverts to formlessness.) One problem with this theory, however, is that the

---

4. The "father" of the *human* way of flexibility, of both leading and yielding to others, is a counterpart of the "mother" of the *cosmic* Way responsible for both Yin and Yang.

5. The number of steps in both chapters 21 and 42 match, though their order does not. Here the (implicit) order is: the Way, semblance, essence, genuineness, thing; there the order is the Way, semblance, thing, essence, genuineness. As I read these, this chapter is talking about all things, the "myriad things," while chapter 21 has a different order to remind readers that, while genuineness may be assumed for all things excepting humans, we humans have to engage in self-cultivation in order to reach genuineness. Alternatively, the "one, two, three" could refer to the *Laozi*'s other cosmogony, in chapter 51, in which the three would be "virtuosity," "(other) things," and "circumstances."

6. Ames and Hall thereby construe the "one, two, three, everything" as "continuity . . . difference . . . plurality . . . multiplicity." See Roger Ames and David Hall, *Dao De Jing: "Making This Life Significant"; A Philosophical Translation* (New York: Ballantine Books, 2003), 143.

174 | The Annotated *Laozi* 老子

"three" is functionally equivalent to the "myriad things" that the "three" is supposed to produce.[7]

"The myriad things carry Yin on their backs and embrace Yang in front and blend these physical energies in order to be harmonious." Here we see that "the myriad things" all make use of both Yin and Yang, and that to properly "blend" them results in a "harmonious" and stable existence.

Chapter 41 began with leadership and then connected it to cosmology; this chapter begins with cosmology and then connects it to leadership. Using locution from chapter 39 (i.e., leaders referring to themselves as "orphaned, widowed, and unfortunate," even if none of these three were literally true), this sentence implies that good leaders "harmonize" the Yin-Yang of office by being simultaneously "elevated" and "lowly." This idea underlies the "servant-leader" idea broached in chapters 7 and 8. Here humility in leadership is fleshed out in the following two sentences.

First, "things can sometimes be added to by being reduced, and sometimes they can be reduced by being added to." That is, sometimes we, when leading, may gain in power by being humble "servant-leaders," and sometimes we may actually lose respect in the eyes of other people by accruing too much power for ourselves, rather than sharing responsibilities. I read this as a nod to what we now call "delegating authority."

Second, the penultimate sentence extends this managerial insight, saying, in effect, that it isn't rocket science: "That which [other] people teach, we also teach it." That is: "stiff and overbearing" leaders "cannot avoid their (untimely) demise." The "this" in "We take this as the father of all teachings" refers to the principles of flexibility, of sometimes yielding to others and sometimes not—of being now Yin and now Yang. This is how leaders and, indeed, all of us, become "harmonious."

The human "way" described in the second and third paragraphs of this chapter are predicated on the cosmic Way described in the first, a Way that (somehow) conveyed or coaxed incipient "semblance(s)" from primal, formless physical energy, which then spontaneously manifested physical

---

7. A fourth theory might be found in the *Huainanzi* chapter 4: "Heaven is one, Earth is two, humans are three" (天一，地二，人三). But I don't know of any evidence for claiming that Heaven "produced" Earth (rather, they spontaneously coalesced from primal physical energies), or for Earth "producing" humans (though this does seem plausible), or for humans "producing" the myriad things (as opposed to, say, "guiding" them), but I suppose it is possible that the author was thinking of the domesticated plants and animals that we humans "produced."

energy's inherent, complementary Yin and Yang states as creative "essence" (of both the physical and mental kinds), which in turn evolved into the "genuineness" of the "forms" of things as we know them. This ontological "genuineness" is, in ethical realist terms, reflected in a leader who suggests, rather than commands; nudges rather than bludgeons; delegates, rather than micromanages, thereby "adding to" their reputations and avoiding their "demise." The implied flexibility in this chapter is made explicit in the opening sentence of the next.

Chapter 43

Key Ideas

Flexibility and non-contrivance are advantageous, but few attain them.

天下之至柔，馳騁於天下之至堅；無有入無間。吾是以知無為
之有益。
不言之教，無為之益：天下希及之。

*The most flexible things in the world run circles around the most
rigid things in the world; the formless can enter even that which
has no fissure. We use these (principles) to know the advantages of
non-contrivance.*

*Wordless teachings and the advantages of non-contrivance:
few people of the world attain these.*

Chapter 43 Explanation

Flexibility in the *Laozi* has a dual meaning: one ontological and one cognitive.
Ontologically, the Yin state is itself "flexible" and receptive, in contradistinction to the rigid and aggressive Yang state. And cognitively, there is a kind
of "meta-flexibility" involved in knowing just when to be Yin and when to
be Yang, both of which are requisite for the "harmonious" Yin-Yang state
described in the previous chapter. The first sentence here addresses both, in
reverse order: first the cognitive, then the ontological.

Cognitively speaking, mentally flexible people "run circles around"
people with "rigid" mindsets and unshakeable biases. The cognitive "meta-

Chapter 43 | 177

flexibility" of knowing when to be flexible and when to exhibit fortitude is implied in other chapters, like the previous one, where both Yin and Yang are described as essential. Here, too, the first part of the first sentence means "the most flexible things in the world" *can* "run circles around the most rigid things in the world," rather than "the most flexible things in the world" *always* "run circles around the most rigid things in the world." This is "the father of all teachings" that we saw in the previous chapter.

We might assume a "(just as)" right after the semicolon, since the ontological foundation for a flexible mindset—via ethical realism—is the primacy (at least from our current point of view) of formlessness, here implied by the example of "formless" air or water penetrating "even that which has no fissure." That is: just as "formless" air or water can, given enough time, "enter" even metal or stone, so a flexible person can overcome the most obstinate people and problems.[1]

The author then extrapolates from the usefulness of flexibility to the advantages of non-contrivance. Non-contrivance, being supremely creative and adaptive, is axiomatically flexible—it cannot *not* be flexible—but the author is extrapolating from the physical realm back to that of human thought and action. This flexible and uncontrived attitude, as we saw in chapter 2 ("sages . . . practice wordless teaching"), implies "wordless teachings" insofar as adaptability is always contingent on circumstance, while "universal teachings" are typically devoid of context. But most people, it seems, prefer abstract, universal teachings, insofar as they are much easier to remember and implement, even if their implementation fails to take into account the situation.[2] The meditation on flexibility in this chapter is continued in the next.

---

1. The example of water is made explicit in chapter 78.

2. As noted in the "key concepts," note 22, *Mengzi* 4A17 relates the story of the teaching "men should not touch women they do not know" that is obviated when a good man is faced with a drowning woman that he does not know. Another example is "Thou shalt not kill," which might be useful as a rule of thumb, but not as useful when it comes to deciding *when* to kill, insofar as all life depends on the death of other living things.

Chapter 44

Key Ideas

Your person is more important than renown or wealth: know contentment and know when to stop.

名與身孰親？身與貨孰多？得與亡孰病？

甚愛必大費，多藏必厚亡。

故知足不辱，知止不殆：可以長久。

Your renown or your person: Which is more dear? Your person or your wealth: Which is worth more? Your getting things or your losing things: Which is the greater bane?

Deep affections may necessitate great expenditures,[1] and excessive hoarding may necessitate much loss.

Therefore, know contentment and do not feel disgrace; know (when and where) to stop and do not fall into danger: then you may live long.

Chapter 44 Explanation

The three rhetorical questions that begin this chapter start out easily enough: clearly, our lives (i.e., our "person") are more important than "renown" or

---

1. YZ and other later exemplars have "This is why" (是故) at the beginning of this sentence, but GD A, MWD A, and HSG do not. Similarly, GD A, MWD A, and YZ have "Therefore" (故) at the beginning of the next sentence, while HSG and many later exemplars do not.

178

"wealth." It is the third question—at least within the context of the *Laozi*—that may make the reader hesitate, but though the "things" that one may "get" are not specified, in the context of this chapter, these "things" are no doubt extravagant possessions that often accompany fame and wealth.

Our "affections" for these three commonly accepted markers of success—renown, wealth, and extravagant material possessions—will likely "necessitate great expenditures" of time and energy to both acquire and maintain them. The reader is implicitly asked: Is it really worth it? We don't even have to go as far as "excessive hoarding" to wonder if the mere pursuit (and then maintenance) of such goals does not "necessitate much loss" of our attention and spirit.

We saw in chapter 33 that "those who know contentment are rich." Here the author adduces two further reasons to "know contentment": first, there is no "disgrace" in not being famous or rich; second, owning lots of material possessions inevitably makes you a target for thieves, which may well put your person "into danger."

We saw in chapter 32 that "knowing when to stop is a means of avoiding danger," and this is reiterated here. But the idea is found throughout the text. In chapter 2, sages are said to "complete tasks, but without dwelling (on them)." Chapter 5 says, "Much speech and frequent exhaustion is not as good as preserving what is within." Chapter 8 says, "In movement, competence lies in timeliness." Chapter 9 says, "When the task is accomplished and you then retire: this is the way of Heaven." All of these, and many more, clearly imply that "knowing (when and where) to stop" is of fundamental importance.

This chapter's theme of "things are not always as they seem" continues in the next.

Chapter 45

Key Ideas

Appearances are sometimes deceiving, but clarity and tranquility can create truth.

> 大成若缺，其用不弊。大盈若沖，其用不窮。大直若屈，大巧若
> 拙，大辯若訥。
> 躁勝寒，靜勝熱。清靜為天下正。

Although great completion may seem flawed, using it does not wear it out. Although great fullness may seem empty, using it will not exhaust it. (Similarly,) great straightness may seem bent, great skill may seem clumsy, and great eloquence may seem stammering.

Movement overcomes cold; tranquility overcomes heat. Clarity and tranquility create truth[1] in the world.

Chapter 45 Explanation

The saying "you can't judge a book by its cover" comes to mind when reading the opening five claims here. Whereas chapter 41 used the "X may sometimes appear as Y" formula to describe the Way, virtuosity, and other things, this chapter uses the same formula to talk about truthfulness, or to describe sages or, at least, some actions of some sages (some of the time).[2] In

---

1. *Zheng* 正 means "correct" or "true" and appears in chapters 18, 39, 45, 57, 58, and 78; I translate it as "correct" in 18, 39, and 57, and as "truth" or "truthful" in 45, 57, 58, and 78.

2. Thus, one might read the first sentence as "Although those who are greatly complete may seem flawed (to you), making use of them will not wear them out."

180

Chapter 45 | 181

the manner of my explanation in chapter 41, I will give some anachronistic but specific examples of these five claims.

"Although great completion may seem flawed, using it does not wear it out." Although your grandpa's advice to "stop and smell the roses" might seem hackneyed and, to one impatient to "get on in the world," even "flawed," it is still an abiding truth.

"Although great fullness may seem empty, using it will not exhaust it." Although the advice to "put out a fire while it is still small" may seem alarmist (i.e., "empty") to those with a higher tolerance for risk, doing so may well pay off in "great fullness" when it saves their houses from burning down. (See chapters 8, 50, 63, and 64 for more on "timeliness.")

"Great straightness may seem bent." One who follows ethical rules (i.e., one who is "straight") may well have to break them sometimes; "obey your parents" is a good rule for children, unless you are unfortunate enough to have parents who ask you to rob a bank for them. "Great skill may seem clumsy." Craftsmen often have "workarounds" that aren't "in the book," and that may appear to an apprentice as "clumsy" or counterintuitive. "Great eloquence may seem stammering." Compare the speech of a (properly) hesitant doctor faced with a patient with a rare medical condition to that of an (overly) confident quack selling snake oil.

The penultimate sentence is an example of deceptively simple advice: if you are cold, get up and move around; if you are hot, maybe stop moving around so much. Although we might debate the individual words of this sentence, since "a name that can be (fully) descriptive is not an abiding name" (ch. 1), these two observations are "true" to the point of being common sense. Thus, the obvious truth of these Yin-Yang (i.e., tranquility-movement) statements is juxtaposed with the preceding truths that we might call *un*-common sense.

Extrapolating from this practical advice, the final sentence returns to the connection between individual self-cultivation and social harmony: "Clarity and tranquility create truth [or, "correctness"] in the world." This "clarity" (清) appears in only two other chapters (chs. 15 and 39); in the first it describes an aspirational figure, and in the latter it describes Heaven, so we might construe this as another example of ethical realism. (For leadership, we might connect it to "transparency.") Here it is implicitly paired with "movement" (which further ties it to Heaven, given the Yang movement of Heavenly bodies), suggesting that we remain clear—a connection to open-mindedness would not be unwarranted—even as we are in the midst of activity. "Tranquility" we have already met several times;[3] here it is the

---

3. Tranquility (靜) appears in chapters 15, 16, 26, 37, 45, 57, and 61.

182 | The Annotated *Laozi* 老子

Yin to the Yang of clarity. The list of counterintuitive truths articulated in this chapter continues in the next.

Chapter 46

Key Ideas

The Way avoids war, reduces desires, and brings contentment.

天下有道，卻走馬以糞；天下無道，戎馬生於郊。
罪莫厚於甚欲，咎莫憯於欲得，禍莫大於不知足。故知足之足，
　恆足矣。

When the world has the Way, then good horses haul dung, and when the world is without the Way, then war horses are bred in the suburbs.

No fault is graver than excessive desire; no calamity is sadder than (always) wanting more; no misfortune is greater than not knowing contentment.[1] Thus, the contentment of knowing contentment is an abiding contentment.

Chapter 46 Explanation

The Way as the ordering principle of the cosmos cannot, by definition, be absent anywhere. Yet the first sentence explicitly says "the world" can be "without the Way." This however is not an ontological description but is rather poetic license, obliquely referring to situations in which human con-

---

1. This sentence derives from GD A; MWD A, YZ, and HSG are similar, but they reverse the second and third phrases (MWD B also reverses them, but it is missing most graphs). Some later exemplars omit the first phrase and simplify the remaining two phrases to "No X is greater than Y" (X 莫大於 Y).

184 | The Annotated *Laozi* 老子

trivance ignores the cosmic principle.[2] Within the cosmogony of chapter 21, it means we humans are uniquely able to fail to realize our "genuineness." Here, one example of such "situations" refers to a militaristic society. As we saw in chapters 30–31, the author sees military action as a regrettable activity and not as a cause for pride and joy. Thus, "when the world is without the Way," and the military is used as an aggressive means of conquest, "then war horses are bred in the suburbs," that is, nearby.

"Excessive desire" is probably the most fundamental problem identified by Laozi, with contrivance being its most salient effect. And it is likely that the author thought these two are closely connected, with contrivance being the result of excessive desire, and the means by which we might get that which we (excessively) desire. As we have seen before with "contentment" (chs. 33 and 44), even if we accept this assessment of the human condition, the inescapable problem comes when trying to decide just what constitutes "excessive" desire. If I desire, for example, to eat, what constitutes an "excessive" meal? The answer will always be context and person specific. Nevertheless, for us as individuals on the path of self-cultivation, "the contentment of knowing contentment" not only "is," but can actually *create*, "an abiding contentment."

The counterintuitive claims of chapter 46 continued in this chapter with "good horses" that "haul dung," and continue in the next with "the farther one goes, the less one knows."

---

2. This is not unlike the problem of using the word "unnatural" to refer to some human activities. In one sense, as natural creatures, humans cannot do anything "unnatural"; nevertheless, we still use the term to refer to some activities, unique to humans, that seem to go against the inclinations of the natural world.

Chapter 47

Key Ideas

Sages can know the Way by inference; they are percipient and complete.

不出於戶，可以知天下；不闚於牖，可以知天道：其出彌遠，
　其知彌少。
是以聖人不行而知，不見而明，不為而成。

Without going out the door, one can know the world, and without looking out the window, one can know the way of Heaven: (indeed, it is possible that) the farther one goes, the less one knows.

This is why sages can know without traveling, can be percipient without inspecting things,[1] and can be complete without contrivance.

Chapter 47 Explanation

The two phrases of the first sentence are a parallelism and, practically speaking, synonymous. "The way of Heaven" is the Yang-active "face" of the Yin-Yang-balanced cosmic Way as it operates in "the world." The author is not claiming that you will be able to learn specific, empirical facts about "the world" by staying indoors. Laozi is not promulgating clairvoyance; rather, he is claiming that the Way, as the organizing principle of things,

---

1. The "can be percipient without inspecting things" (不見而明) derives from *Hanfeizi* chapter 21. MWD B, YZ, and HSG have "can name things without inspecting them" (不見而名). While the latter is plausible, the earlier *Hanfeizi* reading makes more sense to me.

185

186 | The Annotated *Laozi* 老子

operates everywhere, and that we can therefore (sometimes) extrapolate lessons learned in one locale to others. He is talking about theory; gravity operates indoors as well as outdoors.

The third part of the first sentence, "the farther one goes, the less one knows," is both a classic example of memorable hyperbole (hence my added parenthetical) and a warning that the introspective consideration of data is just as important as data collection itself. Noting that observation must be matched with contemplation might point to the phenomenon of being very educated (or "successful") but still rather stupid.

A different way of construing these sentences is to imagine a judge in a courtroom, hearing the details of a case. Gathering evidence might be left to the constables, but the consideration of the evidence, and the weighing of the two sides of the case, can all be done, by a competent judge, without leaving the courtroom.

The final sentence reiterates the first sentence before closing with the observation that the Yang activities of "going out the door" (i.e., "traveling") and "looking out the window" (i.e., "inspecting things") can both be matters of "contrivance" if we divorce them from the Yin task of considering where we have gone and what we have seen. The emphasis on Yin introspection in this chapter is furthered in the next, where we are told that a decrease in a certain kind of Yang activity may lead to success.

Chapter 48

Key Ideas

We should reduce (contrived) learning; leaders should be without (contrived) activities.

為學者日益，為道者日損。損之又損：以至於無為。無為而無不為。

將欲取天下者，恆以無事，及其有事，不足以取天下。

Those who pursue (contrived) learning increase every day, (while) those who pursue the Way reduce every day. Reduce it and reduce it some more: by this one arrives at non-contrivance. Be uncontrived and nothing will be left undone.

Those who want to gain (leadership of) the world usually do so without (contrived) activities,[1] and when they pursue (contrived) activities, it is inadequate to gain (leadership of) the world.

Chapter 48 Explanation

As with so many other instances in the *Laozi*, the added, parenthetical "contrived" must be inferred in order for the sentence to make sense. Without it, the sentence would be tautological and not very interesting.[2] Thus, the

---

1. This locution derives from YZ and FY (and partially from WB's note at chapter 57); MWD A, B, and HSG have a shorter "Gaining control of the world is usually done without (contrived) activities" (取天下常以無事).

2. That is, "Those who pursue learning increase [their learning] every day" is not very interesting, and "Those who pursue the Way reduce [their learning] every day" would be an odd thing to claim in a book about learning about the Way.

187

188 | The Annotated *Laozi* 老子

advice in this chapter does not refer to all learning and activities in general, but only to the contrived sort that leads us away from the contentment and percipience described in the previous two chapters.

The word "learning" (學) appears four times in this text, and it has a negative connotation three of those times. In chapter 20 we were asked to "relinquish (contrived) learning and be without anxiety" (絕學無憂), and here "the pursuit of (contrived) learning" is cast in opposition to "the pursuit of the Way," so it cannot but be bad. In chapter 64 we will meet the interesting idea of sages who "learn to not learn" (學不學), in which the first "learn" must be a good thing, while what is "not learn[ed]" must be "(contrived) learning."

As in the previous chapter, where it is *not* the case that the author is recommending that we never "go out the door" or "look out the window," here too the author is also not saying that we should never "learn" things. If that were the case, we should have to put this book down now. In chapter 47 we are to balance the Yang activity of information gathering with the Yin activity of considering that information with what we might call the "theory of the Way." Here too, a Yang increase in learning—which is unstated, but implied by both the "nothing will be left undone" and the "gain (leadership of) the world"—is balanced with a Yin decrease in *contrived* learning.

But the emphasis on "reduce" here also implies more than just a Yin-Yang balance, or even a slight Yin preference; it also implies a definite plan of "unlearning"—"reducing"—some of the things that we have already learned. This, then, I take to imply a taking stock of what we have learned since childhood and deciding what is and is not "contrived."

The third sentence, "Be uncontrived and nothing will be left undone" (a phrase we saw in chapter 37), serves to remind us that "unlearning" the undesirable, contrived things that we have imbibed from our family and culture will not leave us in a state of deprivation. Rather, it signals a process of coming into our own, of critically examining what we have been taught and taking responsibility for our actions. This is immediately followed by an extreme example of "realizing our destiny," that is, leadership.

"Without (contrived) activities" (無事)[3] is akin to other activities that we should undertake without contrivance, such as being "without (contrived) knowledge" (無知; in chs. 3, 10, 63, and 70) and "without (contrived) desire"

---

3. Although we have seen "activities" (事) in several previous chapters, the phrase "without activities" (無事) appears first here and will appear again in chapters 57 and 63.

(無欲; in chs. 3, 34, and 57). Thus, this second paragraph means that we will only be able to "gain (leadership of) the world" (or the community, or the workplace staff, or the classroom) when we are genuine with others, when we are following principles that we really find useful and inspiring. People, even incompetent people (see the next chapter), often have a good instinct for perceiving insincerity.[4] The pairing of uncontrived learning and uncontrived leadership activities in this chapter continues with the pairing of open-mindedness and unbiased leadership in the next.

---

4. This ability is now often described by psychologists with the idea of "thin-slicing."

Chapter 49

Key Idea

Sages are open-minded and unbiased toward all, even the incompetent and untrustworthy.

聖人恆無心，以百姓心為心。
善者，吾善之；不善者，吾亦善之：德善也。
信者，吾信之；不信者，吾亦信之：德信也。
聖人在天下歙歙，為天下「渾」其心。百姓皆注其耳目，聖人
　　皆孩之。

Sages abide open-mindedly[1] and take the mind of the people as their mind.

Those who are competent: we are competent to them (in return); those who are incompetent: we are nevertheless competent to them (too): this is virtuous competence.

Those who are trustworthy: we trust them (in return); those who are untrustworthy: we nevertheless trust them (too): this is virtuous trustworthiness.

Sages in the world are unbiased, and on behalf of the world keep their own minds "muddled." The people all pay attention with their ears and eyes (only); sages treat them all as children.

---

1. This locution derives from MWD B (恆无心), from the notes of YZ and HSG (both say sages are "open-minded" [無心]), and from the fact—as many scholars have noted—that while "open-minded" is a well-attested phrase, to have "an abiding mind" (常心) is not. Nearly all exemplars say, "Sages are without an abiding mind" (聖人無常心), which, given the evidence in the previous sentence, seems to be a mistaken reversal of the third and fourth graphs.

Chapter 49 Explanation

"Sages abide open-mindedly" is a Yin attitude of fallibilism, and that sages "take the mind of the people as their mind" is a Yang activity of flexibility and ethical pluralism. The claim of this first sentence, which we might call "proto-democratic," however, brings us to the problems of individual flexibility and community democracy. As with other hyperbolic statements in this text, if we were to take the claim that sages "take the mind of the people as their mind" literally, we would have to conclude that sages are spineless and without any original ideas of their own, which, given the *Laozi*'s emphasis on creativity, is untenable.

The next two sentences provide examples of just how sages are objective and impartial, which are akin to being open-minded. With something of a "turn the other cheek" mindset, sages remain "competent" and "trustworthy" even to those who do not return the favor. Precisely just how long a sage would continue to trust a demonstrably untrustworthy person is not articulated (just as Jesus never said how many times we should "turn the other cheek" to those who slap it).

The "unbiased" comportment of sages in the penultimate sentence is yet a third way of saying nearly the same thing. The metaphor of the "muddled" mind (渾心) points to healthy skepticism, to the theme of fallibilism that underlies the entire text.[2] "Muddled," then, is a poetic term for "doubtful," and a doubtful mind is a crucial ingredient for an open mind.

Finally, that most people "pay attention with their ears and eyes (only)" means people, in general, will not be as discerning as sages who use their minds to apprehend the Way in the world. (This is why they can "know the world" without "going out the door" in chapter 47.) But even sages must constantly keep an open mind with all people (and things). The metaphor of "sages" treating the people "as children" should not be taken as arrogant paternalism but rather as fair and impartial treatment of others. Children are famously incompetent and untrustworthy people, yet parents nevertheless (should) treat them impartially. People are to sages as sages are to the Way, which sages treat as "the Mother" (ch. 20), and which was described (via Heaven and Earth) as impartial in chapter 5.

Alternatively, the only other time the word "child / smile" (孩) occurs in this text is in chapter 20, where it clearly means "smile" ("like a baby that has not yet smiled" [如嬰兒之未孩]), so here in chapter 49 the final

---

2. The "muddled" (渾) here is similar to the "muddied" (濁) mind in chapter 15 and the "turbid" (沌沌) mind in chapter 20.

192 | The Annotated *Laozi* 老子

sentence could instead be: "The people all pay attention with their ears and eyes (only), and sages all smile at / with them." Either way, the more important line in this chapter is the first, where "sages . . . take the mind of the people as their mind." Building on this ideal of "proto-democracy," of leaders taking their cues from the people they lead, the next chapter reminds us that "the people" contain different types, competent and incompetent alike.

Chapter 50

Key Ideas

A third of people die old, a third die young, and a third live recklessly: those who die old live carefully.

> 出生入死：「生之徒」十有三；「死之徒」十有三；而「民之生生，動之死地」，亦十有三。夫何故？以其生生之厚。
> 蓋聞善攝生者，陸行不遇兕虎，入軍不被甲兵。兕無所投其角，虎無所措其爪，兵無所容其刃。夫何故？以其無「死地」焉。

In the coming and going of life and death: a third are "disciples of life," a third are "disciples of death,"[1] but also there are a third who, "while living life as people, move toward places of death." Why is this? Because of their excesses in living life.

They should have heard that those competent at assisting life, when walking on land do not encounter rhinoceroses or tigers, and when entering battle do not encounter armed soldiers. (Therefore,) rhinoceroses have no place to stick their horns, tigers have no place to sink their claws, and soldiers have no place to put their blades. Why is this? Because they have no "places for death" in them.

Chapter 50 Explanation

This chapter posits three types of people. The "disciples of life" take care of themselves and live out their natural life spans; thus, "disciples of life"

---

1. Both of these types of people also appear in chapter 76, where "disciples of life" (生之徒) are described as flexible (柔弱) and "disciples of death" (死之徒) are rigid (堅強).

194 | The Annotated *Laozi* 老子

arc those who die old (or, at least, die through no neglect of their own making). The "disciples of death" neither take care of themselves nor live out their natural life spans and thus are those who die young (or, at least, have deaths attributable to their own neglect). Third, those who, "while living life as people, move toward places of death," are the people who live dangerously, not through neglect, as with the "disciples of death," but rather through recklessness, that is, through "excesses in living life."[2] That is, they *could* die old but in fact die young because they live impetuously, foolishly.

In the second paragraph, the "disciples of life" are described as "those competent at assisting life"[3] and are contrasted with the third group, who die because of "excesses in living life." (Or, perhaps, "those competent at assisting life" are a particularly competent subset of the "disciples of life.")[4] How do they "assist life" and avoid "excesses in living life"? While the word "excesses" (厚) might suggest the hoarded possessions of chapter 44, or the extravagant clothes, food, and drink excoriated in chapter 53, here the author gives two examples of simply avoiding danger. "Rhinoceroses" and "soldiers" both have the means to stab you to death, and "those competent at assisting life" are careful to avoid them.[5] Thus, reckless people are here described as having something of an "Achilles' heel" in their penchant for

---

2. This analysis makes "excess" (厚; also: thick / strength / emphasize) the villain, as it is in chapter 75, where bad "leaders seeking to overemphasize (厚) their own lives" results in "the people treating death lightly." But it should be noted that this same word has positive connotations too: "the thick" (厚) that "great people dwell in" in chapter 38, and the "vigorously" (厚) of "those who embody virtuosity vigorously" in chapter 55.

3. "Competence" (善), as we have seen, is a major theme in the *Laozi*, with "those who are competent" (善者) the focus of chapter 49, and people competent at various tasks the focus of chapter 27.

4. Since the locution for "a third" (十有三) is technically "three out of ten," it isn't impossible that the unmentioned "one out of ten" refers to "those competent at assisting life." But I doubt it.

5. Given the obviousness of these two examples, we may be inclined to treat them as metaphors, but this chapter gives no indication of what they might be metaphors for. So if we want to stay within the parameters of this chapter, we must conclude that it is simply advising us to stay away from dangerous things like aggressive animals, including aggressive humans. If we want to look outside this chapter, and are willing to deal with four separate Chinese words that have all been translated in this book as "excess," we might recall chapter 29, where "sages discard excess (甚), discard extravagance, and discard pomposity." Or chapter 44, where "excessive (多) hoarding may necessitate much loss." Or chapter 77, where we are advised to reduce several kinds of "excess" (餘). See the index for disambiguation.

Chapter 50 | 195

excess.[6] Though not mentioned in this chapter, we might notice that "presumptuousness" (敢) was criticized in chapters 3 and 30, and will be again in chapters 64, 67, 69, 73, and 74.[7] Excessive boldness, which is to say, recklessness, may well be considered a type of presumptuousness. The idea that we should be attentive to our surroundings is continued in the next chapter with the introduction of the word "circumstances" (勢).

---

6. *Zhuangzi* chapter 17.1 might be read as a gloss on this *Laozi* chapter: "For people of accomplished virtuosity, fire cannot burn them and water cannot drown them; neither heat nor cold can harm them; neither birds nor beasts can hurt them. This is not to say that they treat these things lightly, but rather that they discern where there is safety and danger, remain calm in both good and bad fortune, are cautious about what to flee and what to approach: thus, nothing can harm them" (至德者，火弗能熱，水弗能溺，寒暑弗能害，禽獸弗能賊。非謂其薄之也，言察乎安危，寧於禍福，謹於去就：莫之能害也).

7. Chapter 73 says: "The courage to be presumptuous may result in death, while the courage to *not* be presumptuous may result in staying alive."

Chapter 51

Key Ideas

Cosmogony no. 2: the Way produces us, virtuosity nurtures us, things shape us, circumstances complete us.

> 道生之，德畜之，物形之，勢成之。是以萬物莫不尊道而貴德。
> 　道之尊，德之貴，夫莫之命而恆自然。
> 道生之，德畜之：長之育之，成之熟之，養之覆之。「生而弗
> 　有，為而弗恃，長而弗宰」：是謂「玄德」。

The Way produces them;[1] virtuosity nurtures them; things shape them; circumstances complete them. This is why all the myriad things venerate the Way and value virtuosity. Venerating the Way and valuing virtuosity is not commanded[2] but abides naturally.

The Way produces them and virtuosity nurtures them, (but we should) raise them and rear them, complete and maturate them,[3] nourish and shelter them. "Produce, but without possessiveness; act,

---

1. The pronoun "them" (之) throughout this chapter refers to "the myriad things" in the second sentence.

2. MWD A and B, and YZ have "enfeoffed" (爵) instead of "commanded" (命); WB notes this variant but chose "commanded," which makes more sense to me, too.

3. YZ, XE, and HSG have "complete and maturate them" (成之熟之), but MWD B, FY, FYY, and other exemplars have "protect and secure them" (亭之毒之); the locution of the latter is obscure.

but without expectation; lead, but without dominating": this is called "mysterious virtuosity."[4]

Chapter 51 Explanation

This chapter is the Yang exterior cosmogony to chapter 21's Yin interior cosmogony. The first sentence describes the creation of things with four factors: "the Way . . . virtuosity . . . things . . . [and] circumstances." In chapter 21, individual things come into being by the Way manifesting a liminal "semblance" on the cusp of formlessness and form; this semblance then grows into a formal "thing," which, if it is a living thing, will have reproductive "essence" (and if it is a sentient thing, will also have cognitive creativity); and after realizing its reproductive fitness, it continues to become what it is in manifesting its individual "genuineness." All of these are interior inclinations. This chapter describes the "nurture" to chapter 21's "nature," that is, how exterior things and events also contribute to our "creation." We begin, again, with the Way: in chapter 21, it "makes" (為) things, while here it "produces" (生) them. It is the ordering principle of the universe that makes our existence possible. Second, "virtuosity nurtures them." If the Way is like gravity, then "virtuosity" is like Newton's "First Law" (in part): an object in motion stays in motion unless acted upon by an external force. I take "virtuosity" here to imply all four of the things subsequent to the Way in chapter 21, and I take the "things" and "circumstances" in this chapter to be the "external forces" that "shape" and "complete" things. That is, our "genuineness," our individual destinies (i.e., the decisions we make about how to live our lives, predicated on, of course, our genetic proclivities), guides us. But these decisions are necessarily influenced by our social and physical environments. Hence, the "things" that fate has surrounded us with (including our parents, the material possessions we inherited, etc.) unavoidably shape us in certain ways. Finally, our "circumstances," our general environment (including where we live and the kind of community we live in) also has an indelible stamp on our growth.

---

4. The three quoted phrases are also in chapter 10; the middle phrase, "act, but without expectation," is also in chapters 2 and 77; "mysterious virtuosity" is also in chapters 10 and 65.

198 | The Annotated *Laozi* 老子

"This" recognition of the Yin-Yang importance of what we now call nature and nurture "is why all the myriad things venerate the Way and value virtuosity." Things and circumstances come and go and are subject to the vicissitudes of life, but the Way and virtuosity are always with us; thus, we "venerate" and "value" them, even though nobody "commanded" us to. One might read this sentence as saying it is the Way and virtuosity that "abides naturally," but grammatically it should be our venerating and valuing of them that so abides; as chapter 62 says: "everyone in the world values" the Way, just as everyone "values" gravity, even if they are unaware of it.

The fourth sentence presents a problem that I think has never been fully solved. It begins by reiterating the importance of the Way and virtuosity, but the role of "things" in shaping us does not occur again, and "circumstances" (勢) appears in this text only in the first sentence. The problem is: What is the grammatical subject of the nine verbs (including those in the fifth sentence) that follows this second articulation of "virtuosity nurtures them"? Some exemplars do not have this "virtuosity," and thus the Way is the subject of all the verbs in the fourth and fifth sentences. (That is, "The Way produces them, nurtures them, raises them . . .") But this reading contradicts the opening sentence that specifies "virtuosity" as that which "nurtures" things. As the last specified subject, "virtuosity" might be the subject of the verbs that come after its nurturing. (That is, "The Way produces them, virtuosity nurtures them, raises them . . .") But this reading also contradicts the opening sentence that specifies "circumstances" as that which "completes" things. So my solution to this problem is to return to the second half of the first sentence (which otherwise would have been mentioned only once and then inexplicably dropped) and infer that it is "things" and, more specifically, us humans, that is the implied subject of these successive verbs. Hence my addition of "(but *we* should)" in the translation. In this reading, we humans are both the "things" and the "circumstances" that "shape" and "complete" things. In the fourth sentence, then, we "raise them and rear them, complete and maturate them, nourish and shelter them." This is particularly true of parents raising children but also may be extended to farmers raising crops and domesticated animals.

Further, given that we humans can in fact "produce" and "nurture" things too, I think the author is implying an overlap between the Way, virtuosity, and ourselves. This implicit anthropomorphizing of the Way helps to articulate Laozi's ethical realist agenda.

The final sentence here describes the attitude with which we should "raise" and "rear" things. This sentence is identical to the end of chapter

Chapter 51 | 199

10, and there too it is we who are the implied subject of these activities. In fact, comparing the last sentence of chapter 10 with the last two sentences in chapter 51 is interesting. In chapter 10, it is we humans who are to "produce things and nurture them: 'produce, but without possessiveness; act, but without expectation; lead, but without dominating': this is called 'mysterious virtuosity.'" Here in chapter 51, it is the Way that "produces," virtuosity that "nurtures," and we who do the "raising" and "rearing," but in the fifth sentence (as I read it), we also "produce" things. So which is it? I think it is not difficult to say "both," insofar as we embody (or can embody) both the Way and virtuosity. This is probably why both chapters end with "mysterious virtuosity," in which the "mysterious" describes our (potential) embodiment of the Way and virtuosity.

The Way is explicit in this chapter, while our following its ways is implicit, but in the next chapter both of these, "the mother" and "her children," are made explicit, albeit through metaphor.

Chapter 52

Key Ideas

Apprehend the mother to know her children; use introspection, then examine things carefully and flexibly.

天下有始，以為「天下母」。既得其母，以知其子。既知其子，
　復守其母，沒身不殆。
塞其兌，閉其門，終身不勤。開其兌，濟其事，終身不救。
見小曰明，守柔曰強。用其光，復歸其明，無遺身殃：是謂
　「襲常」。

The world had a beginning, which can be considered "the mother of the world." Once you apprehend the mother, then you can know her children. Once you know her children, you can return to preserve their mother, and for the rest of your life you will be free from danger.

Block the openings, shut the doors,[1] and for the rest of your life you will not toil. Unblock the openings, multiply your activities, and for the rest of your life you will be beyond saving.

Seeing the small is called percipience, preserving flexibility is called strength. Use the brightness,[2] but return to percipience, to not bring ruin upon yourself: this is called "continuous abiding."[3]

---

1. These two phrases appear again in chapter 56.

2. "Brightness" (光) occurs four times in this text: in chapters 4 and 56, as "glare" that we should "soften"; here in chapter 52; and in chapter 58, where sages are "bright but are not ostentatious" (光而不耀). So it seems to carry both positive and negative connotations: it is sometimes good, but only in measured doses.

3. MWD A, BD, and YZ have "continuous abiding" (襲常), while HSG and other later exemplars have "practicing abiding" (習常). We saw "continuous percipience" (襲明) in chapter 27.

Chapter 52 Explanation

We saw the Way as "the Mother" in chapter 20 and as "the mother of the world" in chapter 25. In chapter 1, the "beginning" (始) correlated with "formlessness" (無) and the "mother" (母) with "form" (有), yet it was said that "the two appear together but have different names." Here, too, they appear together but have different names, but they are also more clearly conflated and equated with the Way. (This conflation is why it is also called the unifying "One.") In the next sentence, a Yin-Yang analysis portrays the Way as the Yin mother, and the myriad things, including ourselves, as the Yang "children." As in chapter 1, where we are to "abide" in both formlessness and form, here the goal is to "apprehend" the mother and "know" her children. And as in chapter 28, where it was slightly more important to "preserve the black" than to "know the white," so too here it is slightly more important to "preserve their mother" than it is to "know her children," though of course, both are important in their own ways.

The means to "apprehend the mother" (which you have to do before you can "preserve" her) is given in the second paragraph: introspection. In chapter 1, again, this introspection was prescribed for us insofar as we should "abide in formlessness"; while in chapter 4 we saw that the Way helps its "children," the "myriad things," insofar as it "blunts their sharpness; untangles their knots; softens their glare; [and] merges with their dust."[4] Meanwhile, here, and again in chapter 56, the responsibility is back on us; it is *we* who are to "block the openings" and "shut the doors" in order to introspect.

This second paragraph is poetically hyperbolic, both with its "for the rest of your life you will not toil" and its "for the rest of your life you will be beyond saving." While the former certainly sounds better than the latter,

---

4. Though the grammar of "Block the openings" (塞其兌) here is the same as chapter 4's "It blunts their sharpness" (挫其銳), determining agency in the form of the grammatical subject is different in these two chapters. This is because the implied subject is derived from context: in chapter 4, the context suggests that the grammatical subject should be the Way, insofar as it is the explicit subject of the first sentence and is the implied subject of the second sentence, which is why I translate "It blunts their sharpness" at the opening of the third sentence. Here in chapter 52 the situation is different, insofar as the implied subjects of the preceding two sentences are those who "apprehend the mother" and "know her children," that is, those readers who aspire to be Daoists. Thus, it is "we" who are to "block the openings." Further, the Way cannot be the subject here because it seems impossible that the Way would ever "unblock the openings," as that would make us "beyond saving." On the other hand, I could be wrong, and we should extrapolate from this chapter back to chapter 4 and infer we humans as the grammatical subject.

202 | The Annotated *Laozi* 老子

the advice, as is clear from chapter 1, is to achieve a balance between Yang activity, when we "unblock the openings," and Yin introspection, when we "block" them. The locution of being "beyond saving" thus refers to those who entirely ignore Yin-receptive introspection.

This alternating, Yin-Yang approach to living is perhaps an obvious observation, but even though it may be a "small" thing, it is nevertheless something often forgotten amid the bustle of everyday life. The "seeing the small" is an allusion to carefully engaging with the world after appropriate introspection, and "preserving flexibility" adds open-mindedness to that carefulness.

The final sentence is precisely a call to this kind of Yin-Yang life: by all means, we should "use the brightness" (similar to "know the white" in chapter 28) of dealing with the world, but we should not forget to "return" to the ideal of balanced "percipience" (a graph that is composed of the Yin-Yang elements of the sun and moon: 明). In this way, we may "not bring ruin upon" ourselves. The translation describes this way of living as "continuous abiding," but it could just as well be translated "continuous abidings," insofar as chapter 1 and this chapter detail two kinds of abiding: in Yang form as well as in Yin formlessness, in the children *and* in the mother. The cosmic mother-children hierarchy in this chapter is expressed in the political ruler-ruled hierarchy in the next, albeit with an unsurprising reversal of respect.

Chapter 53

Key Ideas

The great Way is smooth, but some rulers ignore it to pursue wealth, to the detriment of the people.

> 使我介然有知，行於大道，唯施是畏。大道甚夷，而民好徑。
> 朝甚除，田甚蕪，倉甚虛。服文綵，帶利劍，厭飲食，財貨有
> 餘。是謂「盜夸」；非道也哉！

If we reliably have knowledge at all, then in walking the great Way, only the slanted is to be feared.[1] The great Way is quite smooth, but people like shortcuts.

The government courts are quite well arranged, yet the fields are quite overgrown, and the granaries are quite empty. Their clothes are elegantly colored, they wear sharp swords, are full of food and drink, and have excessive wealth. This is called "thieving lavishly"; it is not the Way!

Chapter 53 Explanation

Chapter 49 said that sages are "unbiased" (歙歙), and here too, "bias" in the idiom of "the slanted" (迆) is eschewed in favor of the "smooth," equal-opportunity Way. Nevertheless, "people like shortcuts." This sentence

---

1. The opening sentence is not very clear and interpretations vary significantly. The overall meaning of the chapter, however, is clear and quite agreed upon.

204 | The Annotated *Laozi* 老子

is the segue between the impartiality of the Way and the obvious partiality of those rulers with ill-gotten wealth in the second paragraph.[2]

It is such rulers whose "courts are quite well arranged," while "the fields are quite overgrown, and the granaries are quite empty." Presumably the people (who till the fields and store the harvest in granaries) have been overtaxed to the point where the author denigrates such policies as "thieving lavishly." This is the opposite of what we shall see in chapter 59: "In organizing the people and serving Heaven, nothing is as good as frugality." But it also foregrounds what is to come in chapter 75: "The hunger of the people is due to their leaders eating too much in taxes." The implication in this chapter is that it is these leaders' bias toward their own socioeconomic class that facilitates (and in their own minds, justifies) their actions. Is it "thieving" or "appropriate compensation"? It is the language skeptic who will ask the question. The answer to the greed depicted in this chapter is the self-cultivation described in the next.

---

2. Thus, it is likely that "people like shortcuts" should be construed as "(*some*) people like shortcuts," meaning greedy rulers in particular.

Chapter 54

Key Idea

Cultivate the Way in your person, family, community, state, and world, so their diverse virtuosities will flourish.

善建者不拔，善抱者不脫：子孫祭祀不輟。
修之於身，其德乃真；修之於家，其德有餘；修之於鄉，其德乃
　長；修之於邦，其德乃豐；修之於天下，其德乃普。
故以身觀身，以家觀家，以鄉觀鄉，以邦觀邦，以天下觀天下。
　吾何以知天下之然哉？以此。

That which is competently established is not (easily) uprooted; that which is competently embraced is not (easily) taken: (thus,) the sacrifices of children and grandchildren will not (easily) cease.

Cultivate it in your person and your virtuosity will be genuine; cultivate it in your family and its virtuosity will be abundant;[1] cultivate it in your community and its virtuosity will be enduring; cultivate it in your state and its virtuosity will be flourishing; cultivate it in the world and its virtuosity will be widespread.[2]

Thus, use the person to observe the personal, use the family to observe the familial, use the community to observe the communal,

---

1. Though it would not affect my translation, GD B, MWD B, and YZ all have "will be abundant" (有餘; literally, "will *have* abundance"), which I follow, while HSG and others use "will be" (乃) in all five cases, instead of just four.

2. This five-step cultivation plan is also used at *Guanzi* 管子 chapter 1, *Mengzi* 孟子 chapter 4A5, and *Liji* 禮記 chapter 42.

205

206 | The Annotated *Laozi* 老子

use the state to observe the regional, and use the world to observe the worldly. How do we know the world is thus? (Precisely) by means of this (Way)![3]

Chapter 54 Explanation

Though "the Way" is not explicitly mentioned in this chapter, I take it to be the implied subject throughout. The first sentence provides a contrast to the preceding chapter: there the Way has been neglected, and the people suffer. Here we turn away from that bleak picture and are given hope, insofar as if the Way is "competently established" and "competently embraced," then, like other cultural traditions, such as ancestral sacrifices, it will "not (easily) cease."[4] This first sentence, then, is about the importance of habit. The Way is not just something to be passively followed but, if our connection to it is to last, we must actively "establish" (建) and "embrace" (抱) it in our community customs and traditions.

The second sentence reminds us that "establishing" the Way is a multilevel effort, and implies that establishing it at the personal, familial, communal, national, and global levels may well require different strategies. The imperative in this sentence to actively "cultivate" (修) the Way in these various arenas is another clear indication that Daoism is not a "non-active" creed. This implication is strengthened in the third sentence, which reminds us to "observe"—that is, evaluate—different contexts on their own terms. The last two sentences seem to be coyly noting that this implication should be somewhat obvious.

The multilevel efforts of establishing the Way in this chapter are focused back into the personal—our immediate concern—in the next.

---

3. The last two sentences (i.e., 吾何以知 . . . 以此), with only slight modifications, are also in chapters 21 and 57.

4. For a modern analogy, instead of "ancestral sacrifices," think "Christmas dinner" or "New Year's Eve party."

Chapter 55

Key Idea

Embody virtuosity like an infant to be safe, essential, and harmonious.

> 含德之厚者，比於赤子。蜂、蠆，虺、蛇不螫；攫鳥、猛獸不搏。
>
> 骨弱筋柔而握固。未知牝牡之合而朘怒：精之至也。終日號而不嗄：和之至也。
>
> 知和曰「常」，知常曰「明」。益生曰「祥」，心使氣曰「強」。
>
> 物壯則老：謂之不道，不道早已。

Those who embody virtuosity vigorously are comparable to infants.[1]
Wasps and scorpions, vipers and snakes do not sting or bite them;
birds of prey and wild animals do not snatch them.[2]

Their bones are supple and their sinews are flexible, but their
grip is firm. They are unaware of the union of female and male,

---

1. "Those who" (者) is in GD A and MWD B; YZ and HSG drop this nominalizer, resulting in the exhortatory "(May) the vigor of your embodiment be like that of an infant" (含德之厚，比於赤子). In keeping with the theme of infants, "embody" (含) might instead be translated as "suckle," thus: "Those who suckle virtuosity vigorously are comparable to infants" or "(May) the vigor of your suckling of virtuosity be like that of an infant."

2. GD A and MWD A and B have this two-phrase locution; YZ, HSG, and many later exemplars have three phrases. YZ, for example, has "Poisonous insects do not sting (them), birds of prey do not snatch (them), wild animals do not strike (them)" (毒蟲不螫，攫鳥不搏，猛獸不據). Incidentally, "sting or bite" (螫) is indicated by a single graph.

208 | The Annotated *Laozi* 老子

but their genitals stir: this is the utmost of essentialness.[3] *They cry all day without getting hoarse: this is the utmost of harmony.*

    To know harmony is called "abiding," and to know how to abide is called "percipience."[4] *That which overwhelms life is called "ominous";*[5] *consciously (over)exerting your physical energies is called being "forced." (Thus,) things that are overbearing get old (prematurely): this is called not (being in accord with) the Way, and things not (in accord with) the Way will come to an early end.*[6]

Chapter 55 Explanation

The "infant" (赤子) image was used in chapters 10 and 28 (albeit as 嬰兒) as a metaphor for flexibility, and in chapter 20 (also as 嬰兒), where it was a metaphor for sedate expressionlessness. Here the metaphor is first for the ability to "embody virtuosity vigorously," which is to say, the tenacity for holding on to the Way. (Recall the "feeding from the 'Mother'" in chapter 20.) This "vigor" is expanded upon in interesting ways in the following four sentences. The second sentence implies that infants are somehow immune from attack from other "animals," the reason for which I infer to be because their mothers (including their meta-mother, the Way) protect them. Also, because *everyone* protects them, since infants do not (typically) alienate anyone. This "ability" of children to avoid danger works as a metaphor for non-contrivance, which is an almost magical ability in the *Laozi*.

    The third sentence revisits the trope of being "flexible," for which the "infant" was used, twice before, as a metaphor. The fourth sentence notes the "essentialness" (精)—the vigor, energy, and creative potential—of (in this

---

3. The word "essentialness" (精), which is used only here and in chapter 21 (as "essences"), refers both to reproductive fitness (one literal meaning is "semen," which infants have not yet "expended") and cognitive creativity.

4. This sentence is reminiscent of a sentence in chapter 16: "To return to destiny is to abide. To know how to abide is percipience" (復命，常也。知常，明也).

5. Similarly, *Zhuangzi* chapter 5 has: "Abidingly rely on the self-so and do not overwhelm life" (常因自然而不益生也). The word for "ominous" (祥) appears in the *Laozi* three times, in chapters 31 (inauspicious), 55 (ominous), and 78 (misfortunes), and though the other two uses are actually accompanied by a negative prefix (i.e., 不祥), all three instances are taken to be negative. None of these examples necessarily imply the supernatural.

6. The last sentence also concludes chapter 30 (with one minor change), and these are both similar to "the father of (all) teachings" (教父) in chapter 42.

Chapter 55 | 209

case, male) infants. The fifth sentence is best understood in comparison with adult crying, which is usually indicative of being out of sorts with the world. An infant, by contrast, cries when it is hungry or physically uncomfortable, so its cries are a natural communication with its parents: crying is thus a kind of "harmony" with the environment.

Such harmony portends an easy "abiding" in the world, and knowing how to so abide is called "percipience." (Chapter 52 also juxtaposes abiding and percipience, but there the safe "return to percipience" was called "continuous abiding," so the one seems to imply the other without strict order.) This insight—this percipience—in which the preceding harmony is implicit, tells us not to forcibly "overwhelm life." Look to the infant metaphor: we were born with what we need: parents, on the one hand, and natural inclinations (including cognitive abilities), on the other. The "physical energies" that we should not "consciously (over)exert," given the context of the previous paragraph, probably primarily refers to our physical bodies, but the advice certainly works with regard to the mind as well.

This paean to infants turns the "wizened *old* sage" trope on its head. It doesn't explicitly preclude us from seeking advice from the elderly, but it does cleverly nudge us to consider the "wisdom" of common traits of the very young: dependence on the parent / Way, flexibility (both physical and mental), potentiality, creativity, and a relatively undemanding harmony with one's surroundings. The metaphor of the infant as a superlative Yin state of body and mind is continued in the next chapter, beginning with the relative unimportance of talking.

Chapter 56

Key Ideas

The Way cannot be articulated; it can be merged with, and valued, though nothing we do will affect it.

> 知者不言，言者不知。塞其兌，閉其門，挫其銳，解其紛，和其
> 　光，同其塵：是謂「玄同」。
> 故不可得而親，亦不可得而疏；不可得而利，亦不可得而害；不
> 　可得而貴，亦不可得而賤。故為天下貴。

> *Those who know do not speak; those who speak do not know. (Thus,)
> block the openings, close the doors, blunt the sharpness, untangle
> the knots, soften the glare, and merge with the dust:[1] this is called
> "mysterious unity."[2]*
>
> *Thus, you cannot attain it and keep it close, nor attain it and
> keep it distant; cannot attain it and benefit it, nor attain it and*

---

1. The six parts of this line appear in two other chapters, in which one has four of the parts and the other has the remaining two. That is, chapter 4 has the last four parts (i.e., 挫其銳，解其紛，和其光，同其塵), while chapter 52 has the first two (i.e., 塞其兌，閉其門). But in chapter 4 the Way is the implied subject, while chapter 52 has the reader as the implied subject and, similarly, here the implied subject is "Those who know" (whom the reader will probably want to identify with).

2. Though the phrase "mysterious unity" (玄同) does not appear elsewhere in the text, chapter 1 said, "This togetherness, we call it mysterious" (同謂之玄), where "togetherness" translates the same word as "unity" in this chapter. There the "togetherness" was of form and formlessness; here it is unstated, but only formless introspection is described, so I suspect the "unity" here is between the Way and those doing the introspecting.

210

harm it; cannot attain and honor it, nor attain it and disgrace it. Thus, it is valued by the world.[3]

Chapter 56 Explanation

The oft-quoted opening sentence has at least two plausible interpretations. If we take the "know" to be intransitive, this yields a "wise people are (usually) quiet types, while chatty people are (probably) not terribly wise" reading. If, on the other hand, we take "know" to be transitive, and assume the unstated object is "the Way," then it would mean "those who know the Way know that it cannot be fully articulated or comprehended, whereas those who do not know the Way claim to be able to do just that." I (slightly) prefer the transitive reading, not least because the third sentence describes something—which I take to be the Way—that is attainable, albeit elusive and ethereal.[4] Thus, the opening sentence is best read not as a logical contradiction, since the author presumably "knows" (something) and is nevertheless "speaking" (about it) but, given the rest of the chapter, as a poetic way of saying that experiencing the Dao is more important than talking about it. This first sentence, then, is about the importance of language skepticism.

The second sentence is a poetic description of introspection, the practice of which is called "mysterious unity." Though "mysterious" (玄) shows up in seven chapters (chs. 1, 6, 10, 15, 51, 56, 65), the phrase "mysterious unity" appears only here. But what is it that is "unified"? I see three answers. First, taking this chapter in isolation, the introspection described here "unifies" us with the Way.[5] Second, the "mysterious" (玄) "togetherness" (同) of chapter 1 referred to the "togetherness" of form and formlessness, so perhaps we should read the introspection of this chapter as referring to "abiding in

---

3. The word "honor / value" (貴) appears twice here, in an apparent contradiction (i.e., we "cannot . . . honor (it)" yet "(it) is valued by the world"), but I think this is a play on the two (related) meanings of this word. The phrase "Thus it is valued by the world" appears again in chapter 62.

4. Also, the GD A text has "know" as clearly transitive, even if it only specifies the object as "it": "Those who know *it* do not speak, those who speak *of it* do not know" (知之者弗言, 言之者弗知).

5. This reading is buttressed by a passage in *Zhuangzi* chapter 10.3: "Reject and disregard goodness and propriety, and the world's virtuosities will begin to have 'mysterious unity'" (攘棄仁義，而天下之德始玄同矣).

212 | The Annotated *Laozi* 老子

formlessness" and infer an implicit "form" (i.e., the tangible things of the world) that constitutes the other part of the "unity" mentioned here. Third, perhaps "this is called mysterious unity" should be read as "*these* are called a mysterious unity," meaning that we should take these six metaphors as describing a single, "unified" enterprise. This would be reminiscent of the locution in chapter 14, where our failure to see, hear, or grasp the Way is noted, and the author concludes that the object of those three (inadequate) perceptions "is unfathomable yet is one" (混而為一). I like all three of these explanations, but am partial to the first, as it is the simplest.

The third sentence says that though we can apprehend (but not fully *comprehend*) the Way, we cannot really affect it, just as we cannot really affect gravity.[6] Chapter 25 already told us that the Way "does not change," in and of itself, and this chapter adds to that by saying we cannot change it either. Perhaps a fourth meaning for the "mysterious unity" in the previous paragraph is our situation of being able to "apprehend" yet not "(fully) comprehend" the Way, or our being able to apprehend it, but not able to affect it. In any case, it is "valued by the world" because it is impartial (ch. 5), useful (ch. 14), it made us (ch. 21), and it is impervious to any attempt to influence it (ch. 56). This attitude of detachment described in the second paragraph is reminiscent of the unbiased sage in chapter 49. Once again, this chapter on the Way is followed by one on how we humans can implement it among ourselves.

---

6. In case anyone mistakenly focuses exclusively on the "you cannot attain it" phrase used repeatedly here and concludes that we cannot in fact attain the Way, chapter 10 has "embrace the One" (抱一); chapter 39 has governors and kings who "attained the One" (得一); and chapter 52 has "Once (you) apprehend the mother" (既得其母). I take "the One" and "the mother" to be metaphors for the Way. So we *can* attain the Way; we just cannot attain it and *change* it. Counterevidence is at chapter 14: "grasping for it without obtaining it, it is called inconspicuous" (搏之不得，名曰微), but I take this to mean that it cannot be *definitively* grasped or cannot *always* be grasped, not that it can *never* be grasped.

Chapter 57

Key Ideas

Sages manage truthfully, wage war with wiliness, rule "without (contrived) activities," and reduce contrivances.

> 以正治邦，以奇用兵，以「無事」取天下。吾何以知其然哉？
> 以此。
> 夫天下多忌諱，而民彌貧。民多利器，而邦滋昏。人多知巧，而
> 奇物滋起。法令滋彰，而盜賊多有。
> 是以聖人之言曰：「我無為而民自化；我好靜而民自正；我無事
> 而民自富；我無欲而民自樸。」

Use truthfulness[1] to organize the state, (even if you) use wiliness[2] in deploying soldiers; (but) be "without (contrived) activities" to gain (leadership of) the world.[3] How do we know it is thus? (Precisely)

---

1. *Zheng* 正 means "correct" or "true," and appears in chapters 18, 39, 45, 57, 58, and 78; I translate it as "correct" in chapters 18, 39, and 57; and as "truth" or "truthful" in chapters 45, 57, 58, and 78.

2. "Wiliness" (奇) directly contrasts with "truthfulness" (正) in a clear Yin-Yang polarity. The term is also in chapters 58 and 74, with either neutral or negative connotations. This ambiguity is similar to that of "cunning" (巧) in the second paragraph, which has a negative connotation in chapter 19 (as "guile"), but a positive one in chapter 45 (as "skill").

3. The phrase "gain (leadership) of the world" (取天下) is also in chapters 29 and 48; chapter 48 similarly connects the phrase to "without (contrived) activities" (無事).

4. This is the third and last use of this locution, "How do we know. . . . (Precisely) by means of (this Way)," which is only slightly modified at the ends of chapters 21 and 54.

214 | The Annotated *Laozi* 老子

by means of this (Way)![4]

The more taboos and prohibitions[5] *there are in this world, the more the people will become poor. The more sharp instruments the people have, the more states*[6] *will become benighted. The more people are (contrivedly) "knowledgeable" and cunning,*[7] *the more wily things will arise. The more laws and statutes are proclaimed, the more thieves and robbers there will be.*

This is why sayings of the sages say: "We are uncontrived, yet the people develop themselves. We prefer tranquility, yet the people correct themselves. We are without (contrived) activities, yet the people become prosperous by themselves. We are without (contrived) desires, yet the people simplify themselves."[8]

Chapter 57 Explanation

This chapter returns to the topic of good government, last broached in chapter 53 (and fleetingly in chapter 54), and begins a six-chapter run on the subject (chs. 57–62). "Truth" (正) was created by "clarity and tranquility" in chapter 45, and the same graph, translated as "correctness," was the result of "governors and kings" who "obtained the One" in chapter 39. Here too it appears to be a human achievement. It is also one of three devices to be used by the ruler: truthfulness for effective government, useful for anyone at any level of government; "wiliness" (奇) for military affairs; and being "without (contrived) activities" (無事), which we saw in chapter 48, for gaining the top governmental post.

"Wiliness," which appears here first (and again in chs. 58 and 74),

---

5. Neither "taboos" (忌) nor "prohibitions" (諱) appear again in this text.

6. GD A only has "states" (邦), while MWD A, YZ, HSG, and others have "states and families" (邦家 or 國家); I follow GD to keep the symmetry of one-word "people" and "states" in this line and of two-word "wily things" and "thieves and robbers" in the next (民, 邦; 奇物, 盜賊).

7. GD A has "wisdom" (智) and MWD A has "knowledge" (知), but these graphs were interchangeable in early China. Symmetry suggests two graphs here, so I added "cunning" (巧), from YZ and HSG, which have "crafty and cunning" (伎巧; "cunning" 巧 was also castigated in chapter 19 as "guile"). FY has "knowledge and intelligence" (知慧), and FYY has "wisdom and kindness" (智慧).

8. Chapter 37 similarly says that good leadership results in the people "developing" (化) and "settling" (定) themselves.

Chapter 57 | 215

is an ambiguous term. In this first sentence it has a positive connotation (or, perhaps, a "lesser of two evils" connotation), but the "wily" in the second paragraph has a negative connotation, while its other two uses are unclear, with either a neutral or a negative connotation. Being "without (contrived) activities," on the other hand, is for Laozi always a good thing. It first appears in chapter 48, then twice in this chapter, then once more in chapter 63. It seems to be nearly synonymous with the more-famous "non-contrivance" that appears in the third paragraph (and throughout the text), but its explicit connection to "gain[ing] (leadership of) the world" (取 天下) here and in chapter 48 indicates that the "activities" in question are stratagems for taking control of a community or state. The advice to be "without (contrived) activities," then, is advice to be genuine: if people want you to lead them, they will let you know.

"The more taboos and prohibitions there are in this world, the more the people will become poor," and the following three sentences, recall the relativity of values first described in chapters 2, 3, and 12, but here it is applied more specifically to the ruler's creation of (contrived or even super-stitious) norms (i.e., "taboos"), weapons (i.e., "sharp instruments"), "wily things" (perhaps ingenious military devices like the catapult, or assassination techniques like poison), and (oppressive) "laws." As in those previous chapters, the author advises a lighter touch: more individuality and less "upward conformance." That is, I do not think that Laozi is saying there is anything inherently wrong with taboos, sharp instruments, wily things, or laws, but their proliferation or misuse should be a matter of concern for everyone.

This advice is developed in four different ways in the final paragraph: were rulers to be "uncontrived . . . prefer tranquility . . . [be] without (con-trived) activities . . . [and be] without (contrived) desires," then the people would respond by becoming citizens who "develop themselves . . . correct themselves . . . become prosperous by themselves . . . [and] simplify themselves." All four pieces of advice we have already met; here they come together specifically under the leadership of an uncontrived ruler. The next chapter continues on with the leadership of sage-rulers.

Chapter 58

Key Idea

Language skepticism: sagely leadership is tentative, in order to avoid deceitful people looking to delude others.

其政悶悶，其民淳淳；其政察察，其民缺缺。
禍兮福之所倚，福兮禍之所伏；孰知其極？其無正：正復為奇，
　　善復為妖。
人之迷，其日固久矣。是以聖人「方而不割，廉而不劌；直而不
　　肆，光而不耀」。

Those governments that are tentative, their people (remain) pure; those governments that are definitive, their people (become) deceitful.[1]
Misfortune is that which fortune relies on, fortune is that which misfortune hides in; who knows their turning points?[2] (Thus,) for those without truthfulness, (even) the truth can be construed as wily, and (even) competence can be construed as uncanny.[3]
The human ability to delude has certainly been around a long time. This is why sages are "upright but not divisive; scrupulous

---

1. Chapter 20 contrasts "hazy" (悶悶; here: "tentative") with "clear" (察察; here: "definitive"), while this chapter contrasts "tentative" (悶悶) with "pure" (淳淳) and "definitive" (察察) with "deceitful" (缺缺).

2. A famous story illustrating this claim is the "old man at the fort" story at *Huainanzi* 淮南子 chapter 18.

3. "Construed as" (復為) in the last two phrases is literally "returned and construed as," where the untranslated "returned" means something like "*counter*intuitively construed as" or "*thrown back* (in your face) and construed as."

216

Chapter 58 | 217

*but not injurious; straightforward but not impudent; bright but
not ostentatious."*

Chapter 58 Explanation

The opening sentence (in the Chinese) reads like a catchy song lyric,[4] and reiterates the main idea of the second paragraph in the previous chapter, which might be summarized as: the spirit of the law is more important than the letter of the law (and: too many laws only benefit lawyers). Here it is made plain that the more detailed a law gets, the more ingenious are the crooks that seek to evade it; better then to articulate only the gist (i.e., the "spirit") of the law.[5] A "tentative" government is quite similar to a "flexible" government, responsive to the changing needs of its citizens (whether they be truthful or wily).

The second sentence that, like the first sentence, reads like it might be a well-known saying, reminds us that things are not always as they seem. A famous (but decidedly later) example of this may be found in the *Huainanzi*, where a series of events confounded a particular father, who was wise enough to not jump to conclusions of whether a given event was "fortunate" (福) or "unfortunate" (禍). First, his horse was lost, but then it returned with a second horse. Then his son broke his leg when he fell off that second horse, but then his injury kept both father and son out of a deadly frontier war that saw ninety percent of their community militia killed.[6] Thus, "fortune is that which misfortune hides in."

The third sentence returns to the subject of wily people, that is, dishonest people: "those without truthfulness." Even well-intentioned claims (and,

---

4. For those who can read the Chinese, there are four sets of reduplicatives, which are relatively rare in this text.

5. This idea is also found in Ruism (Confucianism); cf. *Lunyu* 2.3: "Guide them with regulations, equalize them with punishment, and the people will be evasive and shameless; guide them with virtuosity, and equalize them with protocol, and the people will have both (proper) shame and norms" (道之以政，齊之以刑，民免而無恥；道之以德，齊之以禮，有恥且格). Daoists and Ruists (Confucians) further agree that the answer to this problem is to have leaders lead by example.

6. See John Major, Sarah Queen, Andrew Meyer, Harold Roth, trans., *The Huainanzi: A Guide to the Theory and Practice of Government in Early Han China* (New York: Columbia University Press, 2010), 728–29.

218 | The Annotated *Laozi* 老子

in the context of the previous chapter, laws) can be *intentionally* perverted: "truth" and "competence" can, in the hands of silver-tongued but corrupt people, be turned into their opposites. Construing truth as being "wily" will be familiar to those who know of Orwellian double-speak or even more contemporary campaigns of disinformation. As for "competence" being "construed as uncanny," we might recall the story in the *Zhuangzi* where Woodworker Qing carved such a magnificent bell stand that his competence was "suspected of being the result of spirits" (以疑神) by people who did not understand his skillfulness.[7]

The next sentence, "The human ability to delude has certainly been around a long time," can be read either as commenting on wily people, or as describing those whom wily people dupe. If the latter, then this sentence should instead read "Human delusion has certainly been around a long time." It is probably best to read it both ways, as being about those who delude *and* those who are deluded by them.

Either way, this human proclivity is why sages teach by example and do not rely too much on articulated (or, perhaps, outdated) codes of conduct. They are "upright . . . scrupulous . . . straightforward . . . [and] bright," but even while setting such an example, they are vague enough (as well as truthful enough) in their speech to not be "divisive" or "injurious."

This sagely approach can also be evaluated from another angle: not only does "leading by example" not harm other people, it also means the one doing the leading does not appear "showy" or "ostentatious," as they might, were they to micromanage morality by decree. Daoist rulers, however, are in a tricky situation, because they want to follow the people's (presumed) innate goodness but also want to correct people's inclinations toward selfishness. Ideally the relationship will be like that of athletes to their coaches: the former consent to the "rule" of the latter and expect to be pushed to do things that they themselves *want* to do on their own but cannot quite manage themselves. The theme of leadership continues, again, in the next chapter.

---

7. See Burton Watson, trans., *The Complete Works of Zhuangzi* (New York: Columbia University Press, 2013 [1969]), 152–53.

Chapter 59

Key Ideas

Leaders should use frugality, adaptivity, virtuosity, and possibility to realize ostensible limitlessness.

> 治人事天，莫若嗇。夫唯嗇：是以「早服」。早服：謂之「重
> 積德」。
> 重積德則無不克。無不克則莫知其極。莫知其極，可以有國。
> 有國之「母」，可以長久。是謂「深根、固柢」，長生、久視
> 之道。

In organizing the people and serving Heaven, nothing is as good as frugality.[1] Simple frugality: this uses "early adaptivity."[2] Early adaptivity: (we) call it "emphasizing ingrained[3] virtuosity."

---

1. Despite the importance attached to the virtue of "frugality" (嗇) here, this term does not occur anywhere else in the text, though another word translated as "frugality" (儉) is important in chapter 67.

2. GD B has "preparation" (備) instead of "adaptivity" (服), which MWD B, *Hanfeizi* chapter 20 (鮮老), BD, YZ, HSG, and others have. Some scholars read *fu* 服 as "follow (the Way)" rather than "adaptivity." Wagner says it should be "return" (復); Rudolf Wagner, *A Chinese Reading of the* Daodejing: *Wang Bi's Commentary on the* Laozi *with Critical Text and Translation* (Albany: State University of New York Press, 2003), 320. I prefer "adaptivity" because it implies the simplicity of "frugality" and flexibility we have in discovering our "ingrained virtuosity."

3. The word "ingrained" (積) is used in chapter 81 as "accumulate," which is its primary meaning, but I don't think "virtuosity" is something that one can "accumulate," unless, perhaps, you think of it as potential that you have that you have not yet "expressed" (容; ch. 21) and thus it has "accumulated" within you.

219

220 | The Annotated *Laozi* 老子

If you emphasize ingrained virtuosity, then anything will be possible. If anything is possible, then none will know your limits. If none know your limits, then it will be possible for you to gain (leadership of) the realm.

If you thus have the "mother" of the realm, then you can continue for a long time. This is called having "deep roots and a firm taproot," which is the way of long life and enduring vision.

Chapter 59 Explanation

The theme of "frugality" (嗇) contrasts pointedly with the "thieving lavishly" in chapter 53 and with "the hunger of the people is due to their leaders eating too much in taxes" in chapter 75. It is tangentially related to the theme of unobtrusiveness in the previous chapter, insofar as both prescribe a "less is more" ethic. The second sentence bolsters this line of thought, with "early adaptivity" (早服) presumably referring to our adapting to the vicissitudes of life, or to our own virtuosity, or to the Way, or all three, each of which makes good sense vis-à-vis frugality, insofar as frugal people have less to tie them down and are in that respect more adaptable to change. The third step, "emphasizing ingrained virtuosity," is perhaps less obviously connected to frugality, but we may nevertheless extrapolate from economic frugality and practical adaptivity to fate and the realities of life that we all face, to the "less is more" virtuosities of non-contrivance and open-mindedness.

The fourth and fifth steps might not be steps at all but may only refer to potential optics of "emphasizing ingrained virtuosity." Nevertheless, the fourth step, "anything will be possible," refers to one's own perception of your own potential. The "anything" is of course hyperbole, but the subjective *feeling* of "anything is possible" can be a liberating and motivating state of mind. The fifth step, "none will know your limits," conversely refers to how others perceive one who has emphasized their ingrained virtuosity: such a person may well appear to be a savior figure, or at least to symbolize the possibility of being a great leader.

The first sentence of the final paragraph brings in the Way with the "mother" metaphor that we saw in chapters 20, 25, and 52, and reminds us of its foundational role. The final sentence switches metaphors and articulates two types of root: the "deep roots" that refer to our connection to our individual potentialities, and the "firm taproot" that refers to our connection to the Way. The Yin female and Yang root metaphors were also used together in chapter 6. Thus, connected to both the cosmic Way and our individual virtuosities, we may realize "the way of long life and enduring vision," which, if we take "vision" as a metaphor for the intellect, refer to the body *and* the mind. And, given that this chapter deals primarily with leadership, this "enduring vision" may well refer particularly to a political vision. The focus on politics in this chapter is continued in the next.

Chapter 60

Key Idea

Sagely rulers and spirited ghosts reciprocate their virtuosities so that people are not harmed.

> 治大邦若烹小鮮。以道莅天下，其鬼不神。非其鬼不神，其神
> 不傷人。
> 非其神不傷人，聖人亦不傷人。夫兩不相傷：故德交歸焉。

Organizing a great state is like cooking a small fish. When one governs the world with the Way, its ghosts are not spirited.[1] Or rather, it is not that its ghosts are not spirited, but their spiritedness does not harm people.

Or rather, it is not only that their spiritedness does not harm people: sages also do not harm people. These two not harming one another: thus, their virtuosities are reciprocated and return to each of them.

Chapter 60 Explanation

One of the most memorable lines from this text is the opening sentence here, whereby interfering too much with a small fish when cooking it will

---

1. "Ghosts" (鬼) appear only here, and are presumably the ghosts of the community's dead. "Spirit / spiritous / spirited" (神) appears in this text in chapters 6, 29, 39, and 60; in ch. 6 the "valley spirit" (谷神) is a metaphor for the Way; in ch. 29 the "spiritous vessel" (神器) is a metaphor for the world (like the "small fish" here); in ch. 39 presumably literal "spirits attained the One and become numinous" (神得一以靈); here, "spirited" seems to mean a negative kind of creative: like "wily" or "sneaky."

222

Chapter 60 | 223

make it fall apart, a metaphor for advising a "light touch" from leaders, a theme previously articulated in chapters 57–59.

The next three lines, in what might be construed as slightly comical rhetoric, seek to articulate the supernatural effects of having leaders with light touches. First we are told that in such a situation, "ghosts are not spirited" (i.e., wily or devious), a phrase that is as engaging and delightful as the opening sentence. The author then seems to reconsider the negative connotation that he has implied for "spirited," a term that usually has a very positive connotation, and so restates his claim more clearly: ghosts are clever (*natürlich*), but their cleverness "does not harm people."

But even that phrasing is rejected as being too one-sided, so the author finally settles on wording that combines the insights of the first and third sentences: neither the sagely leaders nor the ghosts that inhabit the communities led by sagely leaders will "harm people."[2] There are two ways that I can see to understand what is going on here. First, Laozi may be talking about literal ghosts, as the post-mortem presence of dead people from the community, and saying that sagely rule will not cause them to become unruly, to bother or "harm" the people. Second, "ghosts" might be a metaphor for "tradition," with the sagely ruler then having the role of (careful) innovator. In this reading, this chapter balances a backwards-looking tradition with forward-looking creativity, much like chapter 20 contextualized (creative) individualism within a (traditional) community.

Finally, we see that both of these potential sources of harm—"these two" referring to sage-leaders and ghosts—when situated within the ideal Daoist community, will create a virtuous circle wherein the "light touch" of the one will reinforce the "light touch" (and, perhaps, even the "blessings") of the other. From the interactions between the community and its ghost population in this chapter, we turn to the interactions between larger and smaller communities in the next.

---

2. Laozi may be arguing against both Kongzi and Mozi here. Kongzi thought ghosts should be respected but kept at a distance. Thus he says, at *Lunyu* 6.22: "Respect ghosts and spirits but keep them at a distance" (敬鬼神而遠之). Mozi, on the other hand, thought the state needs the active participation of ghosts to reward and punish the people. However, this text might precede both of them and so perhaps *they* were reacting to Laozi.

Chapter 61

Key Idea

Great states should be conciliatory toward smaller states so that people are nurtured and served.

> 大邦者：天下之下流也，天下之交也，天下之牝也。牝恆以靜勝
> 牡；以其靜故為下也。
> 故大邦以下小邦，則取小邦；小邦以下大邦，則取於大邦。故或
> 下以取，或下而取。
> 大邦不過欲兼畜人，小邦不過欲入事人。夫兩者各得其所欲，
> 則大者宜為下。

Great states are like the river deltas of the world, are like the intersections of the world, are like the females of the world. Females often overcome males through tranquility; their use of tranquility is the reason for being conciliatory.

Thus, great states, by being conciliatory with smaller states, can thereby accept the smaller states; and smaller states, by being conciliatory with great states, can thereby be accepted by[1] the great states. Thus, one is conciliatory and is accepted, and one is conciliatory and accepts.

---

1. MWD A and B, BD, and FY all have a passive marker (於) that, crucially, appears in the next sentence (as 以) but seems to have dropped out of the YZ and HSG exemplars here.

Great states only want to unite (with smaller states) to nurture the people, and smaller states only want to enter into (this union) to serve the people.[2] *If both are each to obtain what they want, then it is appropriate that the greater be conciliatory.*

Chapter 61 Explanation

Among chapters 57–62, on government, only this chapter targets what we might call "foreign policy." Tangentially related to the "light touch" theme of the preceding chapters, here the message combines three virtues in the metaphors of the opening passage. The three metaphors—"river deltas," "intersections," and "females"—are metaphors for conciliation, reciprocity, and tranquility. A river delta is both low-lying and inclusive (of all the rivers that flow into it): I use "conciliation" to indicate a combination of humility (placing oneself lower than others) and inclusivity. For "intersections," imagine a four-way traffic stop: first one car goes, then another, in turn: hence "reciprocity." That females are a metaphor for tranquility is made clear in the next sentence.[3] But tranquility does not play an obvious role in the rest of the chapter, which is clearly about conciliation and reciprocation, so we presumably take tranquility to be the *manner* in which we are conciliatory and reciprocative.

An unstated premise is that both "great states"[4] and "smaller states" should accept the existence of an unequal hierarchy of power. This chapter aims to make the best of that inequality. Reciprocity vis-à-vis the power hierarchy, through the mechanism of conciliation, is the theme of the third and fourth sentences, with the fifth sentence spelling out why this reciprocity is (or can be) mutually beneficial. This reason does assume, optimistically,

---

2. In chapter 10, the ruler "nurtures" (畜) either the "people" (民) or the "myriad things"; in chapter 51, virtuosity nurtures the myriad things. In chapter 59, rulers "serve" (事) Heaven.

3. The term "river delta" (下流) appears only here; the term "intersection / reciprocate" (交) appears only here and in the last sentence of the previous chapter; for "female" (牝 and 雌), see chapter 6, note 1.

4. By translating this word (i.e., *da* 大) as "great," rather than "large" (which is a more natural antonym to "small"), I can avoid having to add a parenthetical "should," insofar as "great" may be read to imply an aspirational condition. The ambiguity is also in the Chinese.

226 | The Annotated *Laozi* 老子

that leaders of both great and small states primarily want to "nurture the people" or "serve the people" (which I take to be synonymous). But, while the virtues of conciliation and reciprocity are universally applicable, the final sentence makes clear that the onus is upon greater states more than smaller states: it is incumbent upon the more powerful player to not be aggressive or predatory if the hierarchy is to stand. In chapter 60, "ghosts" and sage rulers "reciprocated" their respective virtuosities, while in this chapter greater and smaller states reciprocate theirs.

The theme of being conciliatory comes up again in chapters 66 and 68, but the next chapter deals with being conciliatory (without using that word) to incompetent people.

Chapter 62

Key Ideas

The Way is an inner secret; governing with it helps both the competent and the incompetent.

道者：萬物之奧也，善人之寶也，不善人之所保也。美言可以
市，尊行可以加人：人之不善，何棄之有？
故立天子，置三公：雖有拱璧以先駟馬，不如坐而進此道。
古之所以貴此道者何？不曰：「求以得，有罪以免」邪？故為
天下貴。

The Way is the inner secret[1] of the myriad things, the treasure of competent people, and the protector of incompetent people. Though beautiful words may enable trade and venerable deeds may enable the improvement of people, (still,) how can the incompetent among us be disregarded?[2]

---

1. The word "inner secret / lord" (奧) occurs only here. MWD A and B both have "flowing / focus" (注), which some take to be a graphic variant of "leader / lord" (主), especially since "lord" is one of the meanings of *ao* 奧. Although "lord" conceptually fits with the "Heavenly Scion" in the next paragraph, I follow YZ and all later exemplars in using this graph and do not translate it as "lord" because "lord" here would contradict chapter 34: "The great Way . . . does not make itself lord" (大道 . . . 不為主). However, it is entirely possible that the key term in chapter 34 is *make* itself," and that the text is here saying the Way is, in fact, the "lord" of the myriad things, but that it doesn't force itself upon us.

2. It is also possible to read "incompetent" as "incompetence," which would imply that incompetence persists even among the competent people who exhibit "beautiful words" and "venerable deeds."

228 | The Annotated *Laozi* 老子

> *Hence, in the establishment of the Heavenly Scion and the instituting of the Three Dignitaries: though there be bringing tribute of fine jade and bringing forward teams of horses, these are not as good as sitting and advancing this Way.*
> *Why did those of antiquity value this Way? Did they not say: "Seekers use it to gain, while the guilty use it to escape"?[3] Thus, it is valued by (everyone in) the world.[4]*

Chapter 62 Explanation

This chapter expands upon an idea presented in chapter 27, that "sages are always competent at helping people, without disregarding anyone,"[5] but here this sagely activity is made into both a function of the cosmic Way and good government (and leadership) policy.

The first sentence posits that "the Way" is—or can be, or should be—valuable to everyone: all "the myriad things," including both "competent people" and "incompetent people." The second gives two examples of how competent people flourish: they use "beautiful words" and "venerable deeds" to succeed in life. But this does not mean that "the incompetent among us [should] be disregarded." The third opens with references to the "Heavenly Scion" (meaning the king) and the "Three Dignitaries" (meaning the highest echelon of his government), as they are the ones responsible for avoiding mob rule, the tyranny of the majority, inasmuch as the majority may well want to ostracize the incompetent. (In chapter 74, the author considers the proposition to not just ostracize but kill "wily people," who might be considered a subset of "incompetent" people.) The third sentence goes on to say that though "fine jade" and "teams of horses" (both of which were presented

---

3. It might be tempting to take the last Chinese graph in this sentence (i.e., *xie* 邪: bias) as the object of the verb "escape," but this would (probably) be a mistake because a comparison of other exemplars will show that it should in fact be taken as a grammatical particle that stands in for a modern question mark (i.e., *ye* 邪 = 也乎), as in chapters 7 and 39.

4. This final sentence also appears at the end of chapter 56. I add the parenthetical here to emphasize "everyone," meaning both competent and incompetent people.

5. Also chapter 49: "Those who are competent: we are competent to them (in return); those who are incompetent: we are nevertheless competent to them (too): this is virtuous competence."

as tribute to rulers in antiquity) may also be good and useful, they are still not as good as the tolerant "Way," which accommodates even incompetent people and, perhaps, smaller states that cannot afford such tribute.

The saying from "antiquity" in the penultimate sentence, "Seekers use it to gain, while the guilty use it to escape," can be read either in isolation or as contextualized with the preceding paragraph. In isolation, it means the Way helps anyone seeking anything to be successful—"seek and ye shall find," if you will—while the Way also helps anyone who has broken the rules by making those around "the guilty" to be less vindictive. In the context of the royal court, "seekers" should be understood as "petitioners" to the throne. You could bring tribute to increase your odds of success, or you could pin your hopes on your uncontrived, unselfish, Daoist behavior. The "guilty" would then be those "throwing themselves on the mercy of the court." Rulers with the Way will be more tolerant and thus the "guilty" will be more likely to escape punishment, or at least, overly harsh punishment.

The last sentence recalls the reciprocity of the previous chapter as well as the first sentence here: both competent and incompetent people "value" the Way, the competent because they can rely on it to achieve success, and the incompetent—of which "the guilty" is a subset—because they can count on it to save them despite their incompetence.

Preventing occasionally "guilty" people from snowballing into enduringly "incompetent" people may be a matter of early intervention, which is the topic of the next chapter.

Chapter 63

Key Idea

Non-contrivance, timeliness, and trust are key to dealing with oneself, others, and the world.

> 為無為，事無事，知無知。大小多少：圖難於其易，為大於其
> 細。
> 天下之難事，必作於易；天下之大事，必作於細。是以聖人終不
> 為大，故能成其大。
> 夫輕諾者必寡信，多易者必多難。是以聖人猶難之，故終無難
> 矣。

Be uncontrived, be active without (contrived) activities,[1] know without knowing (contrivedly).[2] Large or small, many or

---

1. The difference between "be" (為) and "be active" (事) is that "be" refers to anything at all that you might do, while "be active" has two qualifying implications to it. One is that "being active" often refers to "being active (in community or government leadership)," which is made clear in chapter 57: "Be 'without (contrived) activities' to gain (leadership of) the world." The second is that the word also means "to serve," which is how it is translated in chapters 59 and 61. So it is possible that the phrase here should mean something like "serve without being servile." But I do not translate it this way here because the "difficult" and "large" "activities" later in this chapter seem to warrant the more expansive meaning of "activities" rather than "service."

2. Nearly all exemplars have "taste without tasting (contrivedly)" (味無味) instead of "know without knowing (contrivedly)" (知無知); GD A has 未亡未 and MWD A has 味无未, but given the graphic similarity of taste (味) and know (知), that three Tang dynasty authors use "know" when (apparently) citing this passage, and that "know" fits better in this chapter (and book) than "taste" (which appears in chapters 12 and 35), I use "know." (*Wei* 未 means "not yet" and so cannot be the intended meaning.) For more on "without knowing (contrivedly)" (無知), see chapters 3, 10, and 70.

230

few:[3] *plan for what is difficult when it is still easy, deal with the large while it is still small.*

The world's difficult activities certainly arose from what was once easy, and the world's larger activities certainly arose from what was once smaller. This is why sages never work on (already) large (activities) but are nevertheless able to complete their large (activities).[4]

Those who lightly assent (almost) certainly lack trustworthiness; those who often think things are easy (almost) certainly will have many difficulties. This is why sages seem to find things difficult, but actually, in the end, do not have difficulties.

Chapter 63 Explanation

This chapter opens with three activities that are important in the *Laozi*: "being" (為), having "activities" (事), and "knowing" (知). They all potentially suffer from the familiar, implied curse of "contrivance." To "be uncontrived" is something that even the Way does (ch. 37); to "be . . . without (contrived) activities" is something that leaders wishing to gain a leadership position should do (ch. 57); and to "know without knowing (contrivedly)" is both a sagely endeavor (ch. 3) and a leadership goal (ch. 10). All three are about genuinely responding to different environments.

The theme of responsiveness underlies the second sentence of the first paragraph. To "plan for what is difficult when it is still easy" seems to be a matter of uncontrived knowing, as it implies *noticing* problems before conventional wisdom might spot a red flag. Next, to "deal with the large while it is still small" is to *respond* perceptively to an incipient situation that others may not have noticed yet. This would be a matter of being uncontrived, which is to be genuine, to be responsive everywhere—not just

---

3. All exemplars from MWD A on have the phrase "requite resentment with virtuosity" (報怨以德) here, but I, following Yan Lingfeng 嚴靈峰 and Chen Guying, have taken this and put it in chapter 79, where it makes better sense. (GD A has chapter 63, but not this line.)

4. As mentioned in chapter 61, note 4, the word *da* 大 means both "large" and "great" (or even "ambitious"); here I strive for a literal translation, but the "large (activities)" that sages are able to "complete" should probably be understood as a double entendre insofar as sages typically work on ethically "great (activities)" too. A very similar sentence appeared in chapter 34 as "This is why sages with it never consider themselves great; thus, they are able to complete their greatness" (是以聖人以其終不自為大，故能成其大).

232 | The Annotated *Laozi* 老子

in your own house and not just in your own community, but everywhere you go—by following your own inclinations, your own destiny (but within reason: "that which people revere must be revered" [ch. 20]).

The theme of responsiveness runs throughout this chapter, but timeliness is a second unstated motif. To be uncontrived, pursue activities, and know things, is good general advice, but there are times when contrivance might be appropriate to the situation: "being" polite in public (e.g., standing in line even when in a hurry), having "activities" at work (e.g., taking on projects assigned to you even though not in your area of expertise), and "knowing" in accord with (contrived) social etiquette (e.g., pretending to know about the latest political outrage). Nevertheless, too much contrivance will preclude us from ever being genuine.

Timeliness is especially clear in "plan for what is difficult when it is still easy," and while timeliness is a theme that was briefly broached in chapter 8, this is the first time we have explicitly encountered the related theme of "act early."[5] The second paragraph takes the generalized timeliness of the first paragraph and contextualizes it for sage-leaders with what I think is an interesting triple entendre (see this chapter's note 4). The first sentence of the second paragraph says, "The world's difficult activities certainly arose from what was once easy, and the world's larger activities certainly arose from what was once smaller." It is possible that "activities" (事) are simply generic activities, but in chapters 48 and 57 the word has a distinct leadership (or political) connotation, which may be implied here. If it does *not* have that connotation, then the third sentence is simply a restatement of the second. If it does, then the third reimagines the second in a leadership context, which is how I take it.

The second sentence of the second paragraph says: "This is why sages never work on (already) large (activities) but are nevertheless able to complete their large (activities)." This reading speaks to the size, or ambition, of one's projects, whether personal or political. As I've translated it, sages do in fact engage in "large" (i.e., ambitious) activities . . . they just do so before anyone else would identify them as "large." A second reading derives from taking "large" as "great" (either or both of which are implied by *da* 大), and construing "large" projects as ethically admirable, as ethically "great." A third reading takes "large" as "great" and "work on" as "seem" (either of

---

5. We can see this "act early" theme *implicitly* in places like chapter 50, where "those competent at assisting life . . . do not encounter" dangerous situations because they perceptively avoid them.

Chapter 63 | 233

which are meant by *wei* 為). Thus: "This is why sages never seem great, but is nevertheless why they are able to complete their greatness" (是以聖人終不為大，故能成其大).[6] This second meaning echoes the final sentence in chapter 34: "This is why sages with it never consider themselves great; thus, they are able to complete their greatness" (是以聖人以其終不自為大，故能成其大).[7]

The two lines of the final paragraph can be read as general advice, like the first paragraph, or as a continuation of paragraph two, with its leadership context. Thus, on the one hand, "Those who lightly assent (almost) certainly lack trustworthiness; those who often think things are easy (almost) certainly will have many difficulties," can be read as a comment on overeager and flippant people in general, or as pertaining specifically to would-be leaders who are willing to bite off more than they can chew in their desire for professional (or political) advancement. Similarly, that "sages seem to find things difficult, but actually, in the end, do not have difficulties," may be read as a comment on the advantages of being cautious and acting early, or as specific advice to leadership candidates to take the job seriously. In any case, these words, like the chapter as a whole, are about responsiveness, timeliness, and caution. It is the timeliness theme that the next chapter expands upon.

---

6. Not to belabor the point, but the "work on" could also be retained: "This is why sages never work on their greatness, but are able to complete their greatness."

7. The difference between "seem great" (為大) and "considers itself / themselves great" (自為大) is the single graph *zi* 自 (self).

Chapter 64

Key Ideas

Timeliness: act early, but always be careful; also: non-contrivance, non-attachment, uncontrived desire, uncontrived learning.

> 其安易持。其未兆易謀。其脆易泮。其微易散。為之於其未有，
> 治之於其未亂。
> 合抱之木，生於毫末。九層之臺，起於累土。百仞之高，始於
> 足下。
> 為者敗之，執者失之。是以聖人無為，故無敗；無執，故無失。
> 民之從事，恆於幾成而敗之。慎終如始：則無敗事矣。
> 是以聖人欲不欲，不貴難得之貨；學不學，復衆人之所過。以輔
> 萬物之自然而不敢為。

That which is steady is easy to grasp. That which is incipient is easy to plan for. That which is brittle is easy to break apart. That which is frail is easy to scatter. (Therefore,) act on things before they become (fully) formed, and organize things before they become (too) disordered.

A tree whose circumference fills one's embrace grew from a downy sprout. A terrace nine stories tall arose from a pile of dirt. (Climbing) a height of a thousand feet began from a single step.[1]

---

1. MWD A, B; BD; YZ have this locution, while from HSG on, the preferred wording is "A journey of a thousand miles began from a single step" (千里之行，始於足下). A *ren* 仞 is about eight feet, so a hundred *ren* (百仞) would be eight hundred feet, but I rounded up for euphony.

Chapter 64 | 235

Those who are contrived will fail in it; those who are attached will lose it.[2] This is why sages are uncontrived and thus do not fail; do not get attached (to things) and thus do not lose (them).

When people pursue activities, often they will be on the cusp of success and yet fail in it. (Therefore,) be as careful at the end as you are at the beginning: then there will be no failure in your activities.

This is why sages desire to not desire (contrivedly), and do not value difficult-to-obtain goods (contrivedly);[3] they learn to not learn (contrivedly), and return to that which has been passed over by the masses. In this way they assist the naturalness of the myriad things, yet do not presume to be contrived.

Chapter 64 Explanation

The theme of timeliness is here carried over from the previous chapter (a theme that partially explains the "light touch" of the ideal leader in the prior chapters). The eight sentences of the first two paragraphs are all easily understood in light of the explanatory fifth sentence, with "(Therefore,) act on things before they become (fully) formed" explaining the first four sentences, and "organize things before they become (too) disordered" commenting on the last three sentences. That is, you want to "grasp . . . plan for . . . break apart . . . [or] scatter" things *before* they become unsteady, complex, hardened, or consolidated. Likewise, when planting a tree, building a terrace, or climbing a height, it is best to figure out exactly—that is, *organize*—where you want to dig a hole, lay a foundation, or make a path, because it's much harder to change your plans once you've gone too far.

In the third paragraph the narrative returns explicitly to non-contrivance and then includes non-attachment, which we saw in chapter 29.[4] The mental

---

2. This sentence is also in chapter 29, where the "it" is, by implication, "gain[ing] (leadership of) the world."

3. The "do not value difficult-to-obtain goods (contrivedly)" is also in chapter 3.

4. "Attachment" (執) is typically used in this text in a value-neutral sense of "holding" on to something; chapters 14, 35, 69, and 79 use it this way, and the things held on to may be good things (chs. 14, 35) or ostensibly bad—or at least unfortunate—things (ch. 69), or completely neutral things (ch. 79). But chapters 29 and 64 both use it, in identical fashion, in a philosophical and decidedly negative way.

236 | The Annotated *Laozi* 老子

attitude of detachment may be connected with the theme of timeliness by again appealing to the "responsiveness" of the previous chapter, insofar as a detached mind will be more responsive than one that is attached to things.

The fourth paragraph adds the advice to remain "careful" (慎) throughout a project, not just at the beginning. This serves as an important corrective to the previous advice of "act on things before they become fully formed," just in case anyone thought this means we can just relax, for example, after taking the first step of "(climbing) a height of a thousand feet."

The last paragraph revisits two pieces of advice from earlier chapters, but in pithier form. That we should "desire to not desire (contrivedly)" is explicit in chapters 3, 19, 34, 37, and 57.[5] That we should "learn to not learn (contrivedly)" is explicit in chapters 20 and 48. Both of these are also implicit in other chapters. That we should not "value difficult-to-obtain goods (contrivedly)" is something we saw in chapter 3, with the parenthetical necessary to remind us that it is not the case that sages disdain all rare or expensive things, but rather that they make up their own minds about *what* to value. (As we saw in the translator's note and throughout the *Laozi*, the idea that sages simply have no values or desires is not tenable.) But the "unlearning" has a new referent here: those who engage in "unlearning" "return to that which has been passed over by the masses." Since what has *not* "been passed over by the masses" can be defined as "the norm," and since Laozi throughout this text clearly wants us to critically examine "the norm" and to weigh it against what we genuinely think (chs. 2, 3, 12, etc.), this is a reworded call to open-mindedness and fallibilism, and a challenge, if not to tradition, then to hidebound traditionalism. It also implies that *after* we "unlearn," we need to go back and relearn things as critical thinking adults, and what we should focus on in that relearning is precisely "that which has been passed over by the masses," the things that are "outside the box."

The final line, "In this way they [i.e., sages] assist the naturalness of the myriad things, yet do not presume to be contrived," says that non-contrivance actually "assists"[6] those around you. But we saw this claim, in other words, in chapters 3, 10, 12, 29, 37, 48, and 57.

---

5. By "pithier," I mean that in the Chinese, this chapter's "desire not to desire" (欲不欲) has a certain ring to it that is not found in chapters 3 (無欲), 19 (寡欲), 34 (無欲), 37 (不欲), and 57 (無欲). The same is true with "learning."

6. The word "assist" (輔) appears only here. The word translated as "assisting" (攝) in chapter 50 is a different, albeit synonymous, word.

Chapter 64 | 237

I think the last three paragraphs of this chapter could serve as a pretty good summary of the text as a whole. The subjects of sages and non-contrivance in this chapter are carried over into the next.

Chapter 65

Key Ideas

Sage-rulers keep people "ignorant" (of contrivance); this "mysterious virtuosity" returns all to "great compliance" with the Way.

古之善為道者，非以明民，將以愚之。民之難治，以其「知」多。

故以「知」治邦，邦之賊也；不以「知」治邦，邦之福也。知此兩者，亦稽「式」也。

恆知稽式，是謂「玄德」。玄德深矣，遠矣，與物反矣，乃至大順。

Anciently, those competent at according with the Way[1] did not use it to make people (contrivedly) percipient,[2] but rather to keep them ignorant (of contrivance). That people are difficult to organize is due to their excessive (contrived) "knowledge."

Thus, to organize a state with (contrived) "knowledge" is to rob the state; while to organize a state without (contrived) "knowledge" is to enrich the state. Knowing these two is also to conform with the "model."[3]

---

1. This opening phrase was also used at the beginning of chapter 15.

2. Since this is the only negative use of "percipience" (明) in the *Laozi*, I suspect it may be a mistake for "knowledgeable" (知), but no exemplars support this.

3. The term "model" (式) also appears in chapters 22 and 28.

238

> *To abidingly know to conform with the model is called "myste-rious virtuosity."[4] Mysterious virtuosity is deep, and wide, and along with (all other) things returns,[5] and then arrives at great compliance.*

Chapter 65 Explanation

This chapter extends ideas in the last two sentences of the previous chapter and connects them explicitly to the topic of good government. Those ideas are to "desire to not desire (contrivedly)" and to "learn to not learn (contrivedly)," but here the activities in question are being "(contrivedly) percipient" and having "(contrived) knowledge." Though both having percipience and knowledge are typically aspirational states in early Chinese texts, in the *Laozi*, the former is always aspirational (except here), while the latter is decidedly ambiguous. On the one hand, suspicion of "knowledge" goes back to chapter 2; on the other, in this very chapter we are asked to "abidingly know to conform with the 'model.'" Thus, the first two sentences here, in keeping with the author's occasional predilection for poetic hyperbole, grab the reader's attention. But they also impel the careful reader to

---

4. The phrase "mysterious virtuosity" also appears in chapters 10 and 51.

5. The word "return / cyclical / contrary" (反) is used four times in the *Laozi*: "going far implies (eventual) return" (遠曰反; ch. 25), "Cyclicality is the movement of the Way" (反者道之動; ch. 40), "Truthful words (can) seem contrary" (正言若反; ch. 78), and here. The "return" in chapter 25 is intransitive (i.e., the verb needs no object), but here, while it is grammatically correct to use it intransitively, the reader may still wonder: "Return" to what? Nothing has been "returned" to in this text using this particular verb. I suspect the implied object is "the Way." Or maybe "the model." However, if we look at two other Chinese verbs translated as "return," then that which has been previously "returned" (歸) to are: "nothingness" (無物; ch. 14); "its root" (其根; ch. 16), "it [i.e., the principle of Oneness]" (之; ch. 22), "being as (flexible as) an infant" (於嬰兒; ch. 28), "the limitless" (無極; ch. 28), "the 'uncarved block' (of potentiality)" (樸; ch. 28), "to it [i.e., the Way]" (焉; ch. 34), and "percipience" (明; ch. 52); and that which has been previously "returned" (復) to are: "fate" (命; ch. 16), "to preserve their mother" (守其母; ch. 52), and "that which has been passed over by the masses" (眾人之所過; ch. 64). At least the first three in this list would also work here. Or perhaps this sentence should be: "Mysterious virtuosity is deep and wide and, along with (all other) things, is cyclical." But I don't see how this would fit into the chapter.

240 | The Annotated *Laozi* 老子

seek clarity in context.[6] Here, it is not that "competent" leaders desire to keep those whom they lead in a state of ignorance, but rather they want to keep everyone (including themselves) "ignorant" of contrived "percipience" and "knowledge." (For example, looking back to the previous chapter, if a person "on the cusp of success" were to think it "wise" of them to think that they could at that point slack off, and then they failed: that would be contrived wisdom.)

"To organize a state with" the so-called "knowledge" of—returning to the examples of chapter 2—what is and is not to be defined as "beautiful" and "competent" would be to set up contrived definitions that are not universally applicable, and would thereby "rob" the people of their individual skill sets, their genuineness. Thus, leaders who "conform with the 'model'" are themselves models of leadership and (if we may draw upon the other uses of the idea of the "model" in this text) may count themselves among sages who "embrace the One" (ch. 22) and those who "know the white, but preserve the black" (ch. 28). Returning to the first sentence of this chapter, they are "those competent at according with the Way."

The locution of "mysterious virtuosity" appears in three chapters, and in all three cases, the phrase describes leaders who do not force things upon those whom they lead. Allowing for individuality among the people should, according to this author, result in people who "return" to the Way, which thereby leads to "great compliance" with it. This "compliance" is not unlike the key idea of "conciliatoriness" in the next chapter.

---

6. In this sense, the challenge of understanding such (overly simplified) hyperbole may be akin to appreciating the now-common trope of master-student narratives in literature and film (especially in East Asia) wherein the student must prove himself to the master via feats of heroic (hyperbolic) perseverance before the master even grants him an initial interview. One early example of this is the story of Huike standing for hours in the snow in order to gain the attention of the wall-gazing Bodhidharma.

Chapter 66

Key Idea

Sage-rulers, like the "great states" in chapter 61, lead by being conciliatory and non-contentious, like "servant-leaders."

江海所以能為百谷「王」者，以其善下之：故能為百谷王。
是以聖人欲上民，必以言下之；其欲先民，必以身後之。故其居
　　上而民不重，其居前而民不害。
是以天下樂推而不厭。以其不爭，故天下莫能與之爭。

The reason why rivers and oceans are able to be "kings" of the hundred valleys is that they are competent at being conciliatory[1] toward them: thus are they able to be kings of the hundred valleys.

This is why sages who want to lead people are always conciliatory toward them in speech; and they who want to guide people always follow them in person. Thus, they are treated as leaders, yet the people are not burdened; and they are situated in the vanguard, yet the people are not harmed.[2]

---

1. As in chapter 61, the Chinese words for "conciliatory" and "lead" have root meanings that are much more stark: *xia* 下 and *shang* 上 are literally "below" and "above," but the semantic evolution probably followed the logic of "below → humble → conciliatory" and "above → commanding → lead." The same is true for "guide" and "follow" in the next sentence, which are literally, foundationally, "before" (先) and "after" (後).

2. There are many variations among the earliest exemplars in these two sentences, but the basic meaning is clear.

241

242 | The Annotated *Laozi* 老子

This is why the world delights in encouraging them and does not tire of them. Because they are not contentious, thus no one in the world is able to contend with them.

Chapter 66 Explanation

This chapter returns to the important idea of being "conciliatory" (下), broached in chapter 61, but here the subject is "sages who want to lead people" and "they who want to guide people" rather than "great states" (though this is probably a distinction without a difference), and the metaphors are low-lying "rivers" and "oceans" rather than low-lying "river deltas," reciprocity-facilitating "intersections," and calm "females." The rhetoric is upped a notch by taking something that is already low-lying—"valleys"—and adducing things that are even lower still: "rivers" and "oceans" (a comparison that we saw in chapter 32).

By the same (counterintuitive) logic of equating "kings" with lowliness, so sage-rulers seek to be good leaders by being good followers. People, in general, are creatures that create social hierarchies in which individuals defer to authority, but simultaneously they are also wary of bullies who want to exert control without their consent. The gist of the second through fourth sentences is that sage-rulers have solved this problem. In modern English, the term "servant-leader" is an appropriate touchstone. The final sentence ties such leadership strategies back to the "non-contentiousness" theme from chapters 3, 8, and 22 (and which will reappear in chapters 68, 73, and 81). This kind of counterintuitive "leading by following" trope is expanded in three ways in the next chapter.

Chapter 67

Key Ideas

Three Treasures: compassion in courage, frugality in generosity, not presuming to lead in leadership.

天下皆謂我道大，似不肖。夫唯不肖，故能大。若肖，其細久矣！
我有三寶，持而保之：一曰慈，二曰儉，三曰不敢為天下先。
夫慈，故能勇；儉，故能廣；不敢為天下先，故能成「器」長。
今舍慈且勇，舍儉且廣，舍後且先，則死矣。
夫慈，以戰則勝，以守則固。天將救之，以慈衛之。

Everyone in the world says our Way is great,[1] and seems to have no likeness. Yet it is precisely because it has no likeness that it is able to be great.[2] If it had a likeness, it would have become trivial long ago!

We have three treasures, and we secure and protect them: the first is called compassion, the second is called frugality,[3] and the third is called not presuming to lead the world.

---

1. GD does not have chapter 67 and MWD A is missing these graphs, but MWD B, YZ, XE, HSG, and FY all have "our greatness" (我大), but the ca. 1445 Daozang exemplar has "our Way is great" (我道大). I follow the later evidence because, otherwise, the first two sentences would constitute the tautology of "our greatness . . . is . . . great."

2. MWD A, YZ, HSG, and most others have the opposite: "(Yet) it is precisely because of this greatness that (it) seems to have no likeness" (夫唯大，故似不肖). This makes less sense to me, so I follow MWD B.

3. "Frugality" (儉) appears only in this chapter, but another word translated as "frugality" (嗇) was important in chapter 59 (and appears only in that chapter).

243

244 | The Annotated *Laozi* 老子

The compassionate are thereby able to be courageous, the frugal are thereby able to be generous, and those not presuming to lead the world are thereby able to become leaders of "vessels."[4]

Now, to reject compassion in courage, reject frugality in generosity, and reject following in leadership will result in death.

Compassion in warfare leads to victory and in defense leads to security. For those whom Heaven saves are safeguarded with compassion.

Chapter 67 Explanation

The importance of humility to "greatness" was conveyed in the last chapter by the counterintuitive image of low-lying "rivers and oceans," but in this chapter Laozi reminds us that the best way to conceive the Way is by rejecting all images.[5] After all, what image comes to mind when you think of "gravity"? If your answer is "nothing," then that is what the author wants. But Laozi is nothing if not a poet, and poets deal in metaphorical imagery, hence the empty vessel (ch. 4), the bellows (ch. 5), the valley and the female (ch. 6) and all the rest. Because "the way that can be (fully) conveyed is not the abiding Way" (ch. 1), and because the Way is "great" (chs. 18, 25, etc.), so "our Way is great, and seems to have no likeness." The "likeness" here implies both that it is invisible and that it isn't "like" anything else.[6] The "Yet it is precisely because it has no likeness that it is able to be great" further implies that truly or abidingly "great" things often cannot be adequately represented visually. And not just great things, but people too: we may all have our own individual ideas about who was a "great leader," but we would never come to an agreement about who is the archetypically *best*

---

4. See chapter 28 for a similar metaphorical use of this otherwise-generic word "vessels" (器). *Hanfeizi* chapter 20 and MWD A have "leaders of activities" (事長) instead of "leaders of vessels" (器長).

5. One might be tempted to refer to the Hindu idea of *neti neti*, or the Christian idea of the *via negativa*, but I shall refrain because otherwise, then the Way would have (something of) a "likeness."

6. Laozi didn't know about gravity, of course, and even though it may be a far from perfect analogy, I wonder if the "seems to" in the first sentence wasn't due to the author wondering if someday someone would come up with a metaphor, a "likeness," that he would be happy with.

Chapter 67 | 245

leader, so perhaps it is better to keep that spot vacant, better to agree that such a person has "no likeness."

The following elucidation of the author's "three treasures" brings our attention back to just what we can *do* with this mysterious Way that has "no likeness." The notion of these "three treasures" is as interesting as it is puzzling. It is interesting because it appears to summarize the author's ideas on ideal leadership, which we might remember is only a subset (albeit an important one) of the larger goal of self-cultivation set forth in this book. It is also puzzling because if these three virtues were as important as the characterization "treasures" implies, then why does this brief list show up only here in chapter 67, and why do the three terms used to describe these virtues not appear in the text more often? The first, "compassion" (慈), appears only here and in chapters 18 and 19, where it is part of a pair—"filiality" (孝), from children toward parents, and "(parental) compassion" (慈), from parents toward their children—that is dismissed as contrived in chapter 18. Thus, the generalized meaning of "compassion" as an unambiguous good appears only in this chapter.

The second treasure is "frugality" (儉), which appears only in this chapter, though another word translated as "frugality" (i.e., 嗇) is emphasized in chapter 59.

"Not presuming to lead the world" (不敢為天下先) uses the verb "lead" (先)—extrapolated from its basic meaning of "before" or "at the fore"—only here and in the previous chapter (and perhaps obliquely in chapter 7).[7] "Not presuming" (不敢) has a somewhat longer pedigree in this text, with presumption having been castigated in chapters 3, 30, and 64 (and will be again in chapters 69 and 73), but in none of these instances is the "not presuming" connected to leading. The paucity of these terms that are here lauded so conspicuously raises the question, Why these three, why now?

I would answer this question by noting that while "compassion" occurs in a clearly positive sense only here, the metaphor of the Way as "mother" appears in chapters 20, 25, and 52 (and probably 59), and "(parental) compassion" is therefore implied in those passages. Furthermore, the importance of compassion is clear, even if not specifically articulated, in chapters 27, 49, and 62, with the theme of protecting "incompetent" people; and in chapters 61 and 66, with the theme of being "conciliatory." Second, while

---

7. Chapter 7: "sages put their persons last yet their persons are brought to the fore" (聖人後其身而身先).

246 | The Annotated *Laozi* 老子

"frugality" appears only in this chapter and in chapter 59, it may also be implied by "simplicity" (樸) and "contentedness" (知足), which are virtues that appear quite often in this work. Finally, the theme of "not presuming to lead the world" is quite clear throughout the text.[8]

After positing these "three treasures," the author, as is his wont, goes on to make some counterintuitive connections. The first connects "compassion" with "courage," a virtue that may be universally admired but that appears (explicitly) only here and in chapter 73. But the exhortation to be compassionate *and* courageous right on the heels of advising leaders to lead by being conciliatory is certainly a timely one, at least if one assumes that the norm for leaders, throughout world history, is to lead with (what they hope to be confidence-building) swagger and aggression.

Similarly, "frugality" is connected to "generosity," and "not presuming to lead the world" is connected to becoming "leaders." The author goes on to assert that courageous compassion, generous frugality, and servant-leadership are not only practically effective leadership strategies, but they will also save the leader who practices them from "death" (literal or metaphorical).

The final two sentences return to the first of the three treasures, noting that compassion is effective in the military as well as in government leadership. It closes with the poetically anachronistic assertion that "those whom Heaven saves are safeguarded with compassion." I say "poetically anachronistic" because the Chinese classics, which are older than the *Laozi*, often characterize Heaven as anthropomorphic. Here Heaven is described this way, insofar as it can ostensibly experience the emotion of compassion, a rhetorical move also made in chapter 5, where "Heaven and Earth are not (contrivedly) good" (天地不仁), and in chapter 73, which refers to "that which Heaven finds repellant" (天之所惡). In these instances, I take "goodness" (仁), "compassion" (慈), and finding something "repellant" (惡) as virtues or states of mind that one typically associates with human agency and not with natural processes. But I think they should all be read metaphorically, as there is no real evidence apart from these three passages that Laozi believed in a conscious Heaven with intentionality. The end of chapter 25, which says that "Heaven complies with the Way" (which "complies with itself"), could, I suppose, be read as Heaven *intentionally* complying with the Way, but I do not think so. The implicit virtuosity of being "conciliatory" in this chapter—via compassion and not being presumptuous—is once again made explicit in the next.

---

8. For example, in chapters 10, 42, 48, 51, 60–62, and 66.

Chapter 68

Key Idea

Competence in being an officer, warrior, victor, or employer lies in being conciliatory and non-contentious.

古之善為士者不武，善戰者不怒，善勝敵者不與，善用人者為
之下。
是謂「不爭之德」；是謂「用人之力」；是謂「配天之極」。

Anciently,[1] competent officers were not martial; competent warriors were not impassioned; competent victors over enemies did not (vindictively) engage with them; and competent employers of people were conciliatory toward them.

This is called "the virtuosity of non-contentiousness"; this is called "the power of employing (competent) people"; this is called "the utmost of cooperating with Heaven."[2]

Chapter 68 Explanation

This chapter continues the trend, in recent chapters, of combining unlikely adjectives (e.g., the "frugal generosity" of chapter 67), and ups the ante by

---

1. The XE, FY, and FYY exemplars begin this chapter with "Anciently" (古之), but many others do not and simply begin with "Competent officers."

2. Most exemplars end this chapter with some form of "this is called 'cooperating with Heaven,' the utmost (aspiration) of the ancients" (是謂「配天」，古之極), but I think this was due to a mix-up whereby the "ancient" (古) at the beginning was accidently moved here. My reading preserves the symmetry of having three four-graph sayings at the end of this chapter. It also makes more sense.

247

248 | The Annotated *Laozi* 老子

bringing in the key adjective "competent." It begins with three military examples before pivoting to leadership in general. That is, "officers," "warriors," and "victors" are usually expected to be "martial," "impassioned," and to "engage with" their "enemies" for vindication. (Vindication, to the degree that it may be performative, or driven by outrage rather than safety, could be another kind of contrivance.) Yet, though somewhat counterintuitive, it is also often expected that military people are more effective when they "keep their cool." The dichotomy between, say, being "impassioned" and "cool" is perhaps primarily a rhetorical one, as these two words indicate subjective points on a spectrum of emotion. The *Laozi* exploits this apparent dichotomy by directly challenging it. And, while military conflict is a relatively minor theme in this book, leadership in general is not.

Thus, after the military examples, we come to leaders who are "employers of people." If such employers are competent at their jobs, then they will also be "conciliatory" (i.e., *xia* 下, from chapters 61 and 66) toward their employees, as well as "non-contentious" (from, most recently, chapter 66) with them. It could be that these four examples constitute a hierarchy, from low to high: an official, a warrior, a general, and a king.

It might be possible to connect the last three phrases that open this chapter with the "three treasures" of the previous chapter. Being "not impassioned" could be construed as being "compassionate"; "not (vindictively) engag[ing]" the enemy could be construed as being "frugal" with one's resources; and being "conciliatory toward" the enemy (if we stay with the military context) or toward those whom we employ (if we do not) could be construed as "not presuming to lead the world."

The final line asserts that such leaders are competent not only at effective leadership but also at tapping into the unrealized potential, or "power," of ordinary people. The flourishing of such non-contentious creativity is then described as "the utmost of cooperating with Heaven."[3] The martial figures that begin this chapter also start off the next.

---

3. The phrase "cooperating with Heaven" (配天) appears in this text only here. It too may bring to mind Xunzi's memorable phrase claiming that humans can "form a triad with Heaven and Earth," noted in chapter 25, note 8.

Chapter 69

Key Ideas

Fight only when necessary; be prepared, but not ostentatiously; do not underestimate the opponent; do not rejoice in victory.

用兵有言曰：「吾不敢為主而為客，不敢進寸而退尺。」
是謂「行無行；攘無臂；執無兵；扔無敵。」
禍莫大於輕敵；輕敵幾亡吾寶矣。故抗兵相若，則哀者勝矣。

Those who deploy soldiers have a saying that says: "Better to act the guest than presume to act the host; better to retreat a foot than presume to advance an inch."

This is called "advancing without advancing (recklessly)"; "rolling up the sleeves without (showing) the arms"; "holding on without soldiers"; and "influencing[1] without making enemies."

No misfortune is greater than underestimating the opponent;[2] underestimating the opponent could bring us near to losing our

---

1. The word "influencing" (扔) fundamentally means to "draw toward oneself." In chapter 38 it is translated negatively as "coerce" and here I used the neutral "influencing."

2. MWD A, B and BD have "having no opponent" (无適 for MWD A; 無敵 for MWD B and BD) rather than "underestimating the opponent" (輕敵), both before and after the semicolon. YZ has "underestimating the opponent," while WB's commentary suggests that his exemplar had "having no opponent," but the HSG commentary makes clear that his had "underestimating the opponent." "Underestimating" makes more sense to me, and it is supported by a majority of the texts that I consulted for the base text. (See the appendix for details.)

249

250 | The Annotated *Laozi* 老子

treasure. Thus, when fighting soldiers are evenly matched, then the sympathetic side will win.

Chapter 69 Explanation

This chapter adds to the counterintuitive military observations that characterize the previous two chapters. It begins with a two-part "saying" that was apparently common within the military but then seems to pile on four more pithy observations that may or may not also have been common sayings. The first part of the explicit saying, "Better to act the guest than presume to act the host," matches the advice to be "conciliatory" and not aggressive in the prior chapters. The key word is "presume," which is something we should never do (as we have seen). In addition to that, however, a "host" assumes they are in charge and prepares things before a "guest" arrives, the implication being a leader should not make obvious preparations for war. It advises against what we might call "saber-rattling" in English.

The "better to retreat a foot than presume to advance an inch" is more practical advice, (sometimes) used by military strategists globally.[3] Insofar as no military leader would *always* rather retreat than advance, this hyperbole assumes a *specific kind* of advancing (i.e., the presumptuous kind) that is reckless, whereby the potential rewards are not worth the implied risk. The saying may thus be summarized as: "be careful," advice that fits well with the entire text.

The second sentence is mostly composed of four, grammatically similar, three-graph sayings. "This" refers to the attitude or strategy of the prior line: non-presumptuous action. All four sayings are brief to the point of requiring parenthetical additions or explanation (like much of the *Laozi*). Hence, I infer the "(recklessly)" in the first and "(showing)" in the second. The meaning of the second I take to be: prepare for war, but do so unobtrusively. That is, I take "(showing) the arms" to be a metaphor for "ostentatiously preparing for a fight," so a non-aggressive leader will, to continue the metaphor, "roll up the sleeves" out of sight (or behind their

---

3. Of course, some strategists will sometimes follow the opposite advice to press one's advantage: when given an inch, take a foot. Here, however, the "inch" in question does not seem to be an advantageous inch but rather a precarious (because "presumptuous") one, hence: better to retreat a foot than to claim an inch that may lead to greater losses later. Some hills are not worth dying for.

Chapter 69 | 251

back) to avoid giving the impression of spoiling for a fight. More generally, it may mean to prepare for a task without drawing attention to the fact that you are preparing. The word for "to roll up the sleeves" also appears in chapter 38, where it also presages violence. The final two, "holding on [to power or territory] without soldiers" and "influencing without making enemies," seem fairly self-evident: diplomacy is better than warfare (as we saw in chapter 30).

All this advice—all of these sayings—are predicated on the central piece of advice: "No misfortune is greater than underestimating the opponent."[4] Be prepared; that is: (if need be,) do advance, do roll up your sleeves, do try to hold on to your state, and do try to influence the neighboring states; but do not advance *recklessly*, do not provoke others by *showing* your bared arms, do not use military troops to *forcibly* maintain your state if it is not under attack (from either within or without), and do not make *needless* enemies.

Not following this advice could result in a loss of one's "treasure," which could simply refer to the "treasure" of having a state, or of having a position of power, or it could refer to the "three treasures" articulated in chapter 67, or even to one's own life. But I think the "treasure" here is a metaphor for the Way, as it was in chapter 62. The author then concludes this chapter by saying the difference between winning and losing may well rest on the attitude of the combatants (or, at least, the leaders of the combatants): the careful military leader will likely be one who feels "sympathetic" to those who have lost life or limb, on both sides of the conflict. We saw this in chapter 31, the only other time "sympathy" (哀) appears in this text.

This chapter concludes a several-chapter run on leadership (and the military). The next admits that the advice proffered in the preceding chapters may be well known—what leader, after all, would not agree that presumption and recklessness are bad—but that does not mean that it is commonly followed.

---

4. Chapter 46 defined "misfortune" (禍) as "not knowing contentment"; chapter 58 noted the changeability of misfortune with "fortune is that which misfortune hides in"; and here "misfortune" is defined as "underestimating the opponent." All three can be usefully connected.

Chapter 70

Key Idea

The Way is easily understood and practiced, but usually ignored, because few are without contrived knowledge.

吾言甚易知，甚易行，而天下莫能知，莫能行。
言有宗，事有君，夫唯「無知」：是以不我知。
知我者希，則我貴矣：是以聖人被褐而懷玉。

Our words are very easy to understand and very easy to practice, but (it seems that) no one in the world is able to know or practice them.

(Our) words have an ancestor and (our) activities have a ruler, which is simply to be "without (contrived) knowledge": this is why they do not know us.

Those who know us are few, and thereby we are valued: this is why sages loosely wear coarse clothing but hide (precious) jade within.

Chapter 70 Explanation

This chapter brings a simple paradox of the author's ideas front and center: the values promoted in this book—introspection, non-contrivance, flexibility, open-mindedness, and so on—are widely acknowledged to be good things (who doesn't want to be open-minded?), but despite this, "(it seems that) no one in the world is able to know or practice them." Why this might be the case, the author does not speculate, but I have two opinions. First, the culprit is excessive desire (chs. 19, 34, 37, 46, 57, 64), one result of which

252

Chapter 70 | 253

is contrivance. Or, second, the author apparently thinks it is simply part of the human condition, albeit a part that can be successfully overcome. This diagnosis is the same as, for example, cognitive bias: it is a human trait, but that does not mean we cannot address it and work to counteract it.

The author does not specify what precisely is the "ancestor" or "ruler" of his teachings, but "the Way" would be a smart bet. Some people believe that the cosmos is created and maintained by an anthropomorphic deity; others think the universe is random chaos. Laozi's Way, as I understand it, simply consists of the claims that the cosmos is orderly, that we can know this order, and that we should order our lives in accordance with that order. If the reader does not know these foundational ideas, then "they do not know us."[1]

Since the number of people who believe in anthropomorphic deity creators far outnumber those who do not, both in antiquity and even today, it is certainly the case that "those who know us are few." Be that as it may, the majority of those people would still probably agree with his ideas (of introspection, non-contrivance, etc.) and find them genuinely aspirational. After all, the Daoist's main goals are to reduce selfishness (which is difficult on an individual level), reduce contrivance (which is difficult on a social level), and try to cultivate servant-leaders (which is difficult on both levels). Thus, though "few," such people—we might even call them "idealists"—are nevertheless "valued." We ordinary folks look to them for inspiration.

But being so outnumbered by the majority will naturally make followers of Laozi mindful of their minority status. Hence, such people may well "wear coarse clothing," as befitting a simple and non-contentious lifestyle, "but hide (precious) jade"—these teachings—"within" those clothes. That sages "loosely wear" (被: to toss on, without buttoning) rather than simply "wear" such clothing indicates that they are not actively trying to hide the precious jade that they are carrying. That many people profess to "know" the value of selflessness and non-contrivance, yet few know what it is like to actually realize those ideals, could be the result of a cognitive bias now called the Dunning-Kruger effect, which is outlined in the next chapter.

---

1. Kongzi, similarly, perhaps, said, "No one knows me!" (莫我知也夫!); see *Lunyu* 14.35.

Chapter 71

Key Idea

Fallibilism: knowing when you do not know is best; thinking you know when you do not is a kind of sickness.

知不知：尚矣；不知知：病矣。聖人不病，以其病病。夫唯病病，是以不病。

> *To know (when you) do not know is best, and to not know but (think that you) do know[1] is a (kind of) sickness. Sages are not sick, by means of their being sick of being sick. So only (when you) are sick of being sick: by this (you can) be not sick.*

Chapter 71 Explanation

Fallibilism (or, if you prefer, humility) is integral to the teachings of this text, and the locution here suggests an early instantiation of what would later become known as the "Dunning-Kruger effect," that is, the human tendency for people who know little about a subject to overestimate their knowledge of said subject.[2] Hence: "To know (when you) do not know is

---

1. MWD A has "to not know (that you) do not know" (不知不知), but no other exemplar supports this.

2. See the "key concepts," note 13. Similarly, Kongzi said: "To take that which you know as that which you know, and to take that which you do not know as that which you do not know: this is wisdom" (知之為知之，不知為不知：是知也). *Lunyu* 2.17. Socrates says much the same in Plato's *Apology* 21a–d.

254

Chapter 71 | 255

best, and to not know (but think that you) *do* know is a (kind of) sickness." The remainder of this short chapter takes the metaphor of "sickness" and runs with it. First comes the clever locution of "Sages are not sick, by means of their being sick of being sick." Then their example is extended to the rest of us: "So only (when you) are sick of being sick: by this (you can) be not sick." Recognition of a problem is the first step in fixing it.

Dunning-Kruger is a kind of presumptuousness, which was vilified most recently in chapter 69. This chapter on sages knowing when they don't know is followed by one where they know themselves, which might be another way of saying the same thing.

Chapter 72

Key Idea

Great authority is neither oppressive nor ostentatious.

民不畏威，則大威至矣。無狎其所居，無厭其所生：夫唯不厭，
　是以不厭。
是以聖人「自知而不自見，自愛而不自貴」。故去彼取此。

When the people do not fear authority, then great authority has (already) arrived.[1] Not constraining them where they live, and not oppressing them where they make their livelihood: simply by not oppressing them, they thus will not oppress you.

This is why sages "know themselves but are not ostentatious, care for themselves but are not self-aggrandizing." Thus, they abandon that and adopt this.

Chapter 72 Explanation

Ideally, leaders should be respected but not feared. If you are a leader, that is, a person with "authority," and "people do not fear" you, then you have,

---

1. MWD B has "(When) the people do not fear authority, then great authority *will soon* arrive" (民不畏威，則大將威至矣), but I take this sentence to mean that "great authority" is, by definition, not fearsome to the people. "Authority" (威) appears only here. *Wei* 畏 means both "fearful" (as in chs. 17, 53, 72, 74) and "reverent" (chs. 15, 20); I chose "fear" here because ch.17 describes four kinds of leaders, and the third kind was the one that people "feared," and I'm not sure what "(When) the people do not revere authority, then great authority has (already) [or 'will (soon)'] arrive" would mean, unless "great" was construed negatively.

256

Chapter 72 | 257

at least in part, succeeded at leadership. Laozi, in chapter 17, described four types of leaders, and the ones that are "feared" were third. (The best are trusted, the second best are praised, the third are feared, and the worst are insulted.) So getting people to fear you is not the goal here.[2] This idea may be connected to the theme of fallibilism in the previous chapter, insofar as leaders who are feared are typically quite confident in their own opinions (even when they are quite unjustified in that confidence). How should leaders ensure that those who are being led do not fear them?

This chapter provides two answers. First, do not "constrain" or "oppress" them, neither at home nor at work. Advising leaders against constraining or oppressing people is related to advising them to be "conciliatory," as in chapters 61, 66, and 68. Second, while leaders should be self-aware and have self-respect,[3] they should not thereby be "ostentatious" (自見, which we saw as "advertise themselves" in chapters 22 and 24) or "self-aggrandizing" (自貴, which appears nowhere else, but literally means to "honor themselves"). This balanced advice seems aimed squarely at authoritarian leaders.

The closing sentence, "Thus, they abandon that [i.e., those ostentatious practices used by bad leaders] and adopt this [i.e., this humble and unassuming Way that nevertheless results in 'great authority']," is the third and final use of this locution (after chapters 12 and 38). Constraining and oppressing people is also a kind of presumptuousness, which is again explicitly criticized in the next chapter.

---

2. This may be directly opposed to Machiavelli's dictum for leaders: "It is better to be feared than loved, if you cannot be both."

3. To have self-respect, that is, to "care for" oneself, was a theme in chapters 13 and 44.

Chapter 73

Key Ideas

Heaven finds presumptuousness repellent; it is not contentious, but it is competent at responding and is inclusive.

勇於敢則殺，勇於不敢則活。此兩者或利或害。天之所惡，孰
　知其故？
天之道，不爭而善勝，不言而善應，不召而自來，默然而善謀。
　「天網」恢恢，疏而不失。

The courage to be presumptuous may result in death, while the courage to not be presumptuous may result in staying alive. Of these two, one is beneficial and one is harmful. About that which Heaven finds repellent: Who knows the reason?[1]

The way of Heaven is not contentious yet is competent at succeeding; does not speak yet is competent at responding; does not beckon yet everything comes to it naturally; and is silent[2] yet competent at advising. "Heaven's net" is wide: it reaches far but does not lose anything.

---

1. Most later exemplars, from HSG on, add "This is why (even) sages seem to find this perplexing" (是以聖人猶難之), which appears in chapter 63 as "This is why sages seem to find things difficult." However, MWD B, BD, YZ, and XE do not have it, so I omit it.

2. Other exemplars say "relaxed" (繟然) instead of "silent" (默然).

258

Chapter 73 Explanation

The target in this chapter is "presumptuousness" (敢), which plays a negative role in several other chapters but here takes center stage as the villain.[3] It is counterintuitively juxtaposed with the (normally) good virtue of "courage," a word that occurs only here and in chapter 67. "Presuming" may not be as ostensibly bad as the "constraining" and "oppressing" people in the previous chapter, but they are surely related. The first sentence makes the claim that, in the natural world—which includes humans—"courage" that has morphed into its related cousin recklessness (a kind of presumptuousness) often results in "death," while being conciliatory often results in a longer life. Though I suspect the primary referent of this "death" is the metaphorical "death" of one's project or career, it probably can also refer to literal, physical death.[4] In any case, the next sentence walks the rhetoric back somewhat by saying "presumptuousness" is, if not a death sentence, then at least "harmful." It is probably no accident that presuming to know things that you do not in fact know was described as a "sickness" in chapter 71 (even though the word "presumptuous" does not occur there).

"Heaven," that is, nature (or at least the Yang-active half of the natural Heaven-Earth cosmos, though sometimes Heaven is used to represent both), according to the author, "prefers" those who are not presumptuous to those who are, much as the text prefers "conciliation" (chs. 66, 68) to "arrogance" (chs. 9, 29, 30). But it is interesting to note that Laozi does not know *why* this should be the case.[5] His "who knows the reason?" for this natural preference is amplified in later exemplars with "(even) sages seem to find this perplexing" (see this chapter's note 1). Nevertheless, according to

---

3. To "presume" (敢) appears in chapters 3, 30, 64, 67, 69, 73, and 74.

4. Since Darwin, "staying alive" translates to greater reproductive fitness, and hence if the author's claim is true, "not presuming" could be considered an adaptive trait that has been naturally selected. I'm not qualified to weigh in on whether "one is beneficial and one is harmful," but the claim does not seem far-fetched to me, especially if one narrows the field of inquiry to human societies.

5. It is interesting because philosophical (and, even more so, religious) ideologies typically seem to present themselves as having all the answers. This confidence is part of their attraction.

260 | The Annotated *Laozi* 老子

Laozi's observations, it is the case, and he proceeds to adduce four claims that he counts as evidence.

"The way of Heaven," code for the natural principles that order the cosmos, "is not contentious . . . does not speak . . . does not beckon . . . and is silent," yet "is competent at succeeding . . . competent at responding . . . everything comes to it naturally; and is . . . competent at advising." That natural principles are not contentious, do not speak or beckon, and are silent, seems uncontroversial; it is the actions ascribed to them that draw our attention.

Of the four things that the "way of Heaven" does, only that its natural principles "succeed" (勝) is unsurprising. The other three are metaphorically anthropomorphic to various degrees. That nature "responds" (應) to things (without talking) is only marginally so: we might say that when I let go of a cup in midair, gravity "responds" by bringing it crashing to the floor. That "everything comes to it naturally" (自來) requires more imagination, insofar as natural principles are inescapable, so there was never a time when anything could be "away" from them such that it could "come back" to them. Still, we might imagine that a given animal will try out various modes of activity—being cautious and then trying out recklessness, for example—and after finding the former to be more effective, it will "come back" to being cautious "naturally."

The final aspect, however, is the most interesting, insofar as it seems to suggest ethical realism rather pointedly. On the one hand, we might construe the "advising" (謀)[6] as a metaphorical way of, to take the example in the previous sentence, impelling the animal to "come back" to being cautious. But on the other, we might take the "advising" to refer to the possibility of extrapolating from one situation to another: that we humans might observe that being cautious and conciliatory simply works better in animal communities and extrapolate from that observation to the "advice" that we "ought" therefore to avoid presumption in our dealings with others.[7] Which is to say, Heaven is "advising" us to emulate it in finding presumptuousness "repellent." Such a reading would be a clear case of ethical realism.

---

6. "Advising" (謀) appears only here and in chapter 64 (as "plan for").

7. A defender of "Hume's guillotine" (see "key concepts," note 18) will object that "works better" is subjective and that there is nothing objectively "better" in a dysfunctional society that soon collapses than in a functional one that persists. A defender of ethical realism will counter that individual well-being and communal harmony are, in fact, objectively "better."

Chapter 73 | 261

The author ends with the (admittedly, question-begging, but still poetic)[8] observation that " 'Heaven's net' is wide: it reaches far but does not lose anything." This veiled advice to extrapolate from "the way of Heaven," from nature, to be socially inclusive and intellectually open-minded, clearly sets the stage for the next chapter.

---

8. Claiming that Heaven, as nature, "does not lose anything" begs the question insofar as the "anything" that nature does not lose are only those things that nature has not, in fact, lost. The things that nature *has* lost—all the mutations that were not naturally selected, all the species that went extinct due to natural causes—might beg to differ with this claim.

Chapter 74

Key Idea

Against capital punishment: do not execute in place of the "chief executioner," not even the wily.

若民不畏死，奈何以殺懼之？若使民恆畏死，而為奇者，吾將得
　而殺之，夫孰敢矣？
恆有「司殺者」。夫代「司殺者」殺：是代大匠斲也。夫代大匠
　斲者，希不傷其手矣。

If the people do not fear death, then how will you scare them with execution? If you want to cause the people to abidingly fear death, then those who are wily,[1] we could seize and kill them, and who would presume (to be wily) then?[2]

But there already is an abiding "chief executioner." To act in place of the "chief executioner" in executing (people): this would be like taking the place of a great carpenter in chopping (wood). Those who would take the place of a great carpenter in chopping (wood) rarely avoid injuring their own hands.

---

1. "Wily" (奇) is also used in chapters 57 (where it seems to be used in both positive and negative senses) and 58 (where it is used in either a neutral or negative sense).

2. Kongzi also rejected the killing of bad people; he was in favor of a charismatic, good leader who will influence bad people like wind on grass. See *Lunyu* 12.19.

Chapter 74 Explanation

The previous chapter was on the natural superiority of caution and concil-iation over presumption, concluding with the image of "Heaven's net" as being so wide that it includes everyone. In this chapter, "everyone" is shown to include even those who might otherwise be killed by the state. It begins with two seemingly enigmatic statements. The first, "If the people do not fear death, then how will you scare them with execution?" immediately raises the question: Who is the author talking about, since everyone fears death? One answer may be found in the following chapter, where "people treat death lightly" because their leaders are selfish and they overtax the people. That is, bad leaders can make life not worth living for those whom they lead.[3] Desperate people take chances, sometimes reckless ones. From the leader's point of view, there are two solutions to such a problem: buckle down or lighten up.

The second sentence hypothesizes the "buckle down" approach: "If you want to cause the people," who currently do *not* fear death, "to abidingly fear death, then" let's lower the bar for applying the death penalty even to "those who are wily." The point of this sentence, then, is: "Rulers, do your citizens not fear you (i.e., your punishments)? Then don't just kill the really bad people, kill *everyone* that dares to even be 'wily.' That'll teach 'em a les-son." If we buckle down like that, "who would presume (to be wily) then?"

That's (the somewhat sarcastic) plan A, but it would require a lot of killing, even including people who are simply "wily." So the author rolls out plan B: systemic capital punishment always runs the risk of executing innocent people, and this risk increases as the bar for applying the death penalty is lowered. In fact, why don't we just eliminate this risk by eliminating capital punishment? The metaphor the author uses might be summarized as "if you play with sharp knives, sooner or later you'll cut yourself." But his metaphor is much grander, with a "chief executioner" instead of a "sharp knife." And thereby a new metaphor for the Way is born. Previous metaphors include the cuddly, comforting image of "the mother," and the lofty, cosmic image

---

3. It is worth remembering that the author was writing about a monarchical political system, so "voting out" a bad leader wasn't an option. Only naked revolution, in which the participants would *really* have to not fear death, was possible for ordinary citizens.

264 | The Annotated *Laozi* 老子

of "the One." Here the Way is "chief executioner," and we would be wise to allow it to make such life-and-death decisions, rather than our (sometimes presumptuous) political leaders. The next chapter continues the theme of why desperate people might sometimes take risky actions.

Chapter 75

Key Ideas

Leaders: do not overtax the people or overemphasize yourselves; the uncontrived life is worthier than just being alive.

> 人之飢，以其上食稅之多：是以飢。
> 百姓之難治，以其上之有為：是以難治。
> 民之輕死，以其上求生之厚：是以輕死。
> 夫唯無以生為者，是賢於貴生。

The hunger of the people is due to their leaders eating too much in taxes: this is why there is hunger.

The difficulty in organizing the people is due to their leaders being contrived: this is why there is difficulty in organizing.

(Thus,) the people[1] treating death lightly is due to their leaders seeking to overemphasize their own lives: this is why there is the treating of death lightly.

Only those who do not live contrivedly are more worthy than those who value life.

Chapter 75 Explanation

If it were up to me, I might reverse the order of chapters 74 and 75, insofar as the latter provides context for the former. (Though the last sentence here

---

1. As previously noted, I translate *ren* 人 (people, humans), *bai xing* 百姓 (the hundred clans), and *min* 民 (the people) all as "the people" in these first three sentences; HSG and many later exemplars use *min* 民 (the people) for all three.

265

266 | The Annotated *Laozi* 老子

does provide an excellent segue to chapter 76.) In any case, this chapter begins by explaining "the hunger of the people," which "is due to" overtaxation by "their leaders." The second sentence assesses the culpability of such leaders when "organizing [i.e., governing] the people" becomes "difficult." The author turns the looking glass around and places the blame on "leaders being contrived," a prognosis one should expect by now from this author. The contrivance of leaders leads to "difficulty in organizing" because such leaders set up contrived ideas as ideals without those ideals being truly universal, or even widespread.[2]

The third sentence directly addresses the premise of the previous chapter. It extrapolates from the specific examples given in the first two sentences—overtaxation and contrivance—and restates the problem more broadly as "leaders seeking to overemphasize their own lives." Thus, the first three sentences provide three answers to the problem of an unhappy populace: overtaxation, contrivance on the part of their leaders, and the selfishness of their leaders.

Similarly, the final sentence echoes the second sentence's theme of non-contrivance but also articulates a "moral" for this story that is as stark as is it generalized: valuing life is normally a good thing—after all, the point of chapters 74–75 seems to be how to get oppressed people to value life again—but it is not the *best* thing. In what might be construed as a twist on Socrates' claim that "the unexamined life is not worth living," Laozi here concludes that "the contrived life is simply not as good as the uncontrived life."[3] This is as blunt as this author ever gets about what is perhaps his central tenet. In the context of citizens who treat "death lightly" in the face of an overbearing ruler or government, perhaps a hyperbolic restatement of the moral of this chapter should be "live free or die." The theme of death is continued in the next chapter.

---

2. For example, chapter 2 referred to contrived ideas of "competence." If we posit a leader who defines "success" solely in terms of "making money," without any ethical component, then that could certainly cause "difficulty in organizing." Chapter 65 says, similarly: "That people are difficult to organize is due to their excessive (contrived) 'knowledge.'"

3. Laozi does not use the word "good" here but rather "worthy" (賢), which appears only in chapters 3, 75, and 77. The Socrates quote is from Plato's *Apology* 38a5–6.

Chapter 76

Key Idea

Supple flexibility is superior to stiff rigidity, though both may have their uses.

人之生也柔弱，其死也堅強。萬物草木之生也柔脆，其死也枯槁。

故堅強者「死之徒」也，柔弱者「生之徒」也。

是以兵強則滅，木強則折。故強大居下，柔弱居上。

People in life are flexible and supple, in death they are rigid and stiff. The myriad things, including plants and trees, in life are flexible and tender, in death they are wilted and withered.

Thus, the rigid and stiff are "disciples of death" and the flexible and supple are "disciples of life."[1]

This is why when soldiers are stiff[2] they are vanquished, and when trees are stiff they fracture.[3] Thus, the stiff and great are situated below, while the flexible and supple are situated above.

---

1. These two phrases, "disciples of life" and "disciples of death," are also used in chapter 50.

2. The word "stiff" (強) here is a double entendre: it means both "stiff," in contrast to "flexible," yet also means "to force" (as in chs. 15, 25, 30, etc.). So soldiers that are inflexible will not succeed, but also soldiers that force themselves on the populace of an occupied territory may not last for long. The word also has a positive sense, as in chapter 3: "*strengthen* the bones" (強其骨), and chapter 33: "those who conquer themselves are *strong*" (自勝者強).

3. This reading derives from *Huainanzi* chapter 1; early *Laozi* exemplars are unanimous in having "do not succeed" (不勝) instead of "are vanquished" (滅), but they differ, incompatibly, on variora for "fracture" (折).

267

268 | The Annotated *Laozi* 老子

Chapter 76 Explanation

The virtue of being "flexible" has been constant throughout this text. It is implicit in the advice to "abide in formlessness" (ch. 1), insofar as the "formless to form and back to formless" cycles[4] require flexibility in dealing with change and the unknown. It is implicit in the "relativity" of beauty and competence (ch. 2), insofar as one must be flexible to acknowledge that different people and cultures may have different ideas of things like beauty and competence. A "flexible will" is specifically articulated in chapter 3, and the metaphors of the "infant" (chs. 10, 28) and "water" (chs. 8, 78) are both employed to denote flexibility. In this chapter, flexibility is associated with "life," an observation that includes "people" as well as "plants and trees" and, indeed, all of "the myriad things."

The author then returns to two phrases used in chapter 50, "the disciples of death" and "the disciples of life," and connects them to flexibility and the lack thereof. Then the virtue of flexibility is applied to the military—a referent in several recent chapters—and to "trees," in both cases decrying inflexibility.

Finally, the chapter closes with what I think is a triple entendre: "Thus, the stiff and great are situated below, while the flexible and supple are situated above." It seems to me that with this simple observation Laozi is simultaneously commenting on trees, armies, and leaders. For trees, the same Chinese graphs (i.e., 強大居下，柔弱居上) can be read: "strong and big (roots and trunks) are below; flexible and supple (branches and leaves) are above." For soldiers (or armies): "inflexible bulkiness is inferior; flexible nimbleness is superior." (Armies, as we saw in chapters 30, 31, 57, and 69, should be unobtrusive and not overbearing.) And for leaders: "the strong and mighty should abide in conciliation; the flexible and supple should abide in leadership." This last reading for leaders, unlike for trees and soldiers, does not contrast the inferior former with the superior latter but reads *both* in a positive manner. For leaders, the more they are in strong and mighty positions, the more they should practice conciliation. (We saw this in chapters 61 and 66.) Conversely, the more flexible and supple a person is, the more they are suited to becoming a leader. Thus, in a neat Yin-Yang balance, both

---

4. "Cycles" in the plural because they are both cosmological and psychological.

Chapter 76 | 269

"conciliation" (下) and "leadership" (上)—literally "below" and "above"—are harmonized.[5] This same rhetorical move of combining opposites is also used in the opening paragraph of the next chapter.

---

5. This triple entendre would be obviated if "great" (大) were removed; XE and FY have "rigid and stiff" (堅強) instead of "stiff and great" (強大), in which case there is only one meaning: rigid and stiff are always bad.

Chapter 77

Key Idea

The way of Heaven, unlike the way of humans, aims at equality: reducing excess and increasing that which is insufficient.

天之道，猶張弓者。高者抑之，下者舉之；有餘者損之，不足
者補之。
天之道，損有餘而補不足。
人之道，則不然：損不足，以奉有餘。
孰能有餘以奉天下？唯有道者。是以聖人「為而弗恃，成功而弗
居」：其不欲見賢。

The way of Heaven is like the stretching of a bow. Those who aim high will lower it, and those who aim low will raise it; just as those who have excessive (tension) will reduce it, and those who have insufficient (tension) will increase it.

The way of Heaven reduces excess and increases what is insufficient.

The way of humans is not like this: it reduces what is (already) insufficient in order to raise up what is (already) excessive.

Who is able to take excess to raise up everyone in the world? Only those with the Way. This is why sages "act, but without expectation; complete tasks, but without dwelling (on them)":[1] they do not desire to show off their worthiness.

---

1. These two phrases also appear in chapter 2; similar phrasing is used in chapters 10 and 51.

270

Chapter 77 Explanation

The theme of flexibility in chapter 76 is immediately conjured here with the image of "the stretching of a bow." But in this chapter, the author extrapolates from the virtue of flexibility to the practical (if unspecified) steps needed to aspire to some kind of egalitarianism. Two steps are noted in the archery metaphor: moving the position of the string-pulling hand and adjusting the tautness of the bowstring. Thus, "Those who aim high will lower it [i.e., the string-pulling hand], and those who aim low will raise it," and "those who have excessive (tension) [in their bowstrings] will reduce it, and those who have insufficient (tension) will increase it." The second articulation of "the way of Heaven" makes clear that it is not only flexible but also equalizing: it "reduces excess and increases what is insufficient." Although we have already seen a metaphorically intentional, anthropomorphic Heaven in this text, this need not be taken as implying intentionality, insofar as there are many self-regulating systems in nature: think ecosystems where animals reproduce to fill their niche but will not succeed if they exceed what the environment has to offer.

The third paragraph contrasts the way of Heaven with "the way of humans" and notes that the latter "is not like" the former. Humans capitalize on natural hierarchies and exacerbate the resulting inequalities.[2] Thus, the second half of the chapter deals with the prospect of egalitarianism in human society. People, the author avers, are "unnatural" in the sense that they are (or can be) egregiously selfish. That is, human selfishness goes well beyond the instinct for self-preservation that characterizes all animals. Humans often do not just take what they need: they (often) take from others even when they already have enough. However, this raises the question: Is Laozi against the hierarchies that result from natural meritocracies, or does he simply think that the inequalities that result from hierarchies can be ameliorated by tweaking the way meritocracies function? I think it must be the latter.

---

2. Cf. Matthew 13:12: "For to those who have, more will be given, and they will have an abundance; but from those who have nothing, even what they have will be taken away." This peculiar idea is repeated in Matthew 25:29. The "Matthew Effect," as a sociological problem, was coined by Robert Merton in 1968. Laozi is referring precisely to this "Matthew Effect," insofar as he is talking about material possessions; Matthew, on the other hand, may have been talking about spiritual understanding.

272 | The Annotated *Laozi* 老子

Laozi has elsewhere excoriated selfishness (chs. 19, 58, 75); here he focuses on a selfishness that perversely "reduces what is (already) insufficient in order to raise up what is (already) excessive."

"Who is able to take excess to raise up everyone in the world? Only those with the Way." The author does not articulate the specific *means* by which a sage-ruler would redistribute "excess" wealth. They seem to be implying that (excessively) unfair economic hierarchies are not the natural consequences of fair play but are rather enabled—or, at least, exacerbated—by selfish leaders. I also don't know the *extent* to which Laozi is advocating the redistribution of wealth, but it is clear that the first step in any such plan is to curb selfishness by curbing ostentatiousness. Thus, the sage's selflessness is described, using two phrases that we saw in chapter 2, in: "This is why sages 'act, but without expectation; complete tasks, but without dwelling (on them).'" The second piece of advice here is akin to that in chapter 9: "When the task is accomplished and you then retire: this is the way of Heaven." Thus, "worthy" people, those who are truly successful, "do not desire to show off their worthiness." As the next chapter shows, good leaders are not only not ostentatious, they also positively accept blame for others.

Chapter 78

Key Ideas

Leaders should be flexible and willing to accept ignominy and misfortune on behalf of the state.

天下莫柔弱於水，而攻堅強者莫之能先：其無以易之。
故柔之勝剛，弱之勝強，天下莫不知，而莫能行。
故聖人之言云：「受邦之垢，是謂社稷之主；受邦之不祥，是
　謂天下之王。」
正言若反。

Nothing in the world is more flexible and supple than water, yet nothing can surpass it for assailing what is rigid and stiff: it has nothing that can replace it.[1]

Thus, the flexible overcomes the inflexible, and the supple overcomes the stiff, and though everyone in the world knows this, none seem to be able to practice it.

Thus, a saying of the sages says: "Those who will accept the ignominies of the state can (truly) be called rulers of the soil and grain altars;[2] while those who will accept the misfortunes of the state can (truly) be called kings of the world."

Truthful words can seem contrary.

---

1. The word "easy / change / replace" (易) occurs eleven times in the *Laozi* (chs. 2, 63, 64, 70, 78), and in every instance except this one, it means "easy." Even here it could be read as "it has nothing that is easier than it."

2. These were the main altars of the state and a symbol of its status. This phrase appears in the *Laozi* only here.

274 | The Annotated *Laozi* 老子

Chapter 78 Explanation

This chapter continues the theme of flexibility in the previous two chapters (and elsewhere). In chapter 76 the image of "flexible and supple" living things was used; here it is water, an image last used in chapter 8. While water's flexibility needs no explanation, that "nothing can surpass it for assailing what is rigid and stiff" directs our attention to how something as apparently flimsy as water can, with time, cut through even solid rock: "the flexible overcomes the inflexible." Persistence pays off. But, as the author notes, this isn't rocket science: "everyone in the world knows this."

Exactly why "none seem to be able to practice it" is hinted at in the following sentence. People are social animals, so no one likes to "accept . . . ignominies," especially when they aren't a result of your own actions. Should you be humble enough to accept responsibility for your own mistakes, that is, of course, great. But should you be humble enough to accept responsibilities for those under your leadership, that is, if you are willing to "accept the ignominies of the state," then you potentially have a career in community leadership.

A third step, however, is reserved for those willing to "accept the misfortunes of the state." That is, for those willing to accept responsibility even for bad luck that may be the fault of no one. There is precedence for such an attitude in early China, but it is still an unusual claim.[3] Although "Heaven" is not here specified as the entity responsible for such "misfortunes," it is nevertheless a reasonable assumption. And whether one takes "Heaven" to be an anthropomorphic entity or to be a cipher for "nature," the message is clear: great leaders take responsibility even for events that are out of their control. Sometimes life isn't fair, and hence this advice may "seem contrary" to our sense of fairness, but retaining the trust of those one leads is crucial for effective leadership. If those you lead want you to retain your leadership role even after an unforeseeable calamity, they will let you know. The leadership advice in this chapter continues in the next.

---

3. *Shang shu* 尚書, chapter 12: In response to an extended drought, Shang King Tang addressed Heaven, and said: "If my person has fault, may it not extend to the myriad directions, and if those in the myriad directions have faults, may my person bear them" (朕身有罪，無及萬方；萬方有罪，朕身受之). Tang's prayer is recorded in many early texts, including the *Lunyu*, *Mozi*, *Shizi*, and *Lüshi chunqiu*.

Chapter 79

Key Idea

Competent people are generous and flexible enough to consider extenuating circumstances to forgive debts.

和大怨，必有餘怨：安可以為善？報怨以德。
是以聖人「執左契」，而不責於人。故有德司契，無德司徹。
天道無親，恆與善人。

In harmonizing great resentment, there always (seems to) be leftover resentment: how can this be considered competent? By requiting resentment with virtuosity.[1]

This is why sages "hold the left tally"[2] but do not (always) hold the people accountable. Thus, those with virtuosity manage tallies, while those without virtuosity manage repayments.

The Heavenly way has no favorites, but it abides with competent people.

---

1. I have taken the phrase "By requiting resentment with virtuosity" (報怨以德) from chapter 63 and inserted it here, where it makes more sense. No exemplars support this move; I am following the suggestion of Yan Lingfeng, who was following the suggestions of Chen Zhu 陳柱 and Ma Xulun 馬敘倫. But Chen and Ma thought the phrase belonged at the beginning of this chapter, while Yan, as well as Chen Guying, thought it belonged after "leftover resentment," and I think it belongs where I put it. I put it there because I think this phrase both answers the question "how can this be considered competent?" and is the referent for "This" in "This is why sages." Yan Lingfeng 嚴靈峰, *Laozi dajie* 老子達解 (臺北: 華正書局, 1992 [1971]), 337, note 3 (where he cites Ma), and 405, note 1 (where he cites Chen).

2. That is, those who are the creditor in a creditor-debtor loan agreement.

276 | The Annotated *Laozi* 老子

Chapter 79 Explanation

This chapter builds on the previous chapter's themes of flexibility and of leaders taking responsibility even for problems they did not create. It opens with a question about conflict resolution—one unenviable task of leaders— where "there always (seems) to be leftover resentment." The "(seems)" must be added, because sometimes conflicts *can* be resolved fairly and amicably. But not always. When there is "leftover resentment," what should competent leaders—or, really, competent people in general, including those involved in potentially resentment-making disputes—do about this? Laozi answers with a rule of thumb: "By requiting resentment with virtuosity."[3] But what does that mean?

The example in the second paragraph is one of debt, and we might suppose that this includes debts both real and imagined. Either way, the best way forward may well be to "not (always) hold the people [i.e., the people who are liable to become resentful] accountable." Which is to say: sometimes generosity and forgiveness are the best solutions.[4]

But the implicit Yin-Yang analytic that permeates this text, as well as the flexibility inherent in individual virtuosity, means that the "requite resentment with virtuosity" rule of thumb is only a rule of thumb, not an immutable rule. In chapter 41, I explained the phrase "established virtuosity may (sometimes) appear lazy" by noting that, in dealing with others (and oneself too), sometimes one needs a "kick in the pants" and other times a "hug." This is certainly the case here: I do not think that Laozi is saying all debts should always be forgiven if those who "hold the right tally," the debtors, display the slightest degree of resentment. One of life's balancing acts involves noting that justice and mercy are not compatible, insofar as justice is when people get what they deserve, while mercy is when people

---

3. *Lunyu* 14.34 has someone ask about a reworded version of this saying (i.e., here it is 報怨以德, while in the *Lunyu* it is 以德報怨, but the meaning is the same), but Kongzi rejects it, saying, "Requite resentment with uprightness, and requite virtuosity with virtuosity" (以直報怨，以德報德). It is possible that Kongzi was responding to Laozi in the *Lunyu*, but it is also possible that this was just a common saying.

4. Cf. *Lunyu* 15.15: "Those who require much of themselves, yet require a lighter responsibility from other people, will keep resentment far away!" (躬自厚，而薄責於人， 則遠怨矣！) This idea also underlies the story of Feng Xuan 馮諼, a tax collector for Lord Mengchang (孟嘗君), in *Zhanguo ce* 戰國策 chapter 11, who "bought" goodwill via forgiving debt.

Chapter 79 | 277

get less (punishment) than they deserve. Circumstances always matter, and "competence," as we saw in chapter 2, will vary from person to person and situation to situation.

This chapter recognizes that not all people are equally responsible-minded, that not everyone can be trusted to complete their tasks in a competent fashion. People fall short for a wide variety of reasons, and no explanation is given for *why* the debtor cannot pay their debt, so the range of possible excuses must remain broad. But sometimes, for some people, their debts should be forgiven. Thus, "those with virtuosity" will be flexible enough to take into account extenuating circumstances, while "those without virtuosity" will not, and, like Dickens's Ebenezer Scrooge, will always demand "repayments."

That the "Heavenly way has no favorites" might, again, be taken as evidence for understanding Heaven as an anthropomorphic entity (given that having "favorites" implies intentionality), but it may equally be taken as evidence that Heaven is another word for "nature" (as nature is, we might say, non-partisan). It is similar to the "Heaven and Earth . . . take the myriad things to be as straw dogs" in chapter 5. If the latter, which is how I take it, then that this way "abides with competent people" is simply another way of saying competent people are flexible, and flexible people are (or, at least, can be) effective and, thereby, long-lasting. Competence is a theme that runs throughout the *Laozi*, and we will meet it again in the final chapter, but first, the next chapter will paint a picture of a simple, but competent, community.

Chapter 80

Key Ideas

Have a small and simple state, with a small and unostentatious army, where people are delightful, safe, and content.

小邦寡民，使民有什伯之器而不用；使民重死而不遠徙。

雖有舟輿，無所乘之；雖有甲兵，無所陳之。使民復結繩而用之。

甘其食，美其服，樂其俗，安其居。鄰邦相望，雞犬之聲相聞，民至老死，不相往來。

In small states with few people, let the people have instruments for a thousand troops, and they will not use them; have the people take death seriously, and they will not move far away.[1]

Then, though they may have boats and vehicles, no one will ride them; and though they may have armor and weapons, no one will display them. Have the people return to knotting rope (for calculating) and use that.

---

1. As I read this sentence, an implied ruler is the subject of "let the people" and "have the people" and the people themselves are the subjects of "will not use" and "will not move." But others read the implied ruler as the subject of all four verbs, such that the ruler "will not (allow the people to) use" their weapons and "will not (allow the people to) move" far away. In this case, change the "and" to "but" in both phrases (i.e., "Let the people have instruments . . . but do not let them use them"). Though the grammar certainly allows it, I find such a dictatorial ruler to be incongruent with the rest of this text.

278

(They will then) make their food tasty, their clothes beautiful, their customs delightful, and their houses safe. Then, though such neighboring states may be mutually visible, with even the sound of their chickens and dogs mutually audible, the people will grow old and die without ever having visited each other.[2]

Chapter 80 Explanation

This brief ode to a simple life lived in a small and simple state begins by stipulating two things fundamental to life and death, Yin and Yang. The first specifies having "instruments [i.e., weapons, armor, etc.] for a thousand troops." These instruments of death provide security for protecting life. Second, "have the people take death seriously," which is to say: value life.[3] A ruler can cause the people to value life precisely by following the advice in this book, advice that includes not glorifying war (ch. 31), leading with non-contrivance and simplicity (ch. 37), being a "disciple of life" (ch. 50), avoiding overtaxation (chs. 53, 75), being frugal (ch. 59), being conciliatory (ch. 61), and being flexible and forgiving (ch. 79).

If the people are secure and value life, then they (hopefully) will not feel the need to "use" their weapons. Neither will they want to "move far away," because they are content where they are. Given the secure and life-affirming foundation laid in the first sentence, the rest of this chapter paints a picture of contentment.

The second paragraph is a little hyperbolic, but nevertheless poetic. In saying "though they may have boats and vehicles, no one will ride them," the author is only exemplifying a kind of perfect contentment and is not saying that content people are not curious about other places. I suspect he means "no one will ride them" *in order to* "move far away," because they like it where they are. The "though they may have armor and weapons, no one will display them," is more realistic, though, because despite having armed troops for protection from external threats, absent such threats, said arms should not be displayed, lest they be mistaken by those neighbors

---

2. These two sentences appear, almost verbatim, in *Zhuangzi* chapter 10.

3. The subject of how people treat death is in chapters 50, 74, 75, and 76, but the subject of valuing life runs throughout the text.

280 | The Annotated *Laozi* 老子

as threatening. Warfare is serious business, and the ruler as well as "the people [should] take death seriously." The reference to "knotting rope (for calculating)" symbolizes a simple life, akin to a modern woodworker using hand tools rather than power tools. I don't think Laozi is antitechnology—he prizes individualism too much for that—but he does value simplicity. I think of the "knotting rope" image as akin to the rustic, *wabi-sabi* type of "imperfect" pottery that is still prized by some today.

Simplicity, however, should not be mistaken for joyless austerity, insofar as "(they will then) make their food tasty, their clothes beautiful, their customs delightful, and their houses safe."[4] The final sentence also should not be taken to imply that such people are incurious or lethargic; rather, this is simply a portrait of rural contentment. It may be romantic, and perhaps even naive, but it is also aspirational. The contentment of this chapter is reiterated with the non-contentiousness of the next, the last.

---

4. It may be worth noting that the "X 其 Y" locution of these phrases is identical to the "blunt the sharpness" or "block the openings" phrases in chapters 4, 52, and 56. If so, then these may be the Yang exterior activities that accompany those Yin interior ones.

Chapter 81

Key Ideas

Competent people are not always eloquent or educated; sages give to others and are not contentious.

信言不美，美言不信。
知者不博，博者不知。
善者不辯，辯者不善。
聖人不積，既以為人，己愈有；既以與人，己愈多。
天之道，利而不害；聖人之道，為而不爭。

Trustworthy words are not (always) beautiful, and beautiful words are not (always) trustworthy.

Those who know are not (always) broadly learned, and those who are broadly learned do not (always) know.

Competent people are not (always) persuasive, and persuasive people are not (always) competent.[1]

Sages do not accumulate, since the more they do for others, the greater their gain; and the more they give to others, the greater their abundance.

---

1. "Persuasive" (辯) also means "eloquent," as it is translated in chapters 19 and 45, in "disregard (contrived) eloquence" (棄辯) and "great eloquence may seem stammering" (大辯若訥), but here I think "eloquence" would be too similar to "beautiful words." The word also means "disputatious," so some read this sentence as "Competent people are not (always) disputatious, and disputatious people are not (always) competent." I went with "persuasive" because "beautiful" and "broadly learned" have positive connotations, while "disputatious" does not, so I think "persuasive" fits the counterintuitive context better.

281

282 | The Annotated *Laozi* 老子

> *The way of Heaven benefits but does not harm; the way of sages acts but is not contentious.*

Chapter 81 Explanation

This text closes on the same note in which it began, with a kind of language skepticism indicated by unusual word pairings.[2] The first point in this chapter is that people sometimes mistake a confident speaker with a truthful one. "Trustworthy words are not" necessarily "beautiful," not necessarily eloquent. The second sentence notes that wisdom is not always dependent on education and that education does not always result in wisdom. Thus, the wise—"those who know"—are not necessarily those with advanced degrees; they in fact "are not (always) broadly learned." The author is not denigrating broad learning but is rather noting that wisdom and education are not *necessarily* linked: there are uneducated wise people and educated stupid people. The same is true for persuasiveness and competence.

After contrasting three pairs of ideas (trustworthiness-beauty, wisdom-education, competence-persuasiveness) that we should associate with one another only with a degree of skepticism, the chapter concludes with the two themes that we have seen throughout the text: selflessness and non-contentious beneficence. This selflessness, however, is not only one that actively helps others but is also one that counts helping others as a measure of one's own success. Here the rhetorical device is a final Yin-Yang pairing—"giving" and "gaining"—that makes for a counterintuitive association. I'm not sure if "the more you give, the more you get" is an established saying in English, but if it isn't, it should be. (Although, in true Yin-Yang style, we might remember that "the more you give, the more they'll take" is also trenchant advice, but Laozi is definitely something of an optimist.) Thus, for sages, "the more they give to others, the greater their abundance," is a fitting penultimate sentence for a text like this one.

The final sentence returns to a couple of common themes in this book: "the way of Heaven" and "the way of sages," which by now should be seen to overlap, in contradistinction to the selfish "way of humans" in chapter 77. The former way "benefits" (利) others (as we saw in chapter 73, there translated as "beneficial"), and the latter way "is not contentious" (不爭)

---

2. In chapter 1, these are "the way" and "the abiding Way," "a name" and "an abiding name," and "form" and "formlessness."

Chapter 81 | 283

(as we saw in chapters 22 and 66). Not being contentious—that is, being agreeable and not antagonistic—is a theme that has run throughout the *Laozi*. Chapter 3 says "not celebrating worthies (contrivedly)" will lead us to "not become contentious." Chapter 8 notes both that "water is competent at benefiting the myriad things while not being contentious" and that "simply not being contentiousness: thus one can be without fault." Chapters 22 and 66 claim that "not being contentious" has the effect that "no one in the world is able to contend with" such people. Chapter 68 connects "non-contentiousness" with being "conciliatory" (下), with being "not martial" (不武) and "not impassioned" (不怒). And chapter 73 says that "the way of Heaven is not contentious yet is competent at succeeding." Thus, reading chapters 73 and 81 together, we see that not being contentious is an attribute of both the way of Heaven *and* the way of sages.

This already is a fitting denouement, but a closer look reveals two final connections. This concluding chapter closes the book with advice for us to be trustworthy, knowledgeable, competent, simple, and generous. Despite beginning the first chapter with "The way that can be (fully) conveyed is not the abiding Way," the Way that Laozi *has* conveyed, even just in this final chapter, is perhaps pretty close to it.

And finally, the first and fourth sentences in this chapter both connect back, ouroboros-like, to chapter 1: language skepticism in the first sentence, and an ethical twist on formlessness in the fourth. That is, in chapter 1, "The way that can be (fully) conveyed is not the abiding Way," is similar to saying the "beautiful words" of the *Laozi* "are not (always) trustworthy." How could they be, given that "a name that can be (fully) descriptive is not an abiding name"? Nevertheless, I suppose many readers will agree that the author made a valiant attempt to create a narrative that is both beautiful and as trustworthy as possible. And in chapter 1, formlessness was connected to introspection (through which we may "observe" the Way's "wonders"), while here in chapter 81, in a final example of ethical realism, the sage's selflessness mirrors that same cosmic formlessness. "This togetherness, we call it 'mysterious'" (ch. 1).

Appendix

The Chinese Text

The *Laozi* is a kaleidoscopic text: its earliest exemplars manifest a dizzying display of variora. I studied biblical text criticism with Hans Dieter Betz at the University of Chicago, a field in which earlier is always better, on the assumption that there is always (or, at least, typically) a single author who wrote an urtext that was subsequently lost and that it was the job of later scholars to reconstruct. I later studied early Chinese text criticism with Li Ling at Beijing University, a field in which earlier is not always better, on the assumption that there (often, maybe even usually) was *not* a single author, and no urtext, but rather "polymorphous" texts that were created over centuries by the hands of several unknown redactors.[1]

As with many other ancient texts, including even the Bible, there is no single, unproblematic, "original" edition of the *Laozi* available to us now, and it's likely that there is not, and perhaps never has been, a single-author urtext that we can "reconstruct."[2] I said in the introduction that I do not see a problem with the theory of a single author based on the content of the text. So what accounts for all the variation? I imagine several possibilities (though there may be more): One, there was a single-author urtext, but later followers and scribes felt free to edit and rewrite the text (perhaps to add "clarity," or to fit changing linguistic expectations, or to fit differing

---

1. For more on this, see Paul Fischer, "Authentication Studies (辨偽學) Methodology and the Polymorphous Text Paradigm," *Early China* 32 (2008–2009): 1–43.

2. For a relatively brief overview of the major exemplars of the *Laozi*, see Bill Boltz's entry in Michael Loewe, ed., *Early Chinese Texts: A Bibliographical Guide* (Berkeley: Society for the Study of Early China, 1993), 269–92. His account does not include the Guodian or Beida exemplars, which were discovered after he wrote it.

286 | The Annotated *Laozi* 老子

philosophical inclinations). Two, there never was a single-author urtext, but rather the text is a compilation by a number of different anonymous authors. Three, there was a single author, but no urtext; rather, Laozi, or some "old scholar," transmitted their thoughts verbally to a number of students, and some of these students took notes and their notes varied. For those who favor an "oral transmission" theory, then teacher(s) and students could have repeated the text orally for decades or even centuries before various people wrote them down. Four, there was a single author, but no urtext; rather Laozi, or some "old scholar," wrote multiple versions of their text over the course of their career (perhaps inadvertently making small changes along the way, or perhaps intentionally catering to different audiences). Perhaps it was a combination of all these scenarios.

In any case, a *Laozi* translator has two options: either choose one exemplar from among many, or consider the variora among a certain number of exemplars and thereby create a base text. Since I don't know how I could justify choosing one exemplar from all the rest, especially given the archeologically recovered finds of the last five decades, I chose the second option.

Some people refer to a more or less "standard" Wang Bi 王弼 (226–249) "edition," but unfortunately there is no agreed-upon Wang Bi edition. I discovered this for myself when I began to create my base text by comparing four exemplars of a putative Wang Bi version: two that are old and authoritative, and two that are from contemporary scholars who both have done careful work on the *Laozi*. These are the Daozang and SBBY exemplars, along with the works of Chen Guying and Rudolf Wagner. While comparing those four, I also brought in six exemplars that have been archeologically recovered in the last fifty years, as well as two traditional exemplars (Yan Zun and Heshang Gong), and a single-volume, side-by-side comparison of about eighteen early exemplars. When relevant, I also considered implicit and explicit *Laozi* quotes in the *Hanfeizi* 韓非子 (ca. 230 BCE), *Huainanzi* 淮南子 (139 BCE), and other early sources. I also have a stack of Chinese translations (that is, translated from ancient Chinese to modern Chinese) and another stack of English translations that I considered.[3] For my translation, the two modern translations that I consulted most often were by Ames

---

3. There is also a mountain of scholarly articles, stretching back decades. If you are a student looking for a place to start, I might recommend Liu Xiaogan 刘笑敢, ed., *Dao Companion to Daoist Philosophy* (New York: Springer, 2015).

4. Roger Ames and David Hall, trans., *Dao De Jing: "Making This Life Significant"; A Philosophical Translation* (New York: Ballantine, 2003).

Appendix | 287

and Hall (2003)[4] and Li Ling 李零 (2008).[5] Thus, while the following list could be much longer, these are the exemplars I compared and considered (remember that older is not necessarily better, except when variora make equal sense, then I usually went with older):[6]

> ca. 300 BCE / 1993 Guodian (GD) A 郭店甲:[7] chapters 2, 5, 9, 15, 16, 19, 25, 30, 32, 37, 40, 44, 46, 55–57, 63, 64, 66 (not in this order).
>
> ca. 300 BCE / 1993 Guodian (GD) B 郭店乙: chapters 13, 20, 41, 45, 48, 52, 54, 59 (not in this order).
>
> ca. 300 BCE / 1993 Guodian (GD) C 郭店丙: chapters. 17, 18, 31, 35, 64 (not in this order).
>
> ca. 230 BCE *Hanfeizi* 韓非子 (HFZ) chapter 20 (解老): chapters 38, 58–60, 46, 14, 1, 50, 53, 54, 67, 53, 54; HFZ chapter 21 (喻老): chapters 46, 54, 26, 36, 63, 64, 52, 71, 64, 47, 41, 33, 27.
>
> ca. 168 BCE / 1973 Mawangdui (MWD) A 馬王堆甲:[8] all eighty-one chapters with chapters 38–81 (with 41–40, 66–80–81–67 order) then chapters 1–37 (with 21–24–22–23–25 order).

---

5. Li Ling 李零 (1948–), *Ren wang dichu zou: Laozi Tianxia diyi* 人往低处走; 老子: 天下第一 (People moving toward the lowly; Laozi: the world comes first) (北京: 三联书局, 2008).

6. Two more works that I found especially helpful were Yan Lingfeng 嚴靈峰 (1904–1999), *Laozi dajie* 老子達解 (*Laozi* thoroughly explained) (臺北: 華正書局, 1992 [1971]), and Zhu Qianzhi 朱謙之 (1899–1972) and Ren Jiyu 任繼愈 (1916–2009), *Laozi shiyi* 老子釋譯 (*Laozi* explained and translated) (臺北: 里仁書局, 1985). In the following list, two dates separated by a forward slash indicate the approximate date of composition followed by the date of discovery (so the Guodian texts date to about 300 BCE and they were excavated in 1993). The list of chapters refers to the chapters that are in each exemplar. The "order" refers to chapter orders that differ from the traditional eighty-one-chapter order (so the Mawangdui texts begin with chapter 38 and end with chapter 37). The "combined" refers to chapters that certain exemplars combine that are not combined in the traditional eighty-one-chapter order (so the Beida text combines what are traditionally chapters 78–79 into one chapter).

7. All three Guodian exemplars are in Jingmen bowuguan 荊門博物館, eds., *Guodian Chu mu zhujian* 郭店楚墓竹簡 (Bamboo texts from a Chu grave at Guodian) (北京: 文物出版社, 1998).

8. Both Mawangdui exemplars are in Guojia Wenwuju Guwenxian yanjiushi 国家文物局古文献研究室, eds., *Mawangdui Han mu boshu* 马王堆汉墓帛书 (Silk texts from a Han grave at Mawangdui), vol. 1 (北京: 文物出版社, 1980). For both Guodian and

288 | The Annotated *Laozi* 老子

ca. 168 BCE / 1973 Mawangdui (MWD) B 馬王堆乙: all eighty-one chapters with chapters 38–81 (with 41–40, 66–80–81–67 order) then chapters 1–37 (with 21–24–22–23–25 order).

ca. 100 BCE / 2009 Beida (BD) 北大:[9] all eighty-one chapters with chapters 38–81 (with 78–79 combined) then chapters 1–37 (with 6–7, 17–19, 32–33 combined).

ca. 24 BCE Yan Zun (YZ) 嚴遵 (ca. 80 BCE–10 CE):[10] chapters 38–81 only (with 39–40, 57–58A, 58B–59, 67–68, 78–79 combined) + fragments from chapters 1–36.

ca. 250 CE Wang Bi (WB) 王弼 (226–249)[11] notes (but notes are contested: compare, for example, SBBY and Wagner).

ca. 250 CE Xiang Er (XE) 想爾 (notes to chapters 3–37 only).

ca. 400 CE Heshang Gong (HSG) 河上公 (dates contested)[12] notes.

ca. 600 CE Fu Yi (FY) 傅奕 (ca. 558–639) "ancient text" (古本) exemplar, possibly dating to ca. 200 BCE.

ca. 700 Jinglong (JL) 景龍 stele (708).

ca. 735 Xuan Zong (XZ) 玄宗 (r. 712–756) exemplar.

ca. 1200 Fan Yingyuan (FYY) 范應元 (thirteenth century) edition of Fu Yi's "ancient text" (古本) exemplar.

ca. 1445 *Daozang* (DZ) 正統道藏 exemplar.[13]

Mawangdui exemplars, I often consulted Daan Publishing 大安出版社, Laozi *sizhong* 老子四種 (Four types of *Laozi*) (臺北: 大安出版社, 1999), the four types being Guodian, Mawangdui, Wang Bi, and Heshang Gong.

9. Beijing daxue chutu wenxian yanjiusuo 北京大學出土文獻研究所, eds., *Beijing daxue zang Xi Han zhushu* 北京大學藏西漢竹書 (Western Han bamboo texts in the Beijing University collection), vol. 2 (上海古籍出版社, 2012).

10. Wang Deyou 王德有, ed., *Laozi zhi gui* 老子指歸 (Pointers on returning to *Laozi*) (北京: 中華書局, 1994 [1983]).

11. This putative "text" is what I was trying to ascertain with my comparison of the DZ, SBBY, Chen, and Wagner exemplars, but another authoritative source is Lou Yulie 樓宇烈 (1934–), *Wang Bi jijiaoshi* 王弼集校釋 (Wang Bi collected, collated, and explained) (臺北: 中華書局, 1992 [1980]).

12. Wang Ka 王卡 (1956–), Laozi Daodejing *Heshang Gong zhangju* 老子道德經河上公章句 (Heshang Gong's notes to Laozi's *Virtuosity of the Way classic*) (北京: 中華書局, 1993; 1997).

13. *Chongbian yingyin Zhengtong Daozang* 重編影印正統道藏 (京都市: 中文發行 and 台北市: 大化經銷, 1986 [昭和61]), vol. 11, 8673–88. The ctext website (https://ctext.org/dao-de-jing/zh) describes its source as the *Daozang* Wang Bi exemplar (i.e., 《正統道藏》本王弼註道德真經), which I think is the same text.

Appendix | 289

ca. 1930; 1980 *Sibu beiyao* (SBBY) 四部備要 exemplar.[14]

1970; 2000 Chen Guying 陳鼓應 (1935–) exemplar and translation.[15]

1973 Shima Kunio 島邦男 (1908–1977) collation of exemplars.[16]

2003 Rudolf Wagner (1941–2019) exemplar and translation.[17]

The following takes the *Daozang* exemplar as a base text and notes my emendations. For reasons of space, I could not explain my reasoning for these emendations. New evidence and new theories will no doubt change my reasoning in the future.

Chapter 1:
   1. 常 → 恆: four times

Chapter 2:
   1. 較 → 形
   2. 傾 → 盈
   3. 前 → 先
   4. 處 → 居
   5. 萬物作焉而不辭，生而不有，為而不恃，成功而弗居。夫唯弗居，是以不去 → 萬物作焉而弗辭，為而弗恃，成功而弗居。夫唯弗居，是以弗去

Chapter 3:
   1. 使心不亂 → 使民心不亂
   2. 常使民 → 恆使民
   3. 天 → 知
   4. 不敢為也 → 不敢不為

---

14. The *Laozi* 老子 and *Zhuangzi* 莊子 volume of the *Sibu beiyao* 四部備要 collection (上海: 中華書局, 1927–1935; rpt. 臺北: 中華書局, 1980).

15. Chen Guying 陳鼓應 (1935–), Laozi *jinzhu jinyi* 老子今註今譯 (臺北: 臺灣商務印書館, 1970; 3rd ed., 2000).

16. Shima Kunio 島邦男 (1908–1977), Laozi *jiaozheng* 老子校正 (*Laozi* collated correctly) (Tokyo: 汲古書院, 1973). He collated two YZ, four XE, three WB, two "ancient text," four HSG, and three XZ exemplars.

17. Rudolf Wagner, *A Chinese Reading of the* Daodejing: *Wang Bi's Commentary on the* Laozi *with Critical Text and Translation* (Albany: State University of New York Press, 2003).

290 | The Annotated *Laozi* 老子

Chapter 5:
1. 不如守中 → 不若守中

Chapter 6:
1. 天地根 → 天地之根

Chapter 8:
1. 處 → 居
2. 故幾於道 → 故幾於道矣
3. 正 → 政

Chapter 9:
1. 如 → 若
2. 堂 → 室
3. 天之道 → 天之道也

Chapter 10:
1. 能嬰兒乎 → 能如嬰兒乎
2. 玄覽 → 玄鑒
3. 國 → 邦
4. 能無知乎 → 能無為乎
5. 生而不有，為而不恃，長而不宰 → 生而弗有，為而弗恃，長而弗宰

Chapter 13:
1. 貴以身為天下 . . . 愛以身為天下 → 貴以身為天下者 . . . 愛以身為天下者
2. 若可寄天下 . . . 若可託天下 → 若可以託天下矣 . . . 若可以寄天下矣

Chapter 14:
1. 能知古始 → 以知古始

Chapter 15:
1. 士 → 道
2. 容 → 客
3. 渙兮若冰之將釋 → 渙兮若釋
4. 孰能安以久動之徐生 → 孰能安以動之徐生
5. 故能蔽不新成 → 故能蔽而新成

Chapter 16:
1. 吾以觀復 → 吾以觀其復
2. 各復歸其根。歸根曰靜，是謂復命 → 各復歸其根，曰靜，靜曰復命

Appendix | 291

3. 復命曰常，知常曰明 → 復命，常也，知常，明也
4. 公乃王，王乃天 → 公乃全，全乃天

Chapter 17:
1. 悠兮 → 猶乎
2. 功成事遂，百姓皆謂我自然 → 成功遂事，而百姓曰我自然

Chapter 18:
1. 智慧出，有大偽 → omit
2. 有仁義 . . . 有孝慈 . . . 有忠臣 → 焉有仁義 . . . 焉有孝慈 . . . 焉有正臣
3. 國 → 邦

Chapter 19:
1. 絕聖棄智 . . . 絕仁棄義 → 絕知棄辯 . . . 絕偽棄詐
2. 此三者 → 此三言
3. 故令有所屬 → 故令之有所屬

Chapter 20:
1. 善之與惡 → 美之與惡
2. 相去若何 → 相去何若
3. 如享太牢，如春登臺 . . . 如嬰兒 → 若享太牢，若春登臺 . . . 若嬰兒
4. 我獨怕兮其未兆 → 我泊焉未兆
5. 我愚人之心也哉 → 我愚人之心也
6. 澹兮其若海 → 忽兮若海
7. 飂兮若無止 → 飂兮若無所止

Chapter 21:
1. 忽兮恍兮 → 惚兮恍兮
2. 其精甚真 → 冥兮窈兮
3. 其中有信 → 其中有真
4. 眾甫之狀哉 → 眾甫之然哉

Chapter 23:
1. 故從事於道者，道者，同於道 → 故從事於道者，同於道
2. 同於道者，道亦樂得之；同於德者，德亦樂得之；同於失者，失亦樂得之 → 故同於德者，道亦得之；同於失者，道亦失之

Chapter 24:
1. 處 → 居

292 | The Annotated *Laozi* 老子

Chapter 25:
1. 獨立不改 → 獨立而不改
2. 強為之名曰大 → 吾強為之名曰大

Chapter 26:
1. 是以聖人終日行 → 是以君子終日行
2. 不離輜重 → 不離其輜重
3. 而以身輕天下 → 而以身輕於天下

Chapter 27:
1. 善行 . . . 善言 . . . 善數 . . . 善閉 . . . 善結 → 善行者 . . . 善言者 . . . 善數者 . . . 善閉者 . . . 善結者
2. 常善救人 . . . 常善救物 → 恆善救人 . . . 恆善救物
3. 故無棄人 → 而無棄人
4. 善人者 . . . 不善人者 → 善人 . . . 不善人
5. 雖智大迷 → 雖知必大迷

Chapter 28:
1. 常 → 恆: three times

Chapter 29:
1. 將欲取天下而為之 → 將欲取天下而為之者
2. 或歔或吹 → 或呴或吹
3. 或挫或隳 → 或培或墮

Chapter 30:
1. 師之所處 → 師之所居
2. 善有果而已 → 故善者果而已

Chapter 31:
1. 夫佳兵者 → 夫兵者
2. 有道者不處 → 有道者不居
3. 恬淡為上 → 恬憺為上
4. 勝而不美，而美之者 → 故不美也，若美之
5. 是樂殺人 → 是樂殺人也
6. 則不可以得志於天下矣 → 不可以得志於天下矣
7. 吉事尚左 → 故吉事尚左
8. 偏將軍居左 → 是以偏將軍居左
9. 言以喪禮處之 → 言以喪禮居之

Chapter 32:
1. 常 → 恆
2. 天下莫能臣也 → 雖小，天下莫能臣

Appendix | 293

Chapter 33:

1. 智 . . . 明 . . . 有力 . . . 強 . . . 富 . . . 志 . . . 久 . . . 壽也 → 智也 . . . 明也 . . . 有力也 . . . 強也 . . . 富也 . . . 志也 . . . 久也 . . . 壽也

Chapter 34:

1. 大道汎兮 → 大道氾兮
2. 萬物恃之而生而不辭 → 萬物恃之以生而弗辭
3. 功成不名有 → 成功而弗名有
4. 衣養 → 愛養
5. 常無欲 → 恆無欲
6. 以其終不自為大 → 是以聖人以其終不自為大

Chapter 35:

1. 安平大 → 安平太
2. 出口 → 出言
3. 用之不足既 → 用之不可既

Chapter 36:

1. 將欲歙之 → 將欲翕之
2. 必固興之 → 必固舉之
3. 將欲奪之 → 將欲取之
4. 國之利器 → 邦之利器

Chapter 37:

1. 道常無為 → 道恆無為
2. 夫亦將無欲 → 夫亦將不欲

Chapter 38:

1. 下德為之而有以為 → omit
2. 忠信之薄，而亂之首 → 忠信之薄也，而亂之首也
3. 前識者，道之華，而愚之始 → 前識者，道之華也，而愚之首也
4. 處其厚不居其薄，處其實不居其華 → 居其厚不居其薄，居其實不居其華

Chapter 39:

1. 萬物得一以生 & 萬物無以生，將恐滅 → omit
2. 侯王得一以為天下貞 → 侯王得一以為天下正
3. 地無以寧，將恐發 → 地無以寧，將恐癈
4. 侯王無以貴高 → 侯王無以正
5. 是以侯王自稱 → 是以侯王自謂

294 | The Annotated *Laozi* 老子

6. 故致數譽無譽 → 故至譽無譽

7. 琭琭如玉，珞珞如石 → 琭琭若玉，珞珞若石

Chapter 40:

1. 反者道之動；弱者道之用 → 反者道之動也；弱者道之用也

2. 天下萬物 → 天下之物

Chapter 41:

1. 勤而行之 → 勤能行之

2. 故建言之 → 是以建言有之

3. 若 → 如: eight times

4. 太白 → 大白

Chapter 43:

1. 馳騁天下之至堅 → 馳騁於天下之至堅

Chapter 44:

1. 是故甚愛必大費 → 甚愛必大費

2. 知足不辱 → 故知足不辱

Chapter 46:

1. 禍莫大於不知足；咎莫大於欲得 → 罪莫厚於甚欲，咎莫憯
於欲得，禍莫大於不知足

2. 常足矣 → 恆足矣

Chapter 47:

1. 不出戶知天下；不闚牖見天道 → 不出於戶，可以知天下；
不闚於牖，可以知天道

2. 不見而名 → 不見而明

Chapter 48:

1. 為學日益，為道日損 → 為學者日益，為道者日損

2. 取天下 → 將欲取天下者

3. 常以無事 → 恆以無事

Chapter 49:

1. 聖人無常心 → 聖人恆無心

2. 德善 ... 德信 → 德善也 ... 德信也

Chapter 50:

1. 人之生 → 而民之生生

2. 動之死地，十有三 → 動之死地，亦十有三

3. 以其無死地 → 以其無死地焉

Chapter 51:
1. 夫莫之命常自然 → 夫莫之命而恆自然
2. 故道生之 → 道生之
3. 亭之毒之 → 成之熟之
4. 生而不有，為而不恃，長而不宰 → 生而弗有，為而弗恃，長而弗宰

Chapter 52:
1. 既知其母 → 既得其母
2. 復知其子 → 以知其子
3. 沒其不殆 → 沒身不殆
4. 是為習常 → 是謂襲常

Chapter 54:
1. 善建不拔 → 善建者不拔
2. 子孫以祭祀不輟 → 子孫祭祀不輟
3. 修之於國 . . . 以國觀國 → 修之於邦 . . . 以邦觀邦
4. 吾何以知天下然哉 → 吾何以知天下之然哉

Chapter 55:
1. 含德之厚 → 含德之厚者
2. 猛獸不據，攫鳥不搏 → 攫鳥、猛獸不搏
3. 全作 → 朘怒

Chapter 56:
1. 解其分 → 解其紛
2. 不可得而疎 . . . 不可得而害 . . . 不可得而賤 → 亦不可得而疏 . . . 亦不可得而害 . . . 亦不可得而賤

Chapter 57:
1. 以正治國 → 以正治邦
2. 天下多忌諱 → 夫天下多忌諱
3. 國家滋昏 . . . 奇物滋起 . . . 盜賊多有 → 而邦滋昏 . . . 而奇物滋起 . . . 而盜賊多有
4. 人多伎巧 → 人多知巧
5. 故聖人云 → 是以聖人之言曰

Chapter 58:
1. 其日固久 → 其日固久矣
2. 光而不燿 → 光而不耀

Chapter 59:
1. 是謂早服 → 是以早服

296 | The Annotated *Laozi* 老子

Chapter 60:
1. 國 → 邦

Chapter 61:
1. 國 → 邦: nine times
2. 大國者下流，天下之交，天下之牝 → 大邦者：天下之下流也，天下之交也，天下之牝也
3. 牝常以靜勝牡 → 牝恆以靜勝牡
4. 以靜為下 → 以其靜故為下也
5. 則取大國 → 則取於大邦
6. 大者宜為下 → 則大者宜為下

Chapter 62:
1. 萬物之奧，善人之寶，不善人之所保 → 萬物之奧也，善人之寶也，不善人之所保也
2. 不如坐進此道 → 不如坐而進此道
3. 以求得 → 求以得

Chapter 63:
1. 味無味 → 知無知
2. 報怨以德 → move to Chapter 79
3. 天下難事 . . . 天下大事 → 天下之難事 . . . 天下之大事
4. 夫輕諾必寡信，多易必多難 → 夫輕諾者必寡信，多易者必多難

Chapter 64:
1. 為之於未有，治之於未亂 → 為之於其未有，治之於其未亂
2. 千里之行 → 百仞之高
3. 常於幾成 → 恆於幾成
4. 則無敗事 → 則無敗事矣

Chapter 65:
1. 智 → 知: three times
2. 國 → 邦: four times
3. 國之賊 . . . 國之福 . . . 亦稽式 → 邦之賊也 . . . 邦之福也 . . . 亦稽式也
4. 常知稽式 → 恆知稽式
5. 然後乃至大順 → 乃至大順

Chapter 66:
1. 欲先民 → 其欲先民

Appendix | 297

2. 是以聖人處上 → 故其居上
3. 處前而民不害 → 其居前而民不害

Chapter 67:
1. 夫唯大，故似不肖 → 夫唯不肖，故能大
2. 若肖久矣。其細也夫 → 若肖，其細久矣
3. 慈故能勇 → 夫慈故能勇
4. 死矣 → 則死矣

Chapter 68:
1. 善為士者 → 古之善為士者
2. 配天古之極 → 配天之極

Chapter 69:
1. 用兵有言 → 用兵有言曰
2. 扔無敵；執無兵 → 執無兵；扔無敵
3. 輕敵幾喪吾寶 → 輕敵幾亡吾寶矣
4. 故抗兵相加 → 故抗兵相若則

Chapter 70:
1. 天下莫能知 → 而天下莫能知
2. 則我者貴 → 則我貴矣
3. 是以聖人被褐懷玉 → 是以聖人被褐而懷玉

Chapter 71:
1. 知不知上 → 知不知尚矣
2. 不知知病 → 不知知病矣
3. 夫唯病病，是以不病。聖人不病，以其病病，是以不病 →
聖人不病，以其病病。夫唯病病，是以不病

Chapter 72:
1. 則大威至 → 則大威至矣
2. 自知不自見，自愛不自貴 → 自知而不自見，自愛而不自貴

Chapter 73:
1. 是以聖人猶難之 → omit
2. 繟然 → 默然

Chapter 74:
1. 民不畏死 → 若民不畏死
2. 奈何以死懼之 → 奈何以殺懼之
3. 常畏死 → 恆畏死
4. 吾得執而殺之，孰敢 → 吾將得而殺之，夫孰敢矣

298 | The Annotated *Laozi* 老子

5. 常有司殺者殺。夫司殺者，是大匠斲 → 恆有司殺者。夫代司殺者殺，是代大匠斲也

6. 希有不傷其手矣 → 希不傷其手矣

Chapter 75:

1. 民之飢 → 人之飢
2. 民之難治 → 百姓之難治
3. 以其求生之厚 → 以其上求生之厚

Chapter 76:

1. 死之徒 . . . 生之徒 → 死之徒也 . . . 生之徒也
2. 兵強則不勝，木強則共 → 兵強則滅，木強則折
3. 強大處下，柔弱處上 → 故強大居下，柔弱居上

Chapter 77:

1. 其猶張弓與 → 猶張弓者
2. 為而不恃，功成而不處 → 為而弗恃，成功而弗居

Chapter 78:

1. 莫之能勝 → 莫之能先
2. 弱之勝強，柔之勝剛 → 故柔之勝剛，弱之勝強
3. 莫能行 → 而莫能行
4. 是以聖人云 → 故聖人之言云
5. 國 → 邦: two times
6. 社稷主 → 社稷之主
7. 受國不祥，是謂天下王 → 受邦之不祥，是謂天下之王

Chapter 79:

1. 報怨以德 → inserted here from Chapter 63
2. 有德司契 → 故有德司契
3. 常與善人 → 恆與善人

Chapter 80:

1. 國 → 邦: two times
2. 使有什伯之器 → 使民有什伯之器
3. 安其居，樂其俗 → 樂其俗，安其居

Chapter 81:

1. 善者不辯，辯者不善。知者不博，博者不知 → 知者不博，博者不知。善者不辯，辯者不善

Index

abandoned (癈): chs. 18, 39

abandon that and adopt this (去彼取此): chs. 12, 38, 72; *also*: discard, dismiss

abide, abiding, always, often, usually (恆): chs. 1, 3, 27 (always), 28, 32, 34, 37, 46, 48 (usually), 49, 51, 61 (often), 64 (often), 65, 74, 79

abide, abiding (常): chs. 16, 52, 55

above, best, high, lead, leader (上): chs. 8 (highest), 14 (above), 17 (leaders), 31 (best; commanding), 38 (lofty), 41 (best, lofty), 66 (lead, leaders), 75 (leaders), 76 (above)

achieve, extensively (致): chs. 10 (achieving), 14 (extensively), 16 (achieve), 39 (achieved)

accomplish (遂): chs. 9 (功遂: task is accomplished), 17 (遂事: accomplishes activities)

accountable (責): ch. 79

accumulate, ingrained (積): chs. 59 (ingrained), 81 (accumulate)

activities, serve (事): chs. 2, 8, 17, 23, 30, 31, 48, 52, 57, 59 (serve), 61 (serve), 63, 64, 70

adaptivity, clothes (服): chs. 53 (clothes), 59 (adaptivity), 80 (clothes)

added to, advantages, more, overwhelms (益): chs. 42 (added to), 43 (advantages), 48 (more), 55 (overwhelms)

advance, advancing (進): chs. 41, 62, 69

advertise, display, manifest, show off (見): chs. 3 (display), 19 (manifest), 22 (advertise), 24 (advertise), 77 (show off); *also*: ostentatious; *note*: 見 also means "see"

advising, plan for (謀): chs. 64 (plan for), 73 (advising)

agitated, movement (躁): chs. 26 (agitated), 45 (movement)

alive (活): ch. 73

alone (or detached) (獨): chs. 20, 25

ambitions, determination, will (志): chs. 3 (will), 31 (ambitions), 33 (determination)

ancestor (宗): chs. 4, 70

ancient, the ancients, antiquity (古): chs. 14, 15, 21, 22, 62, 65, 68

anxiety (憂): ch. 20

arise, incite (作): chs. 2 (arise), 16 (arise, incite), 37 (arise), 63 (arose)

armed, armor (甲): chs. 50, 80

arrogant, arrogance (驕): chs. 9, 30

artifice (詐): ch. 19

299

300 | Index

ascending (登): ch. 20

assailing (攻): ch. 78

assiduously, effort, toil (勤): chs. 6 (effort), 41 (assiduously), 52 (toil)

assist (輔): ch. 64

assisting (攝): ch. 50

attached, grasp, hold, seize (執): chs. 14 (grasp), 29 (attached), 35 (hold to), 64 (attached), 69 (holding on), 79 (hold)

attend to (屬): ch. 19

auspicious (吉): ch. 31

authority (威): ch. 72

battle, military campaign (軍): chs. 30 (military campaign), 31 (將軍: untranslated; part of "general"), 50 (battle)

beauty, beautiful, glorify, glorious (美): chs. 2, 20, 31 (glorify, glorious), 62, 80, 81

beckon (召): ch. 73

before, lead, precede, prior to, surpass (先): chs. 2 (before), 4 (preceded), 7 (to the fore), 25 (prior to), 62 (bringing forward), 66 (lead), 67 (lead, leadership), 78 (surpass)

beginning (始): chs. 1, 2, 14, 32, 38, 52, 64

beginning, front (首): chs. 14 (front), 38 (beginning)

bellows (橐籥): ch. 5

belly (腹): chs. 3, 12

below, conciliatory, low, lowly, subordinate, worst (下): chs. 2 (below), 13 (subordinate), 14 (below), 17 (subordinates), 38 (lowly), 39 (lowly), 41 (worst), 61 (下流: river delta; conciliatory), 64 (足下: a single step), 66 (conciliatory), 68 (conciliatory), 76

(below [in conciliation]), 77 (low); *not counting*: world (天下)

benefit, profit, sharp (利): chs. 8 (benefiting), 11 (profitable), 19 (benefit, profit motive), 36 (sharp), 53 (sharp), 56 (benefit), 57 (sharp), 73 (beneficial), 81 (benefits)

benighted, dim (昏): chs. 18 (benighted), 20 (dim), 57 (benighted)

bent (曲): ch. 22

bent, expended (屈): chs. 5 (expended), 45 (bent)

best, celebrate, even, values (尚): chs. 3 (celebrate), 23 (even), 31 (values), 71 (best)

black (黑): ch. 28

blown about (飂): ch. 20

boast (矜): chs. 22, 24, 30

boats (舟): ch. 80

bones (骨): chs. 3, 55

bow (弓): ch. 77

brag (伐): chs. 22, 24, 30

bright, brightness, glare (光): chs. 4 (glare), 52 (brightness), 56 (glare), 58 (bright)

bright (皦): ch. 14

brittle, tender (脆): chs. 64 (brittle), 76 (tender)

broadly learned (博): ch. 81

by means of this (以此): chs. 21, 54, 57

calm (寧): ch. 39

calmly (徐): ch. 15

calmly (燕): ch. 26

care for, affections (愛): chs. 10, 13, 27, 34, 44 (affections), 72

careful (慎): ch. 64

carriage (車): ch. 11

center (央): ch. 20

change (改): ch. 25

Index | 301

changeable (渝): ch. 41

chariot, ride (乘): chs. 26 (chariot), 80 (ride)

chase, run circles around (馳騁): chs. 12 (chase), 43 (run circles around)

chickens (雞): ch. 80

chief, manage (司): chs. 74 (chief), 79 (manage)

child, children (子): chs. 4 (child), 52 (children), 54 (children)

children, smile (孩): chs. 20 (smile), 49 (treat as children)

circumstances (勢): ch. 51

clay (埴): ch. 11

clear, clarity (清): chs. 15, 39, 45

closes (闔): ch. 10

close, dear, familial relationships, favorites (親): chs. 17 (close to), 18 (familial relationships), 44 (dear), 56 (close), 79 (favorites)

coerce, influence (扔; root meaning: to pull toward oneself): chs. 38 (coerce), 69 (influencing)

compassion (慈): chs. 18, 19, 67

competence (善): chs. 2, 8, 15, 27, 30, 41, 49, 50, 54, 58, 62, 65, 66, 68, 73, 79, 81

complete, become, success (成): chs. 2, 7, 15, 17, 25, 34, 41, 45, 47, 51, 63, 64 (success), 67 (become), 77

complies with, laws (法): chs. 25 (complies with), 57 (laws)

conciliatory: *see* below, conciliatory, low, lowly, subordinate, worst

conquer, overcome, succeed, victory, win (勝): chs. 31 (victory), 33 (conquer), 36 (overcome), 45 (overcomes), 61 (overcome), 67 (victory), 68 (victors), 69 (win), 73 (succeeding), 78 (overcomes)

constraining (狎): ch. 72

contend, contentious, contentiousness (爭): chs. 3, 8, 22, 66, 68, 73, 81

contentment, sufficient, step (足): chs. 28 (sufficient), 33 (contentment), 44 (contentment), 46 (contentment), 64 (step); *not counting*: insufficient (不足)

continuous (襲): chs. 27, 52

contrivance (為): chs. 3, 29, 38, 47, 64, 75; *not counting*: non-contrivance (無為); *note*: 為 also means: as, be, create, make, etc

contrivance (偽): ch. 19

controlling (營): ch. 10

correct, truth, truthfulness (正): chs. 18 (correct), 39 (correct), 45 (truth), 57 (truthfulness, correct), 58 (truthfulness, truth), 78 (truthful)

courage, courageous (勇): chs. 67, 73

crafting, made (制): chs. 28 (crafting), 32 (made)

crazy (狂): ch. 12

creek, creeks (川): chs. 15, 32

crooked (枉): ch. 22

crucially (要): ch. 27

cultivate (修): ch. 54

cunning, guile, skill (巧): chs. 19 (guile), 45 (skill), 57 (cunning)

customs, ordinary (俗): chs. 29 (ordinary), 80 (customs)

danger, endanger (殆): chs. 16, 25 (endanger), 32, 44, 52

dark (昧): chs. 14, 41

decipher (紀): ch. 14

decrease, few, lack, widowed (寡): chs. 19 (decrease), 39 (widowed), 42 (widowed), 63 (lack), 80 (few)

deep (篤): ch. 16

deep (深): chs. 15, 59, 65

302 | Index

deep, depth, deep water (淵): chs. 4
(deep), 8 (depth), 36 (deep water)
delight, delightful, music (樂): chs. 31
(delight), 35 (music), 66 (delights),
80 (delightful)
delude, deluded (迷): chs. 27, 58
deny (辭): chs. 2, 34
description, expression, tolerance (容):
chs. 15 (description), 16 (tolerance),
21 (expression), 50 (put)
desire, may, would (欲): chs. 1 (may),
3 (desire), 15 (desire), 19 (desire),
29 (want), 34 (desire), 36 (to
[implied: "if you want to" or "if you
would"]), 37 (desires), 39 (desire),
46 (desire; wanting), 48 (want to),
57 (desires), 61 (want), 64 (desire),
66 (want), 77 (desire)
destiny, commanded (命): chs. 16
(destiny), 51 (commanded)
detachedly (超然): ch. 26
develop (化): chs. 37, 57
die, death, demise (死): chs. 6, 33, 42
(demise), 50, 67, 74, 75, 76, 80
different (異): chs. 1, 20
difficult (難): chs. 2, 3, 12, 63, 64, 65,
75 (difficulty)
difficult-to-attain goods (難得之貨):
chs. 3, 12, 64
discard, dismiss (去): chs. 2
(dismissed), 21 (discarded), 29
(discard); also: abandon that and
adopt this (去彼取此)
disciples (徒): chs. 50, 76
disgrace, humble (辱): chs. 13
(disgrace), 28 (humble), 41
(disgraceful), 44 (disgrace)
disorder (亂): chs. 3, 18, 38, 64
dispassionate (忽): ch. 20
display (陳): ch. 80; also: advertise,
display, manifest (見)
disregard (棄): chs. 19, 27, 62

dogs (犬): ch. 80; also: straw dogs (芻
狗)
dominating (宰): chs. 10, 51
door (戶): chs. 11, 47
dung (糞): ch. 46
durability, endure, enduring, long
ago, long time, persistent (久): chs.
7 (enduring), 16 (durability), 23
(persistent), 33 (endure), 44 (part of
長久: "live long"), 58 (long time),
59 (long time, enduring), 67 (long
ago)
dust (塵): chs. 4, 56
dwell (處): ch. 26
dwell, houses, occupy, residence,
situated, treated (居): chs. 2
(occupied; dwelling), 8 (dwells;
residence), 24 (occupied), 25
(occupies), 30 (dwell), 31 (occupied;
at home; situated; treated), 38
(dwell), 66 (treated, situated), 72
(where they live), 76 (situated), 77
(dwelling), 80 (houses)

Earth, location, places (地): chs. 7
(Earth), 8 (location), 25 (Earth), 39
(Earth), 50 (places); not counting:
Heaven and Earth (天地)
easy, replace (易): chs. 2 (easy), 63
(easy, easily), 64 (easy), 70 (easy), 78
(replace)
eating, feeding, food (食): chs. 20
(feeding from), 24 (food), 53 (food),
75 (eating), 80 (food)
eloquence, persuasive (辯): chs. 19
(eloquence), 45 (eloquence), 81
(persuasive)
embrace (抱): chs. 10, 19, 22, 42, 54,
64
empty (虛): chs. 5, 22, 53; also: open,
openness (虛)
empty (窪): ch. 22

Index | 303

empty (寥): ch. 25

empty, empty vessel, blend (沖): chs. 4 (empty vessel), 42 (blend), 45 (empty)

encouraging (推): ch. 66

enemies, opponent (敵): chs. 68 (enemies), 69 (opponent)

enjoying (享): ch. 20

enrich, fortune (福): chs. 58 (fortune), 65 (enrich)

equitable (均): ch. 32

err (忒): ch. 28

essence, essentialness (精): chs. 21 (essence), 55 (essentialness)

examine (閱): ch. 21

excess, excessive, et al. (甚; root meaning: extreme): chs. 29 (excess), 44 (deep), 46 (excessive), 53 (quite), 70 (very)

excess, excessive, et al. (多; root meaning: many): chs. 5 (much), 22 (abundant), 31 (great numbers), 44 (excessive, more), 57 (more), 63 (many, often), 65 (excessive), 75 (too much), 81 (more)

excess, excessive, et al. (厚; root meaning: thick): chs. 38 (thick), 44 (much), 46 (graver), 50 (excesses), 55 (vigorously), 75 ([over]emphasize)

excess, excessive, et al. (餘; root meaning: extra): chs. 20 (more than enough), 24 (leftover), 53 (excessive), 54 (abundant), 77 (excess; excessive), 79 (leftover)

execution, death, killing (殺): chs. 31 (killing), 73 (death), 74 (execution)

exhaust, exhaustion (窮): chs. 5, 45

expectation, rely on (恃): chs. 2, 10, 34 (rely on), 51, 77

expenditures (費): ch. 44

extensive, generous (廣): chs. 41 (extensive), 67 (generous, generosity)

extolled, proclaimed (彰): chs. 22 (extolled), 24 (extolled), 57 (proclaimed)

extravagance (奢): ch. 29

fail (敗): chs. 29, 64

father (父): ch. 42

fault (尤): ch. 8

fault, guilt (罪): chs. 46 (fault), 62 (guilt)

fear, revere (畏): chs. 15 (reverent), 17 (fear), 20 (revere), 53 (feared), 72 (fear), 74 (fear)

female (雌; animals): chs. 10, 28

female (牝; birds, small animals): chs. 6, 55, 61

festival (牢): ch. 20

fighting (抗): ch. 69

filiality (孝): chs. 18, 19

fill, fulfill, full, bounteous (盈): chs. 2 (fulfill), 4 (fill), 9 ([over]filling), 15 (full), 22 (full), 39 (bounteous), 45 (fullness)

fissure, space between (間): chs. 5 (space between), 43 (fissure)

flexibility, suppleness (柔 / 弱):[1] chs. 3 (弱), 10 (柔), 36 (柔弱), 40 (弱), 43 (柔), 52 (弱), 55 (骨弱筋柔), 76 (柔弱), 78 (柔弱)

flourishing (豐): ch. 54

flows (氾): ch. 34

focus (專): ch. 10

foolishly (妄): ch. 16

form (有): chs. 1, 2, 11, 14, 40

formlessness, openness (無): chs. 1, 2, 11 (openness), 14 (無物: nothingness), 40, 43 (無有: formless)

---

1. I translate both 柔 and 弱 as "flexible," unless they appear together, in which case I translate 柔 as "flexible" and 弱 as "supple."

304 | Index

founded on (基): ch. 39

four directions (四達): ch. 10

frugality (嗇): ch. 59

frugality (儉): ch. 67

gate, gateway, doors (門): chs. 1
(gateway), 6 (gate), 10 (gate), 52
(doors), 56 (doors)

genuine, genuineness (真): chs. 21,
41, 54

ghosts (鬼): ch. 60

glorious, glorious sights (榮): chs. 26,
28

gold (金): ch. 9

good, goodness (仁): chs. 5, 8, 18, 38

goods, wealth (貨): chs. 3 (goods), 12
(goods), 44 (wealth), 53 (wealth), 64
(goods)

govern (蒞): ch. 60

government (政): chs. 8, 58

governor (侯): chs. 32, 37, 39

grasp, secure (持): chs. 9 (grasping), 64
(grasp), 67 (secure)

great people (大丈夫): ch. 38

guest, travelers (客): chs. 15 (guest), 35
(travelers), 69 (guest)

hack, divisive (割): chs. 28 (hack), 58
(divisive)

harm, harmful (害): chs. 35, 56, 66,
73, 81

harm, injuring (傷): chs. 60 (harm),
74 (injuring)

harmony, harmonize, soften (和):
chs. 2 (harmonize), 4 (softens),
18 (harmony), 42 (harmonious),
55 (harmony), 56 (soften), 79
(harmonizing)

Heaven, Heavenly (天): chs. 7, 9, 10,
16, 25, 39, 47, 59, 62, 67, 68, 73,
77, 79, 81; *not counting*: Heaven
and Earth (天地) *or* world (天下)

Heaven and Earth (天地): chs. 1, 5, 6,
7, 23, 25, 32

Heavenly gate (天門): ch. 10

Heavenly scion (天子): ch. 62

Heavenly way, way of Heaven (天道,
天之道): chs. 9 (天之道), 47 (天道),
73 (天之道), 77 (天之道), 79 (天道),
81 (天之道)

helping, saves (救): chs. 27 (helping),
52 (saving), 67 (saves)

hidden (蔽): ch. 15

hidden (冥): ch. 21

hidden (隱): ch. 41

hoarding (藏): ch. 44

horses (馬): chs. 46, 62

house, room (室): chs. 9 (room), 11
(house)

hub (轂): ch. 11

hunger (飢): ch. 75

ignominies (垢): ch. 78

ignorant, stupid (愚): chs. 20 (stupid),
38 (stupid), 65 (ignorant)

impartiality, dignitaries (公): chs. 16
(impartiality), 42 (dignitaries), 63
(dignitaries)

impassioned, stir (怒): chs. 55 (stir),
68 (impassioned)

impede (妨): ch. 12

impudent (肆): ch. 58

inauspicious, bad (凶): chs. 16
(inauspiciousness), 30 (bad), 31
(inauspicious)

inauspicious, ignominies (不祥): chs.
31 (inauspicious), 78 (ignominies);
also: ominous (祥)

inceptions (甫): ch. 21

incipient, without any (outward) sign
(未兆): chs. 20, 64

inconspicuous, frail, subtle (微): chs. 14
(inconspicuous), 15 (inconspicuous),
36 (subtle), 64 (frail)

Index | 305

increase (補): ch. 77

inevitable, unavoidable, lack of success (不得已): chs. 29 (lack of success), 30 (inevitable), 31 (unavoidable)

infant (嬰兒): chs. 10, 20, 28

infant (赤子): ch. 55

inflexible (剛): chs. 36, 78

injurious (劇): ch. 58

instrument, vessel (器): chs. 11 (vessel), 28 (vessels), 29 (vessel), 31 (instruments), 36 (instruments), 41 (vessels), 57 (instruments), 67 (vessels), 80 (instruments)

insult (侮): ch. 17

interrogated (詰): ch. 14

intersections, reciprocated (交): chs. 60 (reciprocated), 61 (intersections)

jade (玉): chs. 9, 39, 70; *also*: fine jade (璧): ch. 62

king (王): chs. 25, 32, 37, 39, 42, 66, 78

knead (埏): ch. 11

knots (紛): chs. 4, 56

know, knowledge (知): chs. 2–4, 10, 14, 16, 17, 19, 21, 25, 27, 28, 32, 33, 43, 44, 46, 47, 52–59, 63, 65, 70–73, 78, 81

laugh (笑): ch. 41

laws, have, make, statutes (令): chs. 12 (make), 19 (have), 32 (laws), 57 (statutes); *also*: complies with, laws

lead, leader (disambiguation): *see*: above . . . lead (上); before . . . lead (先); dominating (宰: literally, "govern"); govern (茌); government (政); governor (侯); impartialities, dignitaries (公); king (王); leader, lord, host (主); long . . . lead (長); minister (官); ruler (君); (the sort)

that can be entrusted with the world (可以託天下): ch. 13; (the sort) that can be given the world (可以寄天下): ch. 13; those who gain (leadership of) the world (取天下): chs. 29, 48, 57

leader, lord, host (主): chs. 26 (leader), 30 (leader), 34 (lord), 69 (host), 78 (lord)

learning (學): chs. 20, 48, 64

life, bred, grow, produce (生): chs. 2 (produce), 7 (produce, live), 10 (produce), 15 (grow), 25 (production), 30 (grow), 34 (life), 40 (produced), 42 (produced), 46 (bred), 50 (life, living), 51 (produces), 55 (life), 59 (life), 64 (grew), 72 (live), 75 (lives, live, life), 76 (life)

light, lightly, underestimate (輕): chs. 26 (light, lightly), 63 (lightly), 69 (underestimate), 75 (lightly)

like, likely, prefer (好): chs. 30 (likely), 53 (like), 57 (prefer)

likeness (肖): ch. 67

long, long-lasting, endure, lead, leader (長): chs. 2 (long), 7 (long-lasting), 9 (long time), 10 (lead), 22 (endure), 24 (endure), 28 (leaders), 44 (live long), 51 (raise, lead), 54 (enduring), 59 (live long, longevity), 67 (leaders)

lose, loss (亡): chs. 33 (loss), 41 (lose), 44 (losing; loss), 69 (losing)

male (雄: male of birds): ch. 28

male (牡: male of animals): chs. 55, 61

manifestations (徼): ch. 1

many, multitudes (眾): chs. 1 (many), 21 (multitudes), 31 (眾多: great many); *also*: masses (眾人)

306 | Index

martial (武): ch. 68

masses, the (眾人): chs. 8, 20, 64

maturate (熟): ch. 51

metaphorically (譬): ch. 32

mind, consciously (心): chs. 3, 8, 12, 20, 49, 55 (consciously)

minister (官): ch. 28

minister, servant (臣): chs. 18 (minister), 32 (servant)

mirror (鑒): ch. 10

misfortune (禍): chs. 46, 58, 69

model (式): chs. 22, 28, 65

modest, small (小): chs. 32 (modest), 34 (modest), 52 (small), 60 (small), 61 (small), 63 (small), 80 (small)

mother (母): chs. 1, 20, 25, 52, 59

mountain stream (谿): ch. 28

mourning (喪): ch. 31

move, movement (動): chs. 5, 8, 15, 40, 50

muddled (渾): ch. 49

muddy, muddied (濁): ch. 15

myriad things (萬物): chs. 1, 2, 4, 5, 8, 16, 32, 34, 37, 40, 42, 51, 62, 64, 76

mystery, mysterious (玄): chs. 1, 6, 10, 15, 51, 56, 65

name, call, descriptive, renown, reputation (名): chs. 1 (name, descriptive), 14 (part of 名曰 "called"; named), 21 (renown), 25 (name), 32 (nameless [無名], name), 34 (claim, called, said to be), 37 (nameless [無名]), 41 (namelessness [無名]), 42 (describe), 44 (renown)

natural, naturally, naturalness, itself, themselves (自然): chs. 17 (themselves), 23 (natural), 25 (itself), 51 (naturally), 64 (naturalness)

neighbors, neighboring (鄰): chs. 15, 80

new, renewed (新): chs. 15 (renewed), 22 (new)

noble people (君子): chs. 26, 31

non-contrivance, uncontrived (無為): chs. 2, 3, 10, 37, 38, 43, 48, 57, 63, 64

nourish (養): chs. 34, 51

numinous (靈): ch. 39

nurture (畜): chs. 10, 51, 61

observe, behold (觀): chs. 1 (observe), 16 (observe), 26 (behold), 54 (observe)

ocean, oceans (海): chs. 20, 32, 66

officials, officers (士): chs. 41 (officials), 68 (officers)

old (老): chs. 30, 55, 80

ominous (祥): ch. 55

One (一): chs. 10, 22, 39; *note*: this also means "one"

open, openness (虛): chs. 3 (open), 16 (openness); *also*: empty (虛)

open, unblock (開): chs. 10 (opens), 27 (opened), 52 (unblock)

open-minded (無心): ch. 49

oppress, full of, tire of (厭): chs. 53 (full of), 66 (tire of), 72 (oppress)

organize, organization (治): chs. 3, 8, 10, 57, 59, 60, 64, 65, 75

ostentatious (耀): ch. 58

ostentatious (自見): ch. 72; *but* I also translate 自見 as "advertise themselves" in chs. 22, 24

peace (恬): ch. 31

peace (平): ch. 35

penetrating (通): ch. 15

people (百姓): chs. 5, 17, 49, 75

people, human (民): chs. 3, 10, 19, 32 (human), 50, 53, 57–58, 65–66, 72, 74–75, 80

Index | 307

people, humans, others (人): chs. 12, 20, 23 (humans), 25, 27, 30 (untranslated: 人主: "leaders [of people]"), 31 (humans, people), 33 (others), 36, 42, 57, 58 (human), 59–62, 68, 75–76, 77 (humans), 79, 81 (others); *not including* the masses (衆人), sages (聖人)

percipience, perceive, bright, illustrious (明): chs. 10 (perceiving), 16 (percipience), 22 (illustrious), 24 (illustrious), 27 (percipience), 33 (percipience), 36 (percipience), 41 (bright), 47 (percipient), 52 (percipience), 55 (percipience), 65 (percipient)

periphery (荒): ch. 20

persist (存): chs. 4, 6, 7, 41

person, life, themselves, you, yourself (身): chs. 7 (persons), 9 (you), 13 (personal, persons), 16 (life), 26 (person), 44 (person), 52 (life, yourself), 54 (person, personal), 66 (person)

pervasive (孔): ch. 21

physical energies (氣): chs. 10, 42, 55

placid (泊): ch. 20

plants (草): ch. 76

pomposity (泰): ch. 29

poor (貧): ch. 57

practice, actions, go, moves, travel, walk (行): chs. 2 (practice), 12 (actions), 24 (walk, practices), 25 (moves), 26 (travel), 27 (traveler), 29 (go), 33 (untranslated as part of "persevere" 強行, literally: "make [yourself] keep going"), 41 (practice), 47 (traveling), 50 (walking), 53 (walking), 62 (deeds), 69 (advancing), 70 (practice), 78 (practice)

praise (譽): chs. 17, 39

prepared (豫): ch. 15

preserve, safeguard, defense (守): chs. 5 (preserving), 9 (safeguard), 16 (preserve), 28 (preserve), 32 (preserve), 37 (preserve), 52 (preserve), 67 (defense)

presume, presumptuous (敢): chs. 3, 30, 64, 67, 69, 73, 74

Progenitor (帝): ch. 4

prohibitions (諱): ch. 57

propriety (義): chs. 18, 38

prosperous, rich, wealthy (富): chs. 9 (wealthy), 33 (rich), 57 (prosperous)

protect, protector (保): chs. 9, 15, 62, 67

protocol (禮): chs. 31, 38

providing (貸): ch. 41

pure (淳淳): ch. 58

purity (素): ch. 19

purity, clearly, white (白): chs. 10 (clearly), 28 (white), 41 (purity)

quiet (憺): ch. 31

real, fill (實): chs. 3 (fill), 38 (real)

realm (國) ch. 59

reduce (損): chs. 42, 48, 77

relinquish (絕): chs. 19, 20

repayments (徹): ch. 79

resentment (怨): ch. 79

responds, responding (應): chs. 38, 73

results (果): ch. 30

retire, retreat (退): chs. 9 (retire), 41 (retreating), 69 (retreat)

return (歸): chs. 14, 16, 20, 22, 28, 34, 52, 60

return (復): chs. 14, 16, 19, 28, 52, 58 (untranslated as part of 復為: "construed as"), 64, 80

308 | Index

return, cyclicality, contrary (反): chs. 25 (return), 40 (cyclicality), 65 (returns), 78 (contrary)

rhinoceroses (兕): ch. 50

rigid (堅): chs. 43, 76, 78

rivers (江): chs. 32, 66

rob, robbers (賊): chs. 19, 57, 65

root (本): chs. 26, 39

root, roots (根): chs. 6, 16, 26, 59

rope (繩): chs. 27, 79; *also*: as a reduplicative "endless" (繩繩): ch. 14

ruin (殃): ch. 52

ruin, calamity (咎): chs. 9 (ruin), 46 (calamity)

ruler (君): chs. 26, 70; *also*: noble people (君子)

sad (憯): ch. 46

safe, security, settled, how (安): chs. 15 (settled), 35 (security), 64 (steady), 79 (how), 80 (safe)

safeguarded (衛): ch. 67; *also*: preserve, safeguard, defense (守)

sages (聖人): chs. 2, 3, 5, 7, 12, 22, 26–29, 34, 47, 49, 57, 58, 60, 63, 64, 66, 71, 72, 77–79, 81

saying, speak, speaker, speech, talk, word, words (言): chs. 2 ("word" in "wordless"), 5 (speech), 8 (words), 17 (words), 19 (sayings), 22 (talk), 23 (speak), 27 (speakers), 31 (which is to say), 35 (spoken), 41 (saying), 43 ("word" in "wordless"), 56 (speak), 57 (sayings), 62 (words), 66 (speech), 69 (saying), 70 (words), 73 (speak), 78 (saying, words), 81 (words)

scare (懼): ch. 74

scrupulous (廉): ch. 58

seeking (求): chs. 62, 75

seem, as (如): chs. 10 (as), 41, 62 (as; part of 不如: "not as good as"), 64 (as)

seem, like (若): chs. 6, 20, 45, 78; *note*: 若 has other meanings too

seem, seems (似): chs. 4, 20, 67

self, selfishness (私): chs. 7 (part of "selfless" [無私]; "themselves" [其私]), 19 (selfishness)

semblance(s), seems to (象): chs. 4 (seems to), 14, 21, 35, 41

serve (佐): ch. 30; *also*: activities, serve (事)

sharpen, sharpness (銳): chs. 4, 9, 56; *also*: benefit . . . sharp (利)

shortcuts (徑): ch. 53

sick, bane (病): chs. 44 (bane), 71 (sick)

simplicity (樸): chs. 19, 32, 37, 57; *also*: uncarved block (樸)

sincerity (忠): ch. 38

small, trivial (細): chs. 63 (small), 67 (trivial); *also*: modest, small (小)

smooth, unobtrusive (夷): chs. 14 (unobtrusive), 41 (smooth), 53 (smooth)

soil and grain (altars) (社稷): ch. 78

soldiers, weapons (兵): chs. 30 (weapons), 31 (weapons), 50 (soldiers), 57 (soldiers), 69 (soldiers), 76 (soldiers), 80 (weapons)

sorrow (悲): ch. 31

soul, corporeal (魄): ch. 10

sound, chorus (聲): chs. 2 (chorus), 41 (sounds), 80 (sound)

springtime (春): ch. 20

spirit, spirited, spiritous (神): chs. 6, 29, 39, 60

spokes (輻): ch. 11

squares, upright (方): chs. 41 (squares), 58 (upright)

state (邦): chs. 10, 18, 36, 54, 57, 60, 61, 65, 78, 80

steer (御): ch. 14

straight, straightness, straightforward (直): chs. 22, 45, 58

Index | 309

straw dogs (芻狗): ch. 5

strong, strength, strengthen; force, forced, pressed, stiff (強): chs. 3 (strengthen), 15 (forced), 25 (pressed), 29 (strong), 30 (force), 33 (strong, untranslated as part of "persevere" 強行: "make [yourself] keep going"), 36 (stiff), 42 (stiff), 52 (strength), 55 (forced), 76 (stiff), 78 (stiff)

substantial (質): ch. 41

superfluous (華): ch. 38

supply wagon (輜重): ch. 26

surprise (驚): ch. 13

sweet dew (甘露): ch. 32

sympathy, sympathetic (哀): chs. 31, 69

taboos (忌): ch. 57

tallies (籌策): ch. 27

tally, tallies (契): ch. 79

taproot (柢): ch. 59

task, merit, succeed (功): chs. 2 (成功: complete tasks), 9 (功遂: task accomplished), 17 (成功: complete tasks), 22 (有功: succeed), 24 (無功: do not succeed), 34 (成功: completes [its] tasks), 77 (成功: complete tasks)

taste (味): chs.12, 35

taxes (稅): ch. 75

teach, teaching (教): chs. 2, 42, 43

teachers, armies (師): chs. 27 (teachers), 30 (armies)

terrace (臺): chs. 20, 64

thieves, thieving (盜): chs. 3, 19, 53, 57

thin (淡): ch. 35

thin, wearing thin (薄): ch. 38

tigers (虎): ch. 50

timeliness (時): ch. 8

trade (市): ch. 62

tranquility (靜): chs. 15, 16, 26, 37, 45, 57, 61

treasure (寶): chs. 62, 67, 69

tree, trees (木): chs. 64, 76

trust, trustworthiness (信): chs. 8, 17, 23, 38, 49, 63, 81

ugly, repellent, detest (惡): chs. 2 (ugly), 8 (repellent), 20 (ugliness), 24 (detest), 31 (detest), 42 (detest), 73 (repellent)

unbiased (歙歙): ch. 49

uncanny (妖): ch. 58

uncarved block (樸): chs. 15, 28; also: simplicity (樸)

unfathomable, nebulously (混): chs. 14 (unfathomable), 15 (unfathomable), 25 (nebulously)

union, circumference (合): chs. 32 (union), 55 (union), 64 (circumference)

universe (域): ch. 25

utmost, limit, limits, turning points (極): chs. 16 (utmost), 28 (limit [of "limitless"]), 58 (turning points), 59 (limits), 69 (utmost)

valley (谷): chs. 6, 15, 28, 32, 39, 41, 66

value, honor, aggrandizing (貴): chs. 3 (value), 9 (honored), 13 (value), 17 (values), 20 (value), 27 (value), 31 (value), 39 (honored), 51 (value), 56 (honor), 62 (value), 64 (value), 70 (valuable), 72 (aggrandizing), 75 (value); also: best . . . values (尚)

vanquish (滅): ch. 76

vehicles (輿): ch. 80

venerate, venerable (尊): chs. 51, 62

vessel: see: instrument, vessel (器)

vexation (患): ch. 13

virtuosity (德): chs. 10, 21, 23, 28, 38, 41, 49, 51, 54, 55, 59, 60, 65, 68, 79

310 | Index

war (戎): ch. 46

warfare, military, warriors (戰): chs. 31 (military), 67 (warfare), 68 (戰者: warriors)

water (水): chs. 8, 78

Way (道): chs. 1, 4, 8, 14–16, 18, 21, 23–25, 30–32, 34, 35, 37, 38, 40–42, 46, 48, 51, 53, 55, 59, 60, 62, 65, 67, 77; *also*: Heavenly way, way of Heaven (天道, 天之道)

way of humans (人之道): ch. 77

way of sages (聖人之道): ch. 81

we (吾): chs. 4, 13, 16, 21, 25, 29, 37, 42, 43, 49, 54, 57, 69, 70, 74

we (我): chs. 17, 20, 42, 53, 57, 67, 70

weak (羸): ch. 29

weep (泣): ch. 31

who, which (孰): chs. 15, 23, 44 (which), 58, 73, 74, 77

whole, wholeness (全): chs. 16, 22

widespread (普): ch. 54

wilted (枯): ch. 76

withered (槁): ch. 76

wily, wiliness (奇): chs. 57, 58, 74

window (牖): chs. 11, 47

wisdom (智): ch. 33

within, middling (中): chs. 5, 21, 25, 41 (middling)

without (contrived) activities (無事): chs. 48, 57, 63

without (contrived) desires (無欲): chs. 3, 34, 57

without (contrived) knowledge (無知): chs. 3, 10, 63, 70

wonders, wondrous (妙): chs. 1, 15, 27

world (天下): chs. 2, 13, 22, 25, 26, 28–32, 35, 37, 39, 40, 43, 45–49, 52, 54, 56, 57, 60–63, 66, 67, 70, 77, 78

worn-out (敝): ch. 22

worthy, worthies (賢): chs. 3, 75, 77

Yin 陰 and Yang 陽: ch. 42

Ideas *not* mentioned in this text:
essential spirit/ousness (精神): none
Heaven's mandate (天命): none,
    but 命: chs. 16 (destiny), 51
    (commanded)
honesty (誠): none, *but* "truly" ch. 22
(human) nature (性): none
(natural) principles (理): none
spiritous percipience (神明): none